SCC Library
DISCARD
3 3065 00363 7018

Adobe

Santiago Canyon College
Library

TK
6680.5
.D546
2014

Digital Video with
Adobe® Creative Cloud™

D0731521

OCN857706848

CLASSROOM IN A BOOK®
The official training workbook from Adobe Systems

Santiago Canyon College
Library

Digital Video with Adobe® Creative Cloud™ Classroom in a Book®

The official training workbook from Adobe Systems

© 2014 Adobe Systems Incorporated and its licensors. All rights reserved.

If this guide is distributed with software that includes an end user license agreement, this guide, as well as the software described in it, is furnished under license and may be used or copied only in accordance with the terms of such license. Except as permitted by any such license, no part of this guide may be reproduced, stored in a retrieval system, or transmitted, in any form or by any means, electronic, mechanical, recording, or otherwise, without the prior written permission of Adobe Systems Incorporated. Please note that the content in this guide is protected under copyright law even if it is not distributed with software that includes an end user license agreement.

The content of this guide is furnished for informational use only, is subject to change without notice, and should not be construed as a commitment by Adobe Systems Incorporated. Adobe Systems Incorporated assumes no responsibility or liability for any errors or inaccuracies that may appear in the informational content contained in this guide.

Please remember that existing artwork or images that you may want to include in your project may be protected under copyright law. The unauthorized incorporation of such material into your new work could be a violation of the rights of the copyright owner. Please be sure to obtain any permission required from the copyright owner.

Any references to company names in sample files are for demonstration purposes only and are not intended to refer to any actual organization.

Adobe, the Adobe logo, Adobe Audition, Adobe Bridge, Adobe Premiere Pro, Adobe Story, After Effects, Behance, Classroom in a Book, Encore, Flash, Illustrator, Adobe Media Encoder, Photoshop, Prelude, and SpeedGrade are either registered trademarks or trademarks of Adobe Systems Incorporated in the United States and/or other countries.

Apple, Mac OS, and Macintosh are trademarks of Apple, registered in the U.S. and other countries. Microsoft, Windows, and Windows NT are trademarks of Microsoft Corporation registered in the U.S. and/or other countries. All other trademarks are the property of their respective owners.

Adobe Systems Incorporated, 345 Park Avenue, San Jose, California 95110-2704, USA

Notice to U.S. Government End Users. The Software and Documentation are "Commercial Items," as that term is defined at 48 C.F.R. §2.101, consisting of "Commercial Computer Software" and "Commercial Computer Software Documentation," as such terms are used in 48 C.F.R. §12.212 or 48 C.F.R. §227.7202, as applicable. Consistent with 48 C.F.R. §12.212 or 48 C.F.R. §§227.7202-1 through 227.7202-4, as applicable, the Commercial Computer Software and Commercial Computer Software Documentation are being licensed to U.S. Government end users (a) only as Commercial Items and (b) with only those rights as are granted to all other end users pursuant to the terms and conditions herein. Unpublished-rights reserved under the copyright laws of the United States. Adobe Systems Incorporated, 345 Park Avenue, San Jose, CA 95110-2704, USA. For U.S. Government End Users, Adobe agrees to comply with all applicable equal opportunity laws including, if appropriate, the provisions of Executive Order 11246, as amended, Section 402 of the Vietnam Era Veterans Readjustment Assistance Act of 1974 (38 USC 4212), and Section 503 of the Rehabilitation Act of 1973, as amended, and the regulations at 41 CFR Parts 60-1 through 60-60, 60-250, and 60-741. The affirmative action clause and regulations contained in the preceding sentence shall be incorporated by reference.

Adobe Press books are published by Peachpit, a division of Pearson Education located in San Francisco, California. For the latest on Adobe Press books, go to www.adobepress.com. To report errors, please send a note to errata@peachpit.com. For information on getting permission for reprints and excerpts, contact permissions@peachpit.com.

Writers: Adam Shaening-Pokrasso, Sam Young, and Adam Kennedy
Adobe Press Editor: Victor Gavenda
Senior Editor: Karyn Johnson
Production Editor: Maureen Forys, Happenstance Type-O-Rama
Developmental Editor: Corbin Collins
Technical Editor: Simon Walker
Copyeditor: Rebecca Rider
Compositor: David Van Ness
Proofreader: Scout Festa
Indexer: Jack Lewis
Media Producer: Eric Geoffroy
Cover Design: Eddie Yuen
Interior Design: Mimi Heft

Printed and bound in the United States of America

ISBN-13:   978-0-321-93402-4
ISBN-10:   0-321-93402-4

9 8 7 6 5 4 3 2 1

WHERE ARE THE LESSON FILES?

Purchasing this Classroom in a Book gives you access to the lesson files that you'll need to complete the exercises in the book, as well as other content to help you learn more about Adobe software and use it with greater efficiency and ease. The diagram below represents the contents of the lesson files directory, which should help you locate the files you need. Please see the Getting Started section for full download instructions.

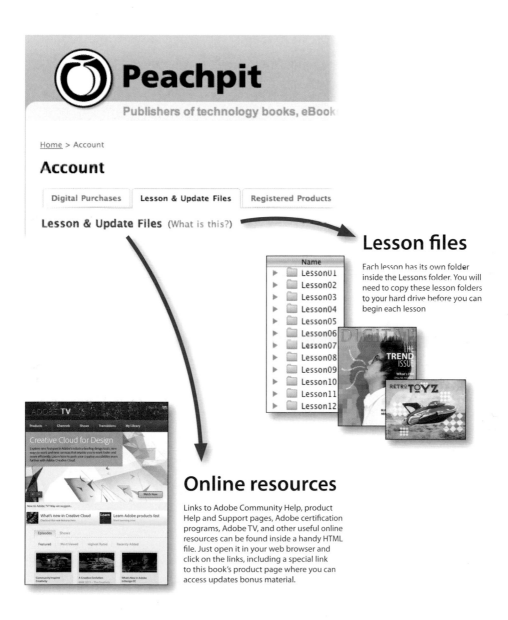

Lesson files

Each lesson has its own folder inside the Lessons folder. You will need to copy these lesson folders to your hard drive before you can begin each lesson

Online resources

Links to Adobe Community Help, product Help and Support pages, Adobe certification programs, Adobe TV, and other useful online resources can be found inside a handy HTML file. Just open it in your web browser and click on the links, including a special link to this book's product page where you can access updates bonus material.

CONTENTS

GETTING STARTED   **xi**

About Classroom in a Book.................................xi

Prerequisites xii

Installing software in Adobe Creative Cloud xii

Hardware requirements.................................... xii

For Windows...xii

For Mac OS... xiii

Optimizing performance...................................xiv

How to use these lessons xiv

Copying the lesson files and bonus chapters................ xv

Relinking the lesson files.................................. xv

Interpreting the frame rate of linked files xvi

Additional resources xviii

Adobe certification xix

1   WORKING IN ADOBE CREATIVE CLOUD   **1**

The "planning to playback" video-production workflow 2

Pre-production.. 2

Production... 3

Post-production... 3

Overview of Creative Cloud 4

Learning the role of each component 4

Understanding the Creative Cloud user interface........................ 5

Using Dynamic Link..................................... 6

Working with media files in video production............... 6

Linking a project with media files...................................... 9

Real-time playback and editing 15

Mercury Playback Engine.................................15

Global Performance Cache 16

Mercury Graphics Engine.................................17

Mercury Performance System..............................17

2 ORGANIZING THE MEDIA FILES FOR YOUR PROJECT   20

About Adobe Bridge 22
Naming and managing your project and media files...................22
Navigating and previewing media.............................22

Working with metadata 26
Adding metadata to your media 26

About Adobe Story 27
Starting a new A/V script in Adobe Story 29
Collaborating with others on your script 34

Planning and managing your production
with Adobe Story 35

About Prelude 37

Ingesting media and working with metadata in Prelude.....37
Adding notes to footage....................................40
Creating bins..41
Assembling a rough cut 41
Adding time-based comments.................................44
Sending your project to Adobe Premiere Pro 46

3 CREATING A BASIC EDIT   50

About Adobe Premiere Pro 52
Optimizing performance 52

Creating a new project in Adobe Premiere Pro 54
Understanding the Adobe Premiere Pro user interface.................56

Importing footage and other media using the
Media Browser...59

Understanding the Project panel 61

Interpreting footage 62

Creating bins 64
Importing assets as a bin 64
Creating a new bin 65

Viewing your footage 67
Listening to your footage...................................68
Viewing your B-roll footage.................................74
Viewing your RED footage..................................77
Music and sound effects...................................79

About subclips. 80
Creating a subclip 80
Editing Interview clips 83
Relinking media with Link & Locate. 84
Creating the first sequence. 88
Using markers 91
Adding a marker to a clip 91
Adding a marker to a sequence 94
Working in the Timeline. 95
Preparing to edit in the Timeline 95
The components of the Timeline 96
Muting and locking tracks. 97
Editing on the Timeline 98
Adding B-roll 102
Reordering clips on the Timeline 108
Using new audio enhancements 111
Using Snap 112
Snapping between edit points 112
Snapping clips into a sequence 112
Snapping clips within a sequence. 115
Refining your story 126
Shorten the music clips. 126
Making an audio gap 130
Adding a reaction shot 131
Adding the last clip. 131
Final marker 133
Finishing your rough edit 134

4   ADVANCED EDITING TECHNIQUES

*Download this lesson and its project files from the Lesson &
Update Files tab on your Account page at www.peachpit.com.
See the "Getting Started" section for more details.*

5   CREATING BASIC MOTION GRAPHICS AND VISUAL EFFECTS   138

Getting started 140
If you are starting here 140
Preserving your rough edit in Adobe Premiere Pro. 140
About After Effects. 143
Creating a new project in After Effects 144
Optimizing performance 144

The Global Performance Cache 145

Understanding the After Effects user interface 147

Creating folders in After Effects 150

Using Dynamic Link: from Adobe Premiere Pro to
After Effects 151

Creating a motion graphic with After Effects 157

Working with layers 157

Understanding keyframes 159

Animating your layers 159

Using RAM Preview 160

RAM Previewing your timelapse 160

Final changes to timelapse 161

Updating a dynamically linkedcomposition 162

About Illustrator 164

Making a new image in Illustrator 164

Overview of the Illustrator interface. 167

Making the lower third background 168

Making the background shape 168

Making a group of shapes 177

Duplicating layers in Illustrator 185

Importing a lower third background to After Effects. 190

Creating a new composition 191

Creating the lower third template composition 191

Create a new text layer 193

Applying the Drop Shadow effect 195

Duplicating a layer 197

Optional exercise: parenting 202

Creating a null object 204

Moving the null into place 205

Using the Pick-Whip 206

Moving and scaling the group 207

Nested compositions 209

Animating the background 212

Animating opacity 217

Verifying updates to a nested composition 219

Animating text in After Effects 220

Animating position 220

Easy Ease interpolation 222

Understanding and applying motion blur 223

Applying motion blur to text layers 223

Working with animation presets in After Effects. 226

Finalizing lower third graphics. 230

Using Dynamic Link: from After Effects to
Adobe Premiere Pro. 235

Importing After Effects compositions in Adobe Premiere Pro. 236

Replacing clips in your Adobe Premiere Pro sequence 239

Dynamic Link updates. 245

6 ADVANCED STILL AND MOTION GRAPHICS TECHNIQUES

*Download this lesson and its project files from the Lesson &
Update Files tab on your Account page at www.peachpit.com.
See the "Getting Started" section for more details.*

7 WORKING WITH AUDIO   **250**

Getting started 252

If you are starting here 252

Making your final edit sequence in Adobe Premiere Pro 252

Monitoring audio. 254

Understanding audio tools in Adobe Premiere Pro
and Adobe Audition 255

Changing your workspace in Adobe Premiere Pro 256

Verifying your preferences 258

Viewing audio waveforms 259

Opening the Audio Mixer 260

Adobe Premiere Pro effects 262

Audio clip editing in Adobe Premiere Pro .266

Automating volume with keyframes 266

Adjusting volume with the Audio Clip Mixer. 270

Audio clip editing in Adobe Audition 272

Examining clips for distractions. 272

Sending audio clips from Adobe Premiere Pro to Adobe Audition
for cleanup. 272

Understanding the Spectral Frequency Display 274

Removing transient sounds using the Spectral Frequency Display 275

Removing background noise from your audio 276

Multitrack mixing and finishing in Adobe Audition. 280

Audio track editing in Adobe Audition. 286

Creating the final audio mix 289

Sending your final audio mix back to Adobe Premiere Pro . .289

8   FINISHING YOUR PROJECT   294

Getting started 296

If you are starting here 296

The basics of color correction 298

Using color-correction techniques in
Adobe Premiere Pro. 299

Setting up for color correction 300

Using the YC Waveform 301

Using the Three-Way Color Corrector 302

Integrating color corrections to RED footage. 315

About SpeedGrade 322

Adjustment layers in Adobe Premiere Pro 323

Lumetri Looks 325

Creating a custom Look in Adobe SpeedGrade 327

Applying your custom Look in Adobe Premiere Pro 329

9   OUTPUT FOR THE WEB AND CREATIVE CLOUD   336

Getting started 338

If you are starting here 338

Final quality control 338

Exporting the final output with Adobe Premiere Pro 341

Understanding compression and other factors
for exporting files. 343

About Adobe Media Encoder. 345

Rendering master files. 345

Saving a preset. 349

Encoding video for web and mobile 350

Introducing Flash Professional 355

Creating interactivity with Flash Professional 355

Uploading and sharing your project using
Creative Cloud. 358

Uploading your work to Creative Cloud 358

Promoting your project 361

Linking Behance with your online social networks 361

Posting an image to Behance. 363

INDEX   368

GETTING STARTED

The tools for creating and broadcasting a professional-quality video have never been as accessible as they are today, thanks to more affordable and powerful recording equipment and computers, broadband Internet, and user-friendly software.

The digital video tools available in Adobe Creative Cloud offer industry-standard applications for project organization, video and audio editing, animation, and final encoding for delivery.

About Classroom in a Book

Digital Video with Adobe Creative Cloud Classroom in a Book® is part of the official training series for Adobe graphics and publishing software. The lessons are designed so you can learn at your own pace. If you're new to the software in Adobe Creative Cloud, you'll learn the fundamental concepts and features you'll need to use the programs. This book also teaches many advanced features, including tips and techniques for using the latest version of this software.

You'll learn how to:

- Format a script in Adobe Story and learn the basics of its online features to collaborate with other members of your creative team

- Ingest footage and add searchable metadata to your video clips with Adobe Prelude

- Use Adobe Premiere Pro as the creative hub in which you'll do a refined edit of your movie and add visual effects and titles

- Use Adobe Photoshop to edit still images with the new Smart Sharpen filter.

- Use Adobe Illustrator to create a lower third graphic

- Create motion graphics in Adobe After Effects and integrate 3D animations with the MAXON CINEWARE plug-in

- Create the final audio mix of your edit using Adobe Audition

- Use the enhanced Three-Way Color Corrector effect in Adobe Premiere Pro to color correct your edit

- Create grading presets with Adobe SpeedGrade

- Create files for the Internet and mobile devices with Adobe Media Encoder

- Apply a media playback skin to your exported movie file with Adobe Flash Professional

- Upload and promote your media with Adobe Creative Cloud

Prerequisites

Before beginning to use *Digital Video with Adobe Creative Cloud Classroom in a Book*, make sure your system is set up correctly and that you've installed the required software and hardware. You can view updated system requirements by visiting the specific software pages in the Video category at www.adobe.com/products/creativecloud.html.

You should have a working knowledge of your computer and operating system. You should know how to use the mouse and standard menus and commands, and also how to open, save, and close files. If you need to review these techniques, see the printed or online documentation included with your Windows or Mac OS system.

Installing software in Adobe Creative Cloud

You must purchase an Adobe Creative Cloud subscription separately from this book. For system requirements and complete instructions on installing the software, visit www.adobe.com/support. You can purchase Adobe Creative Cloud by visiting www.adobe.com/products/creativecloud and following the onscreen instructions.

Hardware requirements

The basic hardware requirements needed to run the software in Adobe Creative Cloud are as follows:

For Windows

- Intel Core™2 Duo or AMD Phenom II processor with 64-bit support; Intel Core i7 processor required for Adobe SpeedGrade

- Microsoft Windows 7 with Service Pack 1 (64 bit)

- 4 GB of RAM (8 GB recommended)

- 21.2 GB of available hard-disk space for installation; additional free space required during installation (cannot install on removable flash storage devices)

- Additional disk space required for disk cache, preview files, and other working files (10 GB recommended)

- 1280×800 display

- 7200 RPM hard drive (multiple fast disk drives, preferably RAID 0 configured, recommended)

- Sound card compatible with ASIO protocol or Microsoft Windows Driver Model

- OpenGL 2.0–capable system

- QuickTime 7.6.6 software required for QuickTime features

- Optional: Adobe-certified GPU card for GPU-accelerated performance

- Internet connection and registration are necessary for required software activation, membership validation, and access to online services

For Mac OS

- Multicore Intel processor with 64-bit support

- OS X v10.7 or v10.8

- 4 GB of RAM (8 GB recommended)

- 21.2 GB of available hard-disk space for installation; additional free space required during installation (cannot install on a volume that uses a case-sensitive file system or on removable flash storage devices)

- Additional disk space required for disk cache, preview files, and other working files (10 GB recommended)

- 1440×900 display

- 7200 RPM hard drive (multiple fast disk drives, preferably RAID 0 configured, recommended)

- OpenGL 2.0–capable system

- QuickTime 7.6.6 software required for QuickTime features

- Optional: Adobe-certified GPU card for GPU-accelerated performance

- Internet connection and registration are necessary for required software activation, membership validation, and access to online services

Optimizing performance

Editing video is memory- and processor-intensive work for a computer. A fast processor and a lot of RAM will make your editing experience faster and more efficient; 4 GB of RAM is the minimum, and 8 GB or more is best for high-definition (HD) media. Adobe Creative Cloud takes advantage of multicore processors on Windows and Macintosh systems.

A dedicated 7200 RPM or faster hard drive is recommended for HD media. A RAID 0 striped disk array or SCSI disk subsystem is strongly recommended for HD. Performance will be significantly affected if you attempt to store media files and program files on the same hard drive. Be sure to keep your media files on a second drive if at all possible.

The Mercury Playback Engine in Adobe Premiere Pro and the Global Performance Cache in Adobe After Effects can operate in software-only mode or in GPU acceleration mode. The GPU acceleration mode provides significant performance improvement. GPU acceleration is possible with select video cards. You can find a list of these video cards on the Adobe website at www.adobe.com/products/premiere/tech-specs.html.

How to use these lessons

Each lesson in this book provides step-by-step instructions for creating one or more specific elements of a real-world project. The lessons stand alone, but most of them build on previous lessons in terms of concepts and skills. So, the best way to learn from this book is to proceed through the lessons in sequential order.

The organization of the lessons is workflow-oriented rather than feature-oriented, and the book uses a real-world approach. The lessons follow the typical sequential steps that creative media makers use to complete a project: writing a script; acquiring video; laying down a cuts-only sequence; adding effects; creating a motion graphic sequence; sweetening the audio track; color-correcting video clips; exporting the project as a movie file for the web, a portable device, or Flash; and ultimately sharing with others online.

Copying the lesson files and bonus chapters

The lessons in *Digital Video with Adobe Creative Cloud Classroom in a Book* use specific source files, such as video clips, audio files, and image files created in Adobe Photoshop CC and Adobe Illustrator CC. To complete the lessons in this book, you must download all the lesson and media files from www.peachpit.com.

Also included with this book are two bonus chapters that cover advanced topics in editing (Chapter 4) and motion graphics (Chapter 6). The lesson files for those chapters are also included at www.peachpit.com (see step-by-step instructions below).

You'll need about 11.4 GB of total storage space. This includes 830 MB for the files from the website in addition to the 10.5 GB you need to install the software used in this book. It is also recommended that you have at least 10 GB of additional storage space for disk cache, preview files, and other working files.

Although each lesson stands alone, some lessons use files from other lessons, so you'll need to keep the entire collection of lesson assets on your hard drive as you work through the book.

To access the Classroom in a Book files:

1 On a Mac or Windows computer, go to www.peachpit.com/redeem and enter the code found at the back of your book.

2 If you do not have a Peachpit.com account, you will be prompted to create one.

   The download files will be listed in the Lesson & Update Files tab on your Account page.

3 Click the lesson file links to download them to your computer.

   This process may take some time to complete, depending on the speed of your computer and Internet connection.

4 Unzip the lesson files and media files.

● **Note:** If updates to this book are posted, those updates will also appear on your Account page at www.peachpit.com.

Relinking the lesson files

It is possible that the file path to the lesson files may need to be updated.

If you open an Adobe Premiere Pro project and it cannot find a media file, a dialog may open and ask *Where is the File MEDIA.mov?* If this happens, you'll need to navigate to one of the offline files to reconnect. Once you've reconnected one file in the project, the rest should reconnect.

If you open an Adobe After Effects project and it cannot find a media file, a window will open telling you that a number of files are missing. Look through your Project panel to find italicized filenames of imported media. Double-click each of these filenames and navigate to the offline files to reconnect them. To find the files:

- You can navigate to the same location where you put the files you downloaded for this book. You may need to look in some of the included folders to find the media file.
- You can use the search field in the OS dialog to search for the file by name.

When you locate a file, just select it and click the Open button.

Interpreting the frame rate of linked files

As of this writing, Premiere Pro project files do not retain their interpret-footage settings on clips that don't require relinking. For the exercises in some lessons in this book to work properly, you must complete the following steps.

All provided RED clips must be modified to have a frame rate of 48 frames per second (fps). They were all shot at 48 fps, but you will be putting them into a sequence that will play at 23.976 fps. If the RED clips play at 23.976 fps, they will play too slowly.

1   In the Premiere Pro Project panel, click in the search field. If there is any text there, select and delete it. Type **.R3D** and press Return (Enter) to search for all clips with the .R3D file extension.

The .R3D clips are revealed.

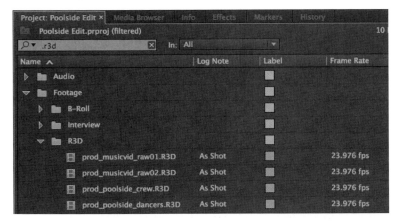

2   With the Selection tool, marquee-select all of these .R3D clips.

3   Choose Clip > Modify > Interpret Footage.

4   In the Modify Clip window, in the Frame Rate settings, select "Assume this frame rate" and enter **48** in the text field.

5   At the bottom of the Modify Clip window, click OK.

Under the Frame Rate column in the Project panel, note the interpreted frame rate of the RED clips.

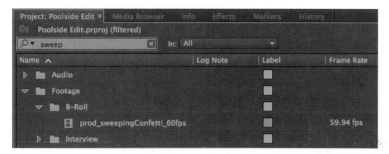

6   In the Project panel search field, click the X button to clear the field. Then type **sweep** into the search field and press Return (Enter) to find the clip prod_sweepingConfetti_60fps.m4v.

This clip was shot at 59.94 fps, but you will want it to play back slowly in your 23.976 fps sequence. Therefore, you want Premiere Pro to interpret its frame rate at 23.976 fps.

7   Select this clip, then choose Clip > Modify > Interpret Footage.

8   In the Modify Clip window, in the Frame Rate settings, select "Assume this frame rate" and enter **23.976** in the text field.

9   At the bottom of the Modify Clip window, click OK.

Note the modified frame rate of this clip in the Project panel.

10 In the Project panel search field, click the X button to clear the field.

Additional resources

Digital Video with Adobe Creative Cloud Classroom in a Book is not meant to replace documentation that comes with the program or to be a comprehensive reference for every feature. Only the commands and options used in the lessons are explained in this book. For comprehensive information about program features and tutorials, please refer to these resources:

Adobe Creative Cloud Help and Support. www.adobe.com/support is where you can find and browse Help and Support content on adobe.com.

Adobe Creative Cloud Learning. For inspiration, key techniques, cross-product workflows, and updates on new features, go to the Creative Cloud Learn page at https://helpx.adobe.com/creative-cloud/tutorials.html. Available only to Creative Cloud members.

Adobe Forums. http://forums.adobe.com lets you tap into peer-to-peer discussions, questions, and answers on Adobe products.

Adobe TV. http://tv.adobe.com is an online video resource for expert instruction and inspiration about Adobe products, including a How To channel to get you started with your product.

Resources for educators. www.adobe.com/education and http://edex.adobe.com offer a treasure trove of information for instructors who teach classes on Adobe software. Find solutions for education at all levels, including free curricula that use an integrated approach to teaching Adobe software and can be used to prepare for the Adobe Certified Associate exams.

Also check out these useful links:

Adobe Marketplace & Exchange. www.adobe.com/cfusion/exchange is a central resource for finding tools, services, extensions, code samples, and more to supplement and extend your Adobe products.

Adobe Creative Cloud product home page. Go towww.adobe.com/products/creativecloud has for more information about this product.

Adobe Labs. labs.adobe.com gives you access to early builds of cutting-edge technology as well as to forums where you can interact with the Adobe development teams building that technology and with other like-minded members of the community.

Adobe certification

The Adobe training and certification programs are designed to help Adobe customers improve and promote their product-proficiency skills. There are four levels of certification:

- Adobe Certified Associate (ACA)
- Adobe Certified Expert (ACE)
- Adobe Certified Instructor (ACI)
- Adobe Authorized Training Center (AATC)

The Adobe Certified Associate (ACA) credential certifies that individuals have the entry-level skills to plan, design, build, and maintain effective communications using different forms of digital media.

The Adobe Certified Expert program is a way for expert users to upgrade their credentials. You can use Adobe certification as a catalyst for getting a raise, finding a job, or promoting your expertise.

If you are an ACE-level instructor, the Adobe Certified Instructor program takes your skills to the next level and gives you access to a wide range of Adobe resources.

Adobe Authorized Training Centers offer instructor-led courses and training on Adobe products, employing only Adobe Certified Instructors. A directory of AATCs is available at http://partners.adobe.com.

For information on the Adobe Certified programs, visit www.adobe.com/support/certification/index.html.

1 WORKING IN ADOBE CREATIVE CLOUD

Lesson overview

Becoming familiar with the applications in Creative Cloud and learning about the basic digital video workflow are essential to successfully completing a project. In this lesson, you will learn about

- The general workflow of creating a video

- The role of each application in Creative Cloud

- The components of the Creative Cloud user interface

- The various types of media files and what they are typically used for in your workflow

- Linking a project with media files

 This lesson will take approximately 20 minutes to complete.

Download the project files for this lesson from the Lesson & Update Files tab on your Account page at www.peachpit.com and store them on your computer in a convenient location, as described in the Getting Started section of this book.

Your Account page is also where you'll find any updates to the chapters or to the lesson files. Look on the Lesson & Update Files tab to access the most current content.

The Timeline and Program Monitor in Adobe
Premiere Pro

The "planning to playback" video-production workflow

The tools for creating and broadcasting a professional-quality video have never been as accessible as they are today, thanks to more affordable and accessible recording equipment and computers, broadband Internet, and user-friendly software.

Creative Cloud offers industry-standard applications for project organization, video and audio editing, animation, and final encoding for delivery.

The lessons in this book take you through the process of creating a short documentary on the making of a music video by the band Poolside. Assets provided include interviews, music clips, and footage of the band and videographers shooting a music video. Using many of the applications in Creative Cloud, you'll assemble the raw video footage and a music track into a rough cut, add some visual effects, animate some motion graphics, create a final audio mix, and then generate exports of the final video.

This book is intended for those who have some experience in the creative process but who have never used Creative Cloud. After completing these lessons, you'll have a basic understanding of the creative process and how the applications in Creative Cloud can play an integral role in that process.

The creative process of making a broadcast-quality video consists of three phases: pre-production, production, and post-production. Each phase has its own procedures.

Pre-production

In pre-production you generate all the big-picture ideas and concepts and establish general creative guidelines and styles. Once you formulate a concept, you then write your scripts and draw your storyboards. These will serve as your points of reference as you proceed to the production phase. As a result, pre-production can be the most creative phase of the entire process, and it establishes a general direction for all the work to follow.

In Lesson 2 you'll learn how to use Adobe Story to create and format a script.

Production

In the production phase you shoot any video footage and record any audio that is unique to a given project. This is also when you gather additional media—stock images, logo graphics, music, and sound effects—that you want to include in your project. You should put just as much care and planning into the production phase as the pre-production phase because if you do not have good video, audio, and other media to work with, you cannot move on to the next phase of the creative process.

Also in Chapter 2 you'll learn how to use Adobe Prelude to ingest raw footage into your computer's hard drive—a task that, thanks to video cameras with tapeless media, is now possible during the production phase.

Post-production

When you have all of your raw media, you are ready to put all of the pieces together. Post-production is when you edit your video, mix your audio, animate your motion graphics, generate final composites, apply color-correcting techniques, output your final video master file, compress your video for web and mobile devices, and deliver your final output to the client or end user.

The lessons in this book use raw video footage and audio that has already been created and provided for you, and so they primarily focus on the post-production phase:

- In Chapter 3 you'll create a rough edit of your movie with Adobe Premiere Pro.

- In Chapter 4 you'll refine your Adobe Premiere Pro edit by applying video effects and transitions.

- In Chapter 5 you'll edit a layered image with Adobe Photoshop and convert that layered image into a motion graphic with Adobe After Effects. You'll add this motion graphic to your edit in Adobe Premiere Pro.

- In Chapter 6 you'll refine your motion graphics sequences in After Effects by incorporating 3D models from MAXON CINEMA 4D by using the new CINEWARE plug-in and CINEMA 4D Lite, which come included with After Effects.

- In Chapter 7 you'll create a final audio mix with Adobe Audition.

- In Chapter 8 you'll use Adobe Premiere Pro and Adobe SpeedGrade to apply color-correcting techniques.

- In Chapter 9 you'll use Adobe Media Encoder to export your final edit for optimized playback on multiple devices. You'll also use SpeedGrade to apply a media playback skin so that your final movie can be embedded in a web page. Finally, you will upload, share, and promote your final movie using Creative Cloud.

Overview of Creative Cloud

Adobe Creative Cloud is an online membership service that allows you to download all of the Adobe applications and install them on your desktop, without requiring a set of install discs. By signing up, you can immediately download and install any Adobe application and start creating content for web, print, mobile devices, and video. Creative Cloud members also have access to both the Windows and Mac OS versions of the applications. These are installed and run locally on your desktop, not in the cloud. A benefit of this is that you could install both the Windows and Mac OS versions of the applications on separate machines but only have to pay for the application suite once.

With Creative Cloud membership, you can save certain application settings, like keyboard shortcuts, layouts, and workspaces, to your Creative Cloud account. That way, if you work on a different machine than the one on which you saved those settings, you can sync your current local Creative Cloud application with the settings in your Creative Cloud account.

As new features and drivers become available in individual Creative Cloud applications, you can download and install these updates without having to wait for a release of the entire software suite. That way, you can ensure that your Creative Cloud applications are always up to date.

Furthermore, Creative Cloud is an online service that gives you 20 gigabytes of storage so that you can store, sync, and share your content. Using Creative Cloud, you can upload your content by simply dragging a file from your desktop directly into the Creative Cloud website. You can also automatically sync the content of a folder on your computer with your Creative Cloud account. All of your content is accessible from any Internet-enabled computer or mobile device through the Creative Cloud web service. Once your content is stored in Creative Cloud, you can share it with colleagues and clients online.

Learning the role of each component

The applications in Adobe Creative Cloud perform different functions in the creative process. The following applications are included when you purchase the entire suite:

Adobe Bridge. Manage all of your digital assets, including photos, video clips, audio clips, and other media.

Adobe Story. Write your script using formatting presets and collaborate online with members of your creative team. Adobe Story Free can be downloaded for free, and Adobe Story Plus is available for purchase at www.adobe.com.

Prelude. Ingest your raw footage and create an assembly edit right away, adding searchable markers and temporal metadata.

Adobe Premiere Pro. The hub of your video-editing processes. Edit your video and audio in a timeline, apply color correction, and create an audio mix.

After Effects. Create motion graphics in 3D space, composite multiple layers of video and images, and generate visual effects.

Photoshop. Create multilayered bitmap image documents, edit still images, and create 3D graphics.

Illustrator. Create multilayered vector image documents and design logo graphics and digital illustrations.

Adobe Audition. Edit, mix, and restore multitrack audio.

SpeedGrade. Color grade your final video edit using presets or customized settings.

Adobe Media Encoder. Create multiple encoded versions of source files, Adobe Premiere Pro sequences, and After Effects compositions.

Flash Professional. Create animation and interactive multimedia content for the Web and mobile devices.

The lessons in this book touch on all of these applications to help you become familiar with them; however, they do not go deeply into using each one. Rather, this book focuses on the essential workflows and the right tools for the job when you use the applications together for your video projects. You'll learn video-making concepts along the way, and this book will point out other *Classroom in a Book* titles for your reference if you want more in-depth information on particular Adobe software applications.

Understanding the Creative Cloud user interface

Although each application performs a different function and features different tools, the overall look and feel of the Creative Cloud applications share many common elements. We touch on these elements here, but you'll learn more about each one in context when that particular application is covered while you go through the lessons in the book:

Toolbars. Each application has its own set of tools located in a toolbar at the top of the interface. The Selection, Hand, Zoom, Pen, and Type tools all work the same way across the suite. By hovering your mouse pointer over a tool in the toolbar, you can see a tool tip that shows the keyboard shortcut to access the tool.

Workspaces. All applications have customizable workspaces that allow you to move interface panels to fit your needs, as well as convenient presets for commonly used workspaces.

Timelines. Time-based applications like Adobe Premiere Pro, After Effects, Adobe Audition, Prelude, and Flash Professional all have a timeline that enables you to play back and quickly scan through layers or footage by adjusting a playhead.

Layers. Image applications like Photoshop and Illustrator allow a single image document to contain a stack of multiple layers of image data; each can have its own unique settings. After Effects compositions also use layers as objects stacked in a timeline.

Folders and bins. These are commonly used across Creative Cloud to organize project media within an application.

Using Dynamic Link

Adobe Premiere Pro, After Effects, and SpeedGrade all feature Dynamic Link, which enables you to send project elements between applications without any intermediate rendering. This greatly speeds up your workflow and saves you time.

For example, if you create a motion graphic in After Effects and want to add it to a sequence in Adobe Premiere Pro, you can import the raw, unrendered After Effects composition into your Adobe Premiere Pro project. Any changes you make to the After Effects composition are automatically reflected in your Adobe Premiere Pro sequence. We explain this in further detail in Chapter 5.

You can also send your projects from Adobe Premiere Pro to SpeedGrade using Dynamic Link without rendering or saving an intermediate file. You'll learn more about this in Chapter 8.

Working with media files in video production

It's important to know the difference between the types of media files and the ideal applications you use to edit them:

Video clips are movie files that originate from a video camera or exist as prerendered animations or other edited videos. Typical formats for these include .mov, .mp4, and .avi. These are typically used in Adobe Premiere Pro, After Effects, SpeedGrade, Flash Professional, and Prelude.

Audio clips are audio files that usually contain music, sound effects, and voice-over recordings. Typical formats for audio clips include .aiff, .wav, and .mp3. Although these can be used in Adobe Premiere Pro, After Effects, and Flash Professional as raw media, editing and mixing of audio clips can be more precisely and professionally edited in Adobe Audition. Be advised that .aiff and .wav formats allow for uncompressed audio data, whereas .mp3 is a compressed format and should not be used for raw audio in your edits. Although .mp3 files are smaller than their .aiff and .wav counterparts, the process of compressing audio to a smaller file removes data from them, resulting in audio that is not an exact copy of the original source.

Bitmap images are still images that are pixel based and are typically photographs or still frames from video. Some bitmap image file formats include .jpg, .tif, .png, and .tga. You should consider a few factors when deciding to using one bitmap image format over another. For instance, consider whether you need a bitmap image format that supports layers (.psd and .tiff support layers, whereas .jpg, .png, and .tga do not); whether you need a bitmap image format that supports embedded transparency, also referred to as an alpha channel (.psd, .tif, .png, and .tga do, whereas .jpg does not); and whether the format supports uncompressed image data (.psd, .tif, .png, and .tga do, whereas .jpg does not). You should use Photoshop to edit bitmap image files. Photoshop's native .psd format can contain layers, alpha channels, and uncompressed image data.

Vector images are still images or graphics that are vector based, meaning they are resolution independent. Because of this versatility, vector images are typically used for logo graphics. Typical vector image formats are .eps and the Illustrator native format, .ai. You should use Illustrator to create or edit vector images. By default, Illustrator will save graphics as .ai files, which may not be compatible on systems that don't have Illustrator installed. However, because the .eps format is not application-specific, these images are good to use as deliverable vector images.

Video format compatibility

Some video files will not play back on your system if the appropriate software is not installed. Formats like .avi and .wmv were developed for playback on the Windows operating system and may not play back on OS X without third-party software such as Flip4Mac (www.telestream.net/flip4mac/). Apple's .mov format is native to the Apple QuickTime media player, and the .mp4 format is cross-platform. They each have different ways of storing video data, which may result in compatibility issues when transferring from one device to another. Fortunately, Apple QuickTime can be downloaded to Windows and Linux machines to provide them with the ability to play .mov files. Media players like VLC by VideoLAN are available for download on Mac computers to provide support for Windows-based .avi files. Adobe Premiere Pro is able to edit nearly any type of video file that is playable on your computer without requiring you to transcode the clips beforehand, and Adobe Media Encoder can convert these playable media files into a grand array of different formats.

Codecs and extensions

The video codec, as its etymology "*compressor-de*compressor" indicates, compresses information into a convenient file and then later reverses the process by decompressing the data for interpretation by a playback system. Codecs are like languages—if your computer does not have a specific codec installed, it will not be able to read or write in that particular language. As newer codecs introduce better ways of encoding and decoding media, older codecs become antiquated and are less commonly used. The most commonly used codec for video sharing today is H.264, which is rooted in the cross-platform MPEG-4 format. Unlike other codecs that were developed for one specific usage, H.264 is renowned for its versatility among web, mobile, Blu-ray, and high-definition recording.

A video's codec relates to its file extension, but they are not synonymous. A video file's extension (like .mp4, .mov, .avi) reflects how data is stored and organized within. The container format also determines how the metadata and audio/video components interrelate. A container format like .mov can be encoded in one of many different codecs. Therefore, the extension does not describe how the file is encoded and decoded but rather how the data is internally structured. Both the codec and the file extension are elements that have a direct impact on the quality and the accessibility of a file.

You'll learn more about the importance of compression and file formats when exporting files in Chapter 9.

Photoshop and Illustrator documents (.psd and .ai, respectively) exist as self-contained files. As new layers and additional graphics are introduced into these multilayered documents, their file sizes will, in turn, get larger.

However, link-based project files, like those generated by Adobe Premiere Pro, After Effects, and Flash Professional, are not self-contained and act as "hubs" for all related project media. Project files exist separately from media files on your computer. This means that for a project file to function properly, it must be linked with all related media on your system.

Self-contained files, like .psd or .ai, can be moved from system to system and edited without requiring linkage to any other media files. Link-based project files, like those used by Adobe Premiere Pro, After Effects, SpeedGrade, and Flash Professional, do require active links to all associated media files. When you're working with link-based project files, it's best to store all associated media in a local project folder accompanied by the project files. This will make it easier to move projects between systems without breaking links to the media files.

Linking a project with media files

Let's do an exercise that will give you a glimpse of working with Adobe Premiere Pro and also show you how to link a project to media files. Make sure you've copied the Adobe Assets folder to your hard drive. You can download the assets from www.peachpit.com.

● **Note:** If you have not already down-loaded the project files for this lesson to your computer from your Account page, make sure to do so now. See "Getting Started" at the beginning of the book.

1   Launch Adobe Premiere Pro. You'll see the Welcome screen with a list of recently opened projects (if any) as well as three buttons at the bottom.

2   Click the Open Project button. Navigate to the Lesson 01 folder (Adobe Project Assets > Lessons > Lesson 01) on your hard drive. Select the Lesson_01 Start.prproj file and click Open.

The Adobe Premiere Pro user interface appears.

At the bottom left of the interface you'll see a Project panel with a list of folders (called bins) that have media organized in them. You'll also see a timeline at the bottom right that has clips in an edited sequence. The Timeline has a playhead that looks like a red vertical line with a yellow handle at the top. At the top right of the interface, you'll see the Program Monitor that shows the frame of your edited sequence where the playhead is currently parked.

Potential error messages

When opening an Adobe Premiere Pro project file that was last saved on a different computer, you may encounter a couple of error messages. Don't panic!

One such error message will tell you that the local scratch disk is not in the same place.

If this happens, choose File > Project Settings > Scratch Disks, then, for all settings in the Scratch Disks window, click the Browse button and navigate to a local folder on your hard drive where you want Adobe Premiere Pro to save your Captured Video and Audio, your Video and Audio Previews, and your Project Auto Saves.

Another error message you may encounter is one that tells you that there is a missing renderer.

This just means that the project file was last saved on a machine that was using a graphics processing unit (GPU) that is not present on the current machine. Again, don't panic. Just click OK and carry on.

3 Click the playhead's yellow handle and drag to the right, thereby moving through time in your sequence. This action is referred to as *scrubbing*. As you do this, notice that the Program Monitor shows many offline clips in the Timeline.

This is a fairly common occurrence, especially if a project file and project media have been copied to a different computer than the one on which the project originated. Although the project file opens and references to the media exist in the project, it still needs to be linked to all of the related media files for you to work with the media in the project.

Fortunately, link-based project files, like those from Adobe Premiere Pro and After Effects, allow you to easily link the clips in the project to the media files on your hard drive.

4 Using the Finder on OS X or Explorer on Windows, navigate to your Adobe Project Assets folder. Notice the subfolders for Audio, Exports, Footage, Graphics, and Lessons. It's good working practice to keep all of your project-related files organized so that they are easy to find when you need them.

5 Switch back to Adobe Premiere Pro.

If you have a project file open and are about to make one or more changes to it, it's also good working practice to save a version of your project file so that the older version is preserved in case you need to reference it later.

▶ **Tip:** Press Command+Tab (Alt+Tab) to switch between open applications quickly.

6 Choose File > Save As. Navigate to your Lesson 01 folder and type **Lesson_01_Relinked** in the Save As dialog. Then click the Save button.

Let's fix the offline media links in this project. You'll first open the bin for the offline media.

● **Note:** When the distinction is required, this book gives Windows keyboard shortcuts in parentheses.

7 In the Project panel, double-click the Footage bin.

It will open as a floating panel in your interface and show a few bins inside it.

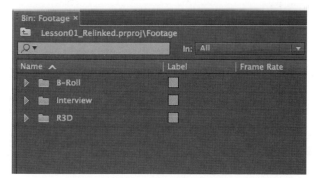

8 Double-click the Interview bin to open it and see a list of all of the Interview clips, which are currently offline. Notice that the icon next to each of these media files, or clips, currently looks like a document with a question mark, indicating that the media is offline.

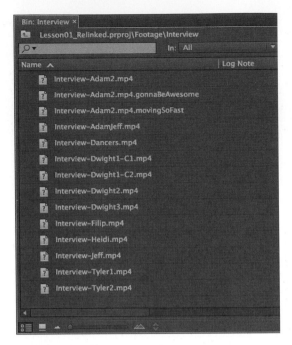

9 Because you need to relink all of these clips to files on your hard drive, select them all by pressing Command+A (Ctrl+A).

All of the clips in the bin will become highlighted, indicating that they are selected. Often, operations can only be performed on project items, such as clips in a bin or in the Timeline, if they are selected. On the other hand, it's important to keep track of what is selected in your interface so that you don't accidentally apply changes to them.

10 With all of the clips in the Interview bin selected, choose Clip > Link Media.

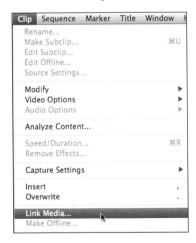

A Link Media window appears, listing all of the unlinked clips.

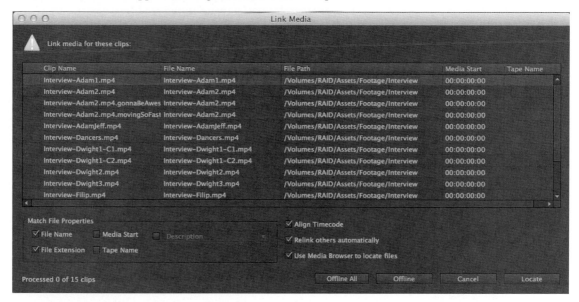

11 Notice the check box at the bottom center of this window, marked "Relink others automatically." If all of the missing clips are in the same folder, relinking one of them relinks all of them.

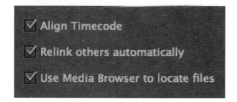

12 If it isn't already selected, choose the first missing clip in the list, Interview-Adam1.mp4, and then click the Locate button at the bottom right of the Link Media window.

13 A Locate File window will open, showing the chosen clip and all other clips in the same folder. Since all of the missing clips were in this folder, Adobe Premiere Pro found the rest, as indicated by the clips' video thumbnails. Click OK. All missing clips in this folder will be relinked, and the Locate File window and the Link Media window will close.

14 Select the Interview bin and press Command+W (Ctrl+W) to close it. Then close the Footage bin.

▶ **Tip:** Press the spacebar to start and stop playback of a sequence in your Timeline.

15 Now scrub the playhead through your Timeline. You should see that all of the B-Roll clips have been relinked and now appear in your Program Monitor.

16 Press the Home key or scrub your playhead all the way to the left to go to the beginning of the edited sequence. Press the spacebar to play the sequence.

▶ **Tip:** It's a good idea to save your work often.

17 Press Command+S (Ctrl+S) to save your Adobe Premiere Pro project file.

You should now be familiar with the concept of linking a project file with project media on your system.

● **Note:** Important! Currently, Adobe Premiere Pro CC does not retain interpret-footage settings on clips even though those clips don't need relinking. Refer to the Getting Started section "Interpret frame rate of linked files" for steps on fixing this issue so that all clips are properly modified in the Timeline.

18 Press Command+Q (Ctrl+Q) to quit Adobe Premiere Pro because you won't need it for the remainder of this lesson.

Real-time playback and editing

Improvements in Creative Cloud yield speed enhancements to Adobe Premiere Pro, After Effects, Photoshop, and Illustrator.

Mercury Playback Engine

The Mercury Playback Engine has brought extraordinary performance to Adobe Premiere Pro since version CS4. In Adobe Premiere Pro, performance and stability have been boosted yet again, thanks to optimizations and enhancements that let you smoothly play and scrub through multilayer, multiformat sequences that include HD, 5K, and even higher-resolution footage. Effects play back in real time, and there are no skipped frames. The enhanced Mercury Playback Engine is dynamically scalable, natively 64-bit, GPU-accelerated, and optimized for today's multicore CPUs—and it has improved support for third-party hardware. Although having a supported GPU is ideal, you can still work on a computer without one. This allows you to work on dense, complex projects using a fast, GPU-enabled workstation, and then bring them onto a lesser-powered computer and continue working.

To check whether you are using GPU acceleration in Adobe Premiere Pro, under Video Rendering and Playback, choose Project > Project Settings > General.

Under Video Renderer and Playback, click the menu for Renderer. If Mercury Playback Engine GPU Acceleration (OpenCL) is not grayed out, then choose it. Otherwise, choose Mercury Playback Engine Software Only. Click OK.

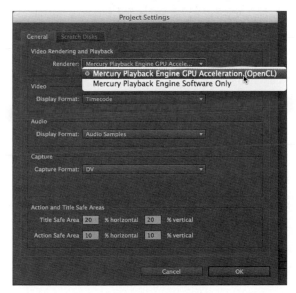

Systems with GPUs that support CUDA (Compute Unified Device Architecture) or OpenCL technology allow Adobe Premiere Pro to fully utilize the Mercury Playback Engine.

For more information on the Mercury Playback Engine and supported GPUs, go to www.adobe.com/products/premiere/mercury-playback-engine.html.

For more information on CUDA and OpenCL technologies in general, go to http://blogs.adobe.com/premiereprotraining/2011/02/cuda-mercury-playback-engine-and-adobe-premiere-pro.html.

GPU cards

Video editing and motion graphics can take a toll on your computer if you're using dated hardware, so it is important to be mindful of the video card specifications that will help to boost your experience with the Creative Cloud software. Many effects in Adobe Premiere Pro are GPU accelerated, and rendering 3D scenes in After Effects is greatly enhanced when the GPU is enabled. Unfortunately, not every GPU card is supported by the Adobe software. Most of the latest Nvidia cards are supported for GPU acceleration, specifically the Nvidia GeForce and Nvidia Quadro series. PC users will find an easier time choosing a graphics card than Mac users, because only a small handful of GPUs are currently available for Macs. Check the Previews tab in your Adobe After Effects preferences to check whether your current video card supports GPU acceleration.

CUDA vs. OpenCL

The video community is involved in a contentious debate as to whether CUDA or OpenCL is the best option for a computing platform within the scope of video editing. Both are processing languages that have different ways of dealing with image data. Graphics-intensive software is often built from the ground up with only one of these languages in mind, and in the case of the Creative Cloud applications, only CUDA acceleration is currently supported. However, as updates and workarounds continue to become available, you will continue to find a wealth of resources online to help you configure your hardware to work with the latest Adobe software, or to help you figure out which graphics card you should purchase given the system you are working on.

Global Performance Cache

The Global Performance Cache feature is a revolution "under the hood" that makes After Effects faster and more responsive by taking full advantage of your computer's hardware. The Global Performance Cache comprises a set of technologies: a global RAM cache, a persistent disk cache, and a new graphics pipeline.

The Global Performance Cache is covered in more depth in Chapter 5.

Mercury Graphics Engine

The Mercury Graphics Engine in Photoshop uses the power of your computer's GPU to speed up the performance of Photoshop. Many features in Photoshop take advantage of the Mercury Graphics Engine, including the all-new Crop tool, Puppet Warp, Liquify, Adaptive Wide Angle, and the Lighting Effects Gallery. Doing 3D work in Adobe RayTrace mode in Photoshop is also quickened thanks to the Mercury Graphics Engine.

Mercury Performance System

The Mercury Performance System in Illustrator speeds up your workflow when creating and editing your vector graphics. Native 64-bit support on Mac OS and Windows provides access to all available RAM on your system. Overall performance optimization is apparent when you open, save, and export large files. Previews are faster, and interaction in general is more responsive.

Creating a disk image to back up your system regularly

Your system hard drive holds your operating system files and your applications. After continual use of the applications, cached data and preference files tend to accumulate and slow your computer's performance. We recommend that you create an archive of your system hard drive that has a fresh install of the operating system and all regularly used applications. Such an archive can be saved as a disk image file on a separate hard drive.

To do this, first create a fresh install of your operating system and applications on your system hard drive. Don't copy any project files or media to your system drive after you do this. Your system drive should only have the operating system and applications, nothing else. Then create an archive of your system drive. On OS X, you can use Disk Utility to create a disk image of your system drive. On Windows, you can use the "Back up your files" feature to create a system image.

In the event that you need to restore your operating system and applications due to unbearably slow performance or a complete hard drive failure, all you need to do is simply restore your system drive from your system archive rather than reinstall your operating system and applications one at a time.

To go one step further, if your computer allows you to easily remove the physical system hard drive and replace it with another, we recommend that you have at least one spare hard drive that has your operating system and applications already installed on it. You should restore your system hard drive monthly or on an otherwise regular basis.

Review questions

1   What is the difference between a timeline and a bin?

2   What is Dynamic Link?

3   What are some common file formats for video clips?

4   What is a codec?

5   In Adobe Premiere Pro, how do you relink offline media in your project?

Review answers

1 A bin is used to store raw project media that can be included in multiple timelines, whereas a timeline contains instances of project media that were added from bins.

2 Dynamic Link is a feature that enables users to send project elements between Adobe Premiere Pro, After Effects, and Encore without any intermediate rendering.

3 Common file formats for video clips include .mov, .avi, and .mp4.

4 A codec is a compression/decompression algorithm that allows a video file size to be shrunk so that the video clips are more manageable on a wider range of computer systems.

5 To relink media, select the clips in a bin that need to be relinked (a document with a question mark indicates the media is offline) and choose Project > Link Media. In the Link & Locate window, select the media item you want to relink then click Locate. The clip and any other missing items will relink and appear in your Program Monitor.

2 ORGANIZING THE MEDIA FILES FOR YOUR PROJECT

Lesson overview

The way you plan and organize your media files at the beginning of a project affects how easily and efficiently you can work in the later phases. In this lesson, you'll learn how to

- Use Adobe Bridge to manage, preview, and add metadata to your media files
- Understand basic film script page elements
- Use Adobe Story to write and collaborate on a script
- Use Prelude to ingest and add comments to video clips
- Create bins to organize your media files
- Assemble a rough cut
- Add time-based comments
- Export your Prelude project for use in Adobe Premiere Pro

 This lesson will take approximately 50 minutes to complete.

Download the project files for this lesson from the Lesson & Update Files tab on your Account page at www.peachpit.com and store them on your computer in a convenient location, as described in the Getting Started section of this book.

Your Account page is also where you'll find any updates to the chapters or to the lesson files. Look on the Lesson & Update Files tab to access the most current content.

Clip thumbnails in Adobe Bridge

About Adobe Bridge

Adobe Bridge is an application available with your Creative Cloud subscription. It is digital asset management software that provides integrated, centralized access to your project files and enables you to quickly browse through your creative assets visually—regardless of what format they're in—making it easy for you to locate, organize, and view your files.

In addition, Adobe Bridge allows you to add searchable keywords to your files to make these files easier to find. You can add frequently accessed folders on your system to a Favorites list as well. Adobe Bridge also can do batch processing of media files, such as applying a Photoshop Action to a folder of images or renaming several files for more efficient organization.

Naming and managing your project and media files

Having a strategy for how you name and organize your files is fundamental. When possible, use clear, simple naming that describes what is in the file or folder. Organize your media files into folders based on category.

You'll use Adobe Bridge to browse through the media files that we've included for you to work with in this *Classroom in a Book*. We've named the files and organized them into folders based on a simple, effective strategy that you can use in your own productions.

Navigating and previewing media

When you're beginning the post-production of a video project, it's good working practice to look at all of the footage and media before you start editing. You become familiar with the material you'll be working with and also discover anything that might be wrong with the footage.

Adobe Bridge allows you to browse through your footage and other media, and it can provide technical details about your footage and media.

Note: If you have not already downloaded the project files for this lesson to your computer from your Account page, make sure to do so now. See "Getting Started" at the beginning of the book.

1 Launch Adobe Bridge.

   At the top left of the interface, you will see two tabs, Favorites and Folders.

2 Click the Favorites tab, and navigate to the Assets folder.

▶ **Tip:** You can drag a folder from a Finder (or Explorer) window to the Favorites panel in Adobe Bridge to add it to your Favorites.

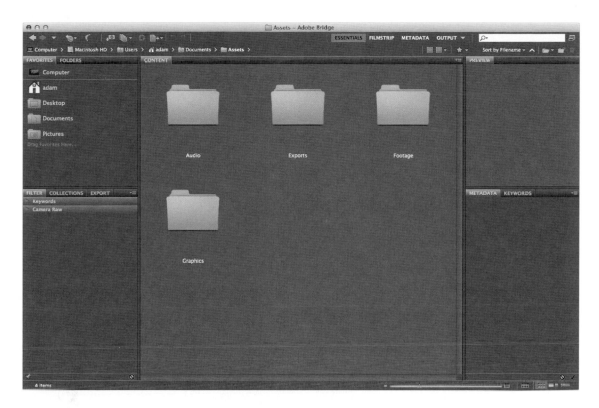

3 Choose Window > Workspace > Reset Standard Workspaces.

4 Then choose Window > Workspace > Essentials.

5 Double-click the Assets folder to reveal its contents.

The assets are organized by category: Audio, Exports, Footage, and Graphics. This is a simple way to organize assets at a high level in any video project.

6 Double-click the Footage folder and then double-click the Interview folder to reveal its contents.

You can adjust the size of the clip thumbnails by using the slider at the bottom-right of the interface.

The interview clips are all named "Interview" with the name of the person interviewed. They are grouped together in this folder for easy access later in the editing process.

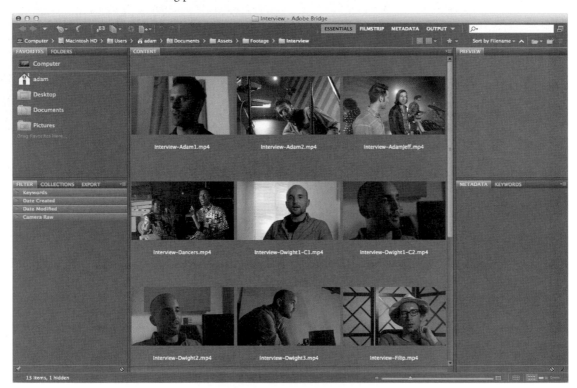

7 Click the clip Interview-Dwight1-C1.mp4 to select it.

The clip is now visible in the Preview panel.

8 In the Preview panel, click the Play button to preview the clip. When you're finished, click the Pause button to stop playback.

▶ **Tip:** You can also drag the playback bar to scrub forward and backward through the video, which is useful when you're choosing which clips to use.

Media asset management storage and integration

If you work in a facility with other video professionals, it is usually advantageous to have a shared asset management and storage system to streamline workflow and minimize costs.

Many Adobe partners offer products and services to help you do just that, such as online storage, asset management, hardware solutions for video acquisition and conversion, and software solutions for creating broadcast graphics.

You'll find a current list on the Adobe website at www.adobe.com/solutions/broadcasting/partners.html.

Working with metadata

Simply put, *metadata* is data about your data.

Looking at a video file, you'd have no idea what is contained within the file without metadata. For example, what video format is it? What are the frame size and frame rate? What is the duration? Is this a good take or a bad take? Metadata describes these and other attributes of the media files you use in video production.

One of the advantages of using Adobe Bridge as a file-management tool is that you can create custom metadata fields and then add them to your media files. Because the metadata stays with the media, it will be usable in all facets of your workflow down the line. For example, if you enter comments about the video in Adobe Bridge, you'll be able to see those comments when you're working with that video later in the other components of Creative Cloud.

In the Metadata panel in Adobe Bridge, you'll see some of the metadata attached to the Interview-Dwight1-C1.mp4 clip that you currently have selected.

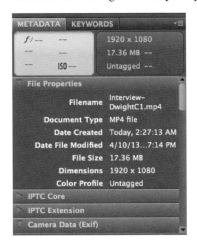

You can add your own metadata to any file using Adobe Bridge.

Adding metadata to your media

Adobe Bridge provides an easy way to add metadata to your footage for future reference when editing.

Metadata can include information like scene description, shot number, and shooter's name. You can also add a comment about qualitative information, such as whether a take is usable or not, which can help streamline the editing process. This process of adding comments to your media is known as *logging clips*.

Let's look at the basics on adding metadata by adding a "Best Take" comment.

1   Using the scroll bar in the Metadata panel, scroll down until the Video category is visible.

2   Click the gray space directly to the right of Log Comment.

3   Type **Best Take**.

4   Press Enter.

The comment is now attached to the file and will stay with it throughout the rest of the workflow.

▶ **Tip:** When you're logging clips, it's very useful to add notes about camera angles or different takes, making it much easier to find and work with your clips.

About Adobe Story

Now that we've discussed some basics about naming files and adding metadata, let's change gears and talk about Adobe Story, which is an application that simplifies formatting scripts for film, television, and other outlets so that you can focus on writing your story.

Adobe Story is more than just a scriptwriting application. During the pre-production phase of a project, scriptwriters can use Adobe Story to store their scripts in the cloud. After all of the footage has been shot, video editors can import an Adobe Story Script format file to Adobe Premiere Pro to compare the dialogue in the script with a speech analysis of selected clips. This makes it easier for editors to locate segments of footage with certain dialogue.

With a paid subscription to Adobe Story Plus, you can automatically sync scripts and other Adobe Story documents with other collaborators. Because scenes are numbered in the script, this information can be used during the production phase.

Producers can use Adobe Story Plus to automatically generate production reports and schedules that relate to certain scenes.

The first exercise in this section is intended to give you a brief overview of how to properly format audio/visual (A/V) script page elements with Adobe Story, and the subsequent exercise covers some of the collaboration features found in Adobe Story Plus.

Basic film script page elements

A screenplay is more than just a script with scene descriptions and character dialogue: It's also a blueprint for producers and directors that makes it easy for them to break down what is needed to shoot a movie and helps them to budget costs for equipment, actors, locations, and so on. A screenplay follows a certain format that is based on standards that were established in the 1980s. These standards have been adopted in screenwriting software and are still in use today.

The following is a brief list of screenplay formatting elements that you can use in your script when you're writing with Adobe Story:

Scene heading. This is a brief indicator of the location of a scene and what time of day it takes place. Interior and exterior locations are denoted by the abbreviations INT and EXT.

Character. When a character is introduced in a screenplay, it is important to clearly indicate this to the reader, which is why the character's name is written in capital letters. This element also allows a producer to see at a glance how many actors will be needed to shoot a scene or a movie when a script is being budgeted.

General. At the beginning of a scene, it's a good idea to describe what you intend the viewer to see. If your script needs to indicate the presence of props, visual effects, sound effects, or anything that the producer might need to include in the production's budget, indicate those items with capital letters.

Dialogue. When a character has a spoken line of dialogue, the character's name (using capital letters) and the dialogue are indented to the center of the page.

Action. When something happens in a scene that is not dialogue, write a brief visual description of it. Be as concise as possible; a screenplay is not a novel.

Parenthetical. This element is brief stage direction that is indented on the page with dialogue so that the flow of the scene is not interrupted with a separate general description. Keep parenthetical directions very brief.

Shot. Whenever a specific camera direction (pan, zoom, dolly, etc.) is needed for a shot, indicate this using capital letters. The producer can then see at a glance if any extra camera equipment (special lenses, camera crane, etc.) will be required and needs to be included in the production budget.

Transition. This element indicates a specific type of transition (cut, dissolve, wipe, etc.) at the end of a scene as a general guideline for the editor(s).

Starting a new A/V script in Adobe Story

To get a taste of what Adobe Story can do, let's write a sample page of A/V script.

Briefly, an A/V script is a standard for scripts that are used for TV broadcasts, documentaries, commercials, and other non-film productions. An A/V script page is divided into two columns, with visuals on the left and audio on the right. Each row in the script page describes what is seen and heard at any given time. As when writing any kind of movie script, you want to keep your descriptions as brief as possible, as each page of script is intended to represent a certain amount of screen time (usually one page represents one minute of screen time).

Let's begin!

1 Open your web browser.

2 In the Address field, type the URL **story.adobe.com** and press Return (Enter).

3 On the Adobe Story home page, click Sign In.

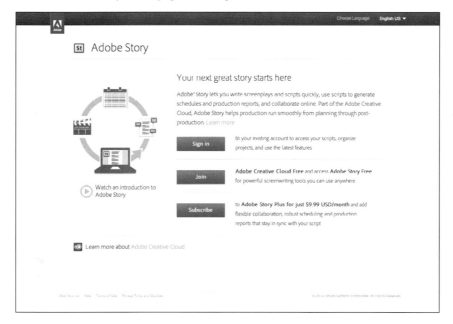

4 In the Sign In window that appears, enter your Adobe ID and Password and then click Sign In. If you don't already have an Adobe ID, follow the onscreen instructions to create one, being sure to accept the terms of use.

Your web browser loads the Adobe Story interface.

5 Click the Projects menu at the top left of the interface and choose New Project.

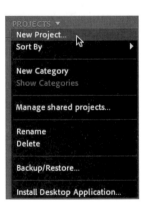

6 In the Create New Project dialog, enter **Making of If We Make It** as the name for your project and then click Create.

7 At the top of the Story interface, click the + New button to create a new script in your project.

8 In the Create New Document - Adobe Story window, click the Type menu and choose A/V Script (Two Columns).

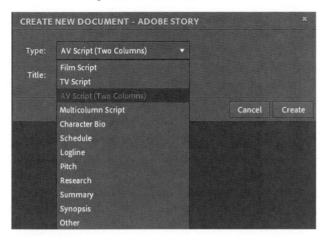

9 Double-click in the Title field and type **Making of If We Make It**.

10 Click Create. The script's first blank page appears.

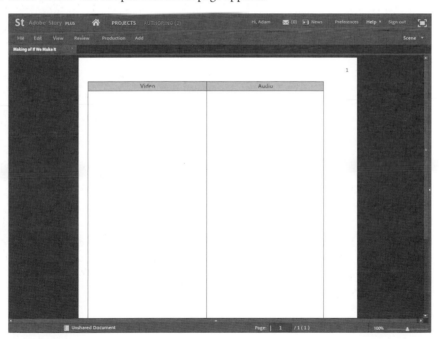

11 Notice that Adobe Story has formatted your page by automatically splitting it into two columns, with headers for Video and Audio.

Choose the left column and begin writing.

Note: GFX is A/V shorthand for "graphics."

12 Type **GFX: MAKING OF IF WE MAKE IT, THE LATEST MUSIC VIDEO BY POOLSIDE**.

13 Press the Tab key to move your cursor to the right column. Here, as a description of what we will hear as the intro graphics are shown, type **MUSIC BEGINS: "IF WE MAKE IT" BY POOLSIDE**.

14 Create a new row in the script page below the current one by pressing the Tab key twice.

Note: MCU is short for the photography term *medium close up*, which denotes a shot of someone from the chest up, typically used in documentary interview footage.

15 In this new row, type the description of what the documentary will show next. Type **MCU ON DWIGHT FROM 12FPS**.

16 Press the Tab key to move your cursor to the Audio column of this row. Here, type **DWIGHT INTRODUCTION, TALKING ABOUT POOLSIDE, MAKING THEIR NEW MUSIC VIDEO**.

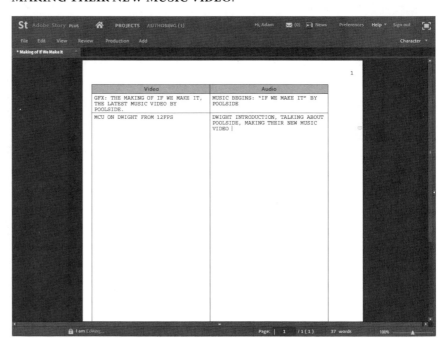

Obviously, before shooting a documentary, you won't know exactly what your interview subjects are going to say, and therefore you cannot write it into the script! But an A/V script is useful to help plan what your documentary needs to show and what kind of sound bites to capture during production.

17 Press the Tab key to create a new row. Now type **B-ROLL: 12FPS AND POOLSIDE, TALKING AND PLANNING.** *B-roll* is footage shot with the intent to show the viewer a variety of different things, which gives editors more options when they want to cut away from the interview subject and to obscure cuts in the edit that they don't intend the viewers to see.

18 Copy the remainder of the script, as shown in the figure here. If you need to edit text, choose the cell that contains that text and then edit.

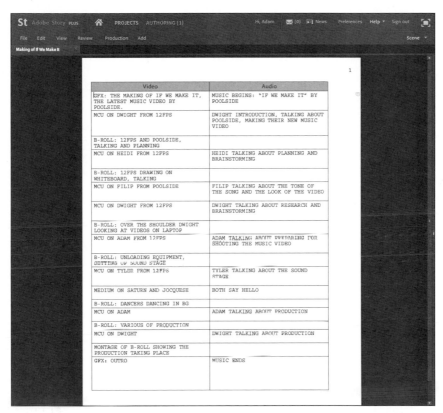

19 Be sure to save your script! Choose the Save Now button at the bottom of the Story interface.

Collaborating with others on your script

The free version of Adobe Story, which is available with your Adobe ID account, gives you the ability to craft your story using industry-standard formatting. However, many collaboration features are only available with a paid subscription to Adobe Story Plus.

The following exercise takes advantage of these collaboration features. If you do not have a paid subscription to Adobe Story Plus, proceed to the next section, "Planning and managing your production with Adobe Story."

Adobe Story Plus

If scriptwriting is a regular part of your workflow, it might make sense to upgrade to Adobe Story Plus. Not only does it feature enhanced scriptwriting tools—like trackable history of changes, customizable script templates, and industry-standard formatting—it also allows you to collaborate with project team members online. Many of the online features include tools for scheduling and reporting, such as permission assignment, email notifications, and the ability to organize and sync scene elements like props and costumes.

One of the primary advantages of using Adobe Story Plus to write your scripts is that it enables you to collaborate with others and track changes in a single interface. This removes the "what version is this?" factor of sharing and working on the same document with multiple contributors.

Adobe Story Plus helps to ensure that any changes to dialogue, shot lists, or other copy in a script are associated with a specific user and tracks when those changes were made.

1   Choose File > Share.

2 In the dialog that appears, enter the email addresses of people you want to collaborate with and assign them roles (co-author, reviewer, or reader).

3 Select the Send E-Mail Notification check box.

4 Click OK to add your collaborators and send them an email inviting them to collaborate on your script.

5 Choose Review > Start Tracking Changes.

6 Choose View > Track Changes Toolbar.

Now you'll be able to see, in red text on your script, what changes have been made and by whom.

Planning and managing your production with Adobe Story

Adobe Story is more than just a collaborative screenwriting application. It is also a production-management tool that allows production managers, assistant directors, and other production team members to coordinate schedules, as well as generate lists and production reports.

For example, a director can generate a shooting schedule based on scenes that are shot at a location or at a studio. Any changes to a schedule are automatically updated for other project team members.

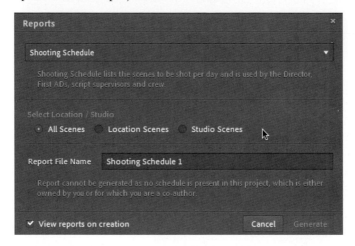

Or a production manager can generate a list of all characters, all actors, or all sets to be used.

A script from Adobe Story can also be used in the post-production phase of a project.

Since a script written in Adobe Story can store information about specific characters and locations, that information is saved as embedded metadata that can be read by Adobe Premiere Pro to quickly attach scene data to video clips, generate text from speech using the script as reference, and streamline the editing process.

About Prelude

With modern digital video cameras that use memory cards, it has become possible during the production phase of a project to not only view footage immediately after it is shot, but to transfer the footage to a computer's hard drive while on set.

Prelude allows you to begin organizing your footage right after the footage has been transferred to a computer from a camera. Prelude was also designed for producers (and non-editors) to be able to mark up clips for their editors as part of a collaborative workflow. You can ingest entire raw clips or selected portions of clips to a Prelude project. Once clips are ingested to Prelude, you can add descriptive metadata to them, mark subclips, and insert searchable comments. This added metadata will be saved with the clips when you send your rough cut from Prelude to Adobe Premiere Pro, which can help streamline the editing process.

In this exercise you'll ingest the interview raw clips to a project in Prelude, apply metadata to some clips, create a rough cut of the clips, and then send the rough cut to Adobe Premiere Pro.

Ingesting media and working with metadata in Prelude

Let's go through the process of ingesting the raw footage for the project into Prelude so that you can begin logging and commenting on the footage.

1   Launch Prelude and click New Project.

2   By default, Prelude saves a new project to its own Projects folder. But instead, navigate to the Lesson 02 folder (Assets > Lessons > Lesson 02) and open it.

3   Name your project **Poolside Ingest** and click Save.

4 Click the Ingest button. The Ingest panel opens.

As with Adobe Bridge, you'll see a list of the contents of your computer's hard drive(s) on the left of the interface.

▶ **Tip:** Click the dropdown menu at the top left of the interface to quickly display the Home Directory.

5 Navigate to the Assets folder, then the Footage folder, and finally the Interview folder to reveal its contents.

You can hover your mouse pointer over a thumbnail and scrub through it to preview its contents.

▶ **Tip:** Use the search box to quickly find files and items in folders with lots of content.

6 Drag your mouse pointer to one of the thumbnails and park it there, but do not click the thumbnail.

Interview-Adam2.mp4   Interview-

7 Move your mouse pointer left and right to scrub through the video.

If you want to ingest just a portion of a video clip, set In and Out points, defining the portion of the video to be ingested.

8 Click any of the thumbnails in the Ingest panel.

9 Drag the scrubber to a frame toward the beginning of the clip.

10 Press the I key to set an In point.

The thumbnail now shows a shortened Timeline, indicating that the portion of the video prior to the In point will not be ingested.

11 Drag the scrubber to a frame toward the end of the clip.

12 Press the O key to set an Out point.

Interview-Adam2.mp4   Interview-I

Note that to ingest only part of a clip, Prelude would need to make a trimmed copy of the file and it would only do that if the Transfer Clips to Destination check box is selected along with Transcode.

Because you actually want to ingest this entire clip, reset the In and Out points to their original locations.

13 Drag the scrubber to the beginning of the clip and press the I key.

14 Drag the scrubber to the end of the clip and press the O key.

15 You can select which clips and folders you want to ingest simply by selecting the check box under their corresponding thumbnails. Deselected clips and folders will not be ingested into your project. However, in this exercise you'll be ingesting all the clips and folders contained within the Footage folder.

16 Navigate to the Footage folder at the left of the Ingest interface.

17 Click the Check All button at the bottom of the Ingest window to select all the clips.

pre_filip_laughing.m4v

Check All   Uncheck All

▶ **Tip:** The shortcut for marking clips is to press the V key. You can then select multiple clips and press the V key to mark all selected clips for ingest.

18 Click the Ingest button to ingest your selected clips.

Cancel   Ingest

Copying and transcoding footage to a new location

In most scenarios you'll be ingesting media from memory cards (such as SD or CompactFlash) or a hard drive and copying it to a different location. Prelude can automatically copy your media to your destination of choice as part of the ingest process.

To set Prelude to do that, locate the Transfer Options on the right side of the Ingest dialog and select the Transfer Clips to Destination check box. Then choose a Primary Destination folder on your computer. You can add more destinations by clicking the Add Destination button.

In some cases you may receive media that needs to be transcoded—or saved as a different file format and/or with different video and audio settings—to work with Adobe Premiere Pro. If this is the case, select the Transcode check box in the Ingest dialog and use the Transcode presets to save the media with your desired settings upon ingest.

Adding notes to footage

The log comment you added in Adobe Bridge, in the earlier section "Adding meta-data to your media," remains attached to the file as metadata. You can view this comment in Prelude and add new comments.

A typical workflow involves ingesting files and then adding the notes or log comments. Prelude is perfectly suited for this.

1 In the Project panel, double-click the clip Interview-Dwight1-C1.mp4.

2 Choose Window > Metadata. Click the disclosure triangle next to Dynamic Media and then scroll down the list until the Log Comment field is visible.

   Note that the comment you entered in Adobe Bridge is still attached to the file.

3 In the Project panel, double-click the clip Interview-Dwight1-C2.mp4.

4 In the Metadata panel, type **Second Camera** in the Log Comment field and press Return (Enter). Close out of the Metadata panel in preparation for the next lesson.

The comment is added to the file and will be attached to the clip throughout the rest of the workflow.

Creating bins

In film and video production, the folders you create to organize your media files are called *bins*. The term *bins* dates back to traditional film editing when you literally sorted your physical clips of film into actual bins.

It's essential when starting a video editing project to organize your media into bins. This will help you to quickly locate specific clips when the editing process is underway.

1   In the Project panel, click the New Bin icon. A new bin appears in the Project panel.

2   Name the bin **Interviews** and press Return (Enter) to confirm.

3   Click the Interview-Adam1.mp4 clip to select it. Then hold down the Shift key and click the Interview-Tyler2.mp4 clip to select it, thus selecting all clips in between. Drag these selected interview clips into the Interview bin.

Assembling a rough cut

You can begin creating simple assembly edits in Prelude, either to get a head start on editing or to assemble clips for another editor if you're working on a project as part of a team.

1   Click the Create a New Rough Cut icon.

2   In the Create Rough Cut dialog, enter the name **Interview Assembly** and save the rough cut to your Lesson 02 folder.

3   Make sure you switch from Thumbnail view to List view in your Project panel by clicking the List View icon.

The rough cut should now be visible in your Project panel.

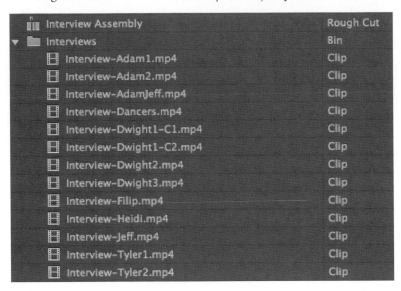

Interview Assembly	Rough Cut
▾ Interviews	Bin
Interview–Adam1.mp4	Clip
Interview–Adam2.mp4	Clip
Interview–AdamJeff.mp4	Clip
Interview–Dancers.mp4	Clip
Interview–Dwight1–C1.mp4	Clip
Interview–Dwight1–C2.mp4	Clip
Interview–Dwight2.mp4	Clip
Interview–Dwight3.mp4	Clip
Interview–Filip.mp4	Clip
Interview–Heidi.mp4	Clip
Interview–Jeff.mp4	Clip
Interview–Tyler1.mp4	Clip
Interview–Tyler2.mp4	Clip

4   Double-click the Interview Assembly rough cut to open it in the Timeline.

Let's add some clips to the rough cut.

5   Open the Interviews bin and drag the clip Interview-Filip.mp4 to the Timeline.

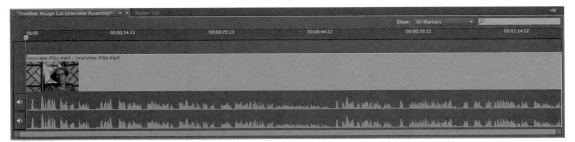

6   Drag the clip Interview-Adam1.mp4 to the right of the first clip in the Timeline and drop it there. The second clip is now inserted after the first clip.

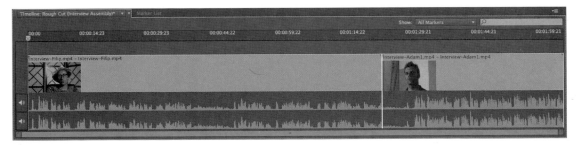

7 Drag the clip Interview-Dwight1-C1.mp4 to the left of the first clip in the Timeline panel and drop it there. The third clip is now inserted before the first clip.

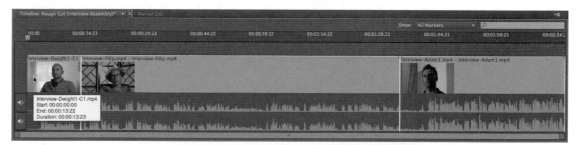

8 Drag the clip Interview-Heidi.mp4 in between the first two clips on the Timeline. The fourth clip is now inserted in between the existing clips.

9 Press the spacebar to play back your rough cut.

10 Choose File > Save to save your project.

Adding time-based comments

You may want to specify which segment of a clip you want to use in the edit. You can enter comments on clips in your Prelude Timeline that pertain to specific parts of your clips. These comments will be available in Adobe Premiere Pro when you move to the editing part of the workflow.

1   In your Timeline, double-click the clip Interview-Filip.mp4.

2   In the Marker Type panel, click the Comment button.

3   Type **use this section** to enter the comment, and press Return (Enter).

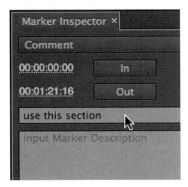

You'll see the comment in the Timeline starting at whatever frame your playhead was parked on. You can adjust the In and Out points of the comment to indicate which portion of the clip it pertains to.

4 In the Timeline, play the Interview-Filip.mp4 clip. Set the playhead to 00:00:10:17, when Filip starts to say, "with this particular song…." Drag the left edge of the comment to this frame to set its In point.

5 Play the Interview-Filip.mp4 clip in the Timeline. Find the frame, at approximately 00:00:29:00, when Filip says, "accent that contrast through the video." Drag the right edge of the comment to this frame to set its Out point.

▶ **Tip:** It's helpful to add comments about camera movements and live audio.

It's also possible to set comment In and Out points by scrubbing your playhead in the Timeline and then clicking the In and Out buttons in the Marker Inspector panel.

6 To return to the rough cut, click the Timeline: Interview-Filip.mp4 text at the top of the Timeline and then choose Timeline: Rough Cut (Interview Assembly) from the menu.

Sending your project to Adobe Premiere Pro

All of the work you've done so far is prep work for the next step of the workflow, which is to edit your project in Adobe Premiere Pro. A single menu selection is all it takes to move your project from Prelude to Adobe Premiere Pro.

1   Click the Project panel.

2   Choose Edit > Select All to select all of the items in the project.

If you want to send just certain items to Adobe Premiere Pro, not your entire project, simply select those items in the Project panel. Any items not selected will not be sent to Adobe Premiere Pro.

▶ **Tip:** You can also right-click a clip or sequence in your Project panel and choose Send to Premiere Pro from the menu.

3   Press Command+S (Ctrl+S) to save your project. Then choose File > Send to Premiere Pro.

Adobe Premiere Pro will launch, if it is not already open, and will create a new project for you.

● **Note:** If Adobe Premiere Pro is already open when you send a rough cut from Prelude, the currently open Adobe Premiere Pro project will receive the rough cut.

4 In the New Project dialog, click the Browse button.

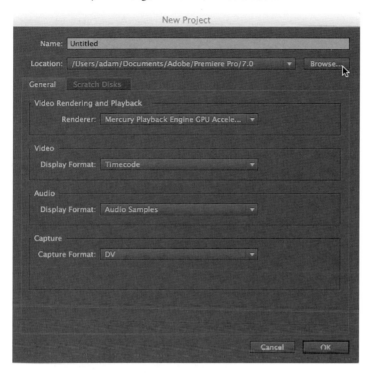

5 Navigate to your Lesson 02 folder and click Choose.

6 In the Name field, type **Poolside Edit 01** and click OK.

All of your footage (with metadata still attached), the bin you created, and the rough cut you created are now in your Adobe Premiere Pro project.

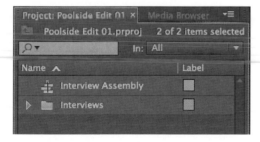

7 Press Command+S (Ctrl+S) to save your Adobe Premiere Pro project.

8 Press Command+Q (Ctrl+Q) to quit Adobe Premiere Pro.

Although it is important to demonstrate how to bring a rough edit from Prelude to Adobe Premiere Pro, the next lesson in this book shows you the essential workflow, and more likely scenario, of creating a new project from scratch in Adobe Premiere Pro.

Review questions

1 What is a simple and effective way of organizing your media into folders?

2 What is metadata, and why is it useful?

3 How do you format text in a script?

4 How do you collaborate with others on your script?

5 When ingesting media, how do you ingest only a portion of a clip?

6 How do you send footage and rough cuts from Prelude to Adobe Premiere Pro?

Review answers

1 Organizing your media by asset type (Footage, Audio, Graphics) is simple and effective.

2 Metadata is information about your data. It contains information such as frame resolution, frame rate, clip duration, and so on. Metadata provides useful information to streamline your video production workflow.

3 The Formatting menu in Adobe Story lets you easily format your script the preferred, industry-standard way.

4 Choosing File > Share in Adobe Story lets you invite and assign roles to collaborators.

5 Setting In and Out points on a clip in the Prelude Ingest panel lets you specify which portion of the clip is ingested, but only if it's marked for transcoding.

6 Select all desired clips and rough cuts in the Prelude Project panel, and then choose File > Send to Premiere Pro.

3 CREATING A BASIC EDIT

Lesson overview

The editing tool is the hub of the video post-production workflow, so understanding how to do basic editing with the Adobe Premiere Pro component of Creative Cloud is a fundamental skill. In this lesson, you'll learn how to

- Create a new project and import media files with the Media Browser
- Interpret and view footage
- Organize your project by creating bins
- Create subclips
- Use the Timeline to create and edit a sequence
- Work with tracks on the Timeline
- Reorder and remove clips from your sequence
- Adjust audio levels
- Trim your edit points and use the Dynamic Timeline Trimming feature in Adobe Premiere Pro
- Add markers to clips and sequences
- Use the Snap feature in the Timeline

 This lesson will take approximately 180 minutes to complete.

Download the project files for this lesson from the Lesson & Update Files tab on your Account page at www.peachpit.com and store them on your computer in a convenient location, as described in the Getting Started section of this book.

Your Account page is also where you'll find any updates to the chapters or to the lesson files. Look on the Lesson & Update Files tab to access the most current content.

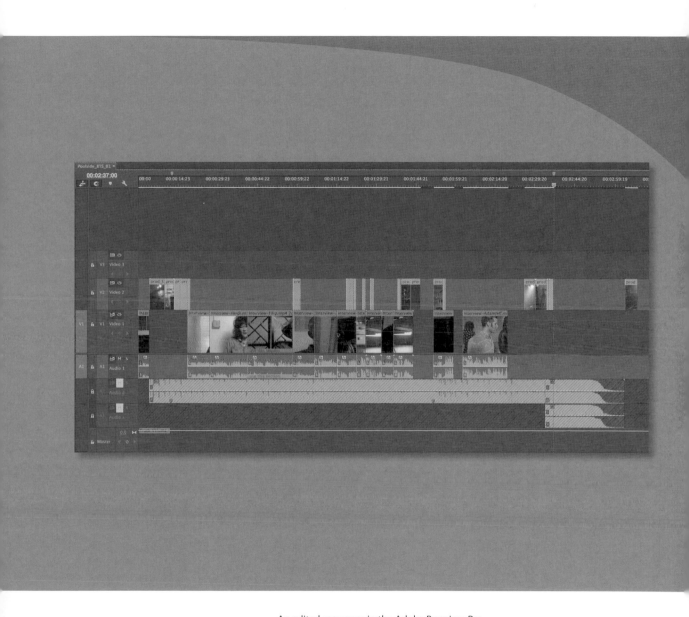

An edited sequence in the Adobe Premiere Pro
Timeline

About Adobe Premiere Pro

Adobe Premiere Pro is your nonlinear video editing system. It offers lots of intuitive and powerful features that simplify the post-production phase of your project.

As the hub of your post-production workflow, Adobe Premiere Pro is not only where you compose your edited piece, it's also where you bring together the rest of the work that you will create in the other components of Creative Cloud.

In addition, Adobe Premiere Pro allows you to link dynamically to project assets from other applications in Creative Cloud so that intermediate rendering is not required.

Linear editing vs. nonlinear editing

Linear editing is a method of editing video using a system in which you record each edit sequentially onto videotape. If any changes are required to an edit that has already been recorded to tape, all edits after that change need to be re-recorded in sequence onto the tape. Linear editing systems are largely obsolete now due to the introduction of nonlinear editing systems in the 1990s.

Nonlinear editing is a method of editing video using computer software that enables you to manipulate the sequence of digitized video clips before exporting the entire sequence to videotape or as a digitized movie file. You can easily make changes in the software before output, allowing for maximum flexibility. Adobe Premiere Pro is an example of nonlinear editing software.

One way to summarize the difference between linear video editing and nonlinear video editing is to compare them, respectively, to typing onto a piece of paper with a typewriter versus using a word processor on a computer.

Optimizing performance

Your hardware requirements for running Adobe Premiere Pro largely depend on which video file formats you will be editing, as well as the types of tasks you are performing. Adobe Premiere Pro is able to perform well on high-end systems as well as lower-spec machines, such as laptops, thanks to the Mercury Playback Engine (see Chapter 1 for more details).

The video files we've provided for you to work with in this *Classroom in a Book* are H.264 files, which were encoded to a bitrate that will play back in real time on most computers. However, in film production, you'll likely encounter other video formats, such as 2K and 4K, which require much more horsepower to play back in real time.

What is H.264?

H.264 has become widely used as a standard of video compression for web video on sites such as YouTube and Vimeo, allowing high-definition (HD) video to play online with smaller file sizes. H.264 is also a standard compression used on Blu-ray Discs. Modern video cameras commonly use H.264 as a means of internally compressing raw footage.

2K, 4K, and high frame rates

The terms 2K and 4K refer to video standards that describe the pixel width of a digitized frame of film. For example, a 4K frame can have 4096×3072 pixels, whereas a 2K frame can have 2048×1080 pixels.

Many cameras on the market today can acquire imagery at high frame rates and at a resolution that is higher than standard HD.

Acquiring video footage at resolutions higher than the standard 1920×1080 pixel frame size gives you the flexibility to crop regions of the frame in post-production and create simple post-production pans and zooms. High frame sizes may also be required when producing movies for theatrical release. However, as a result of having more pixels per frame, 2K and 4K footage can be a bit unwieldy and require more storage space, transfer speed, and processing power.

Shooting at a high frame rate yields more frames per second (fps) of playback, which can be interpreted in Adobe Premiere Pro or After Effects to achieve a dramatic slow-motion look. When shooting at a high frame rate, there is less time to capture each frame; therefore, more light is required.

Many of the cameras made by RED can shoot at frame rates of up to 300 fps; cameras manufactured by Phantom HD can shoot close to 10,000 fps. These cameras tend to be more expensive than digital SLR (single-lens reflex) cameras (which can shoot at up to 60 fps) and require more camera support, such as rigging and additional crew assistance.

The most current tech specs for Adobe Premiere Pro can always be found on the Adobe website at www.adobe.com/products/premiere/tech-specs.html.

Here are the general rules of thumb for improving performance in Adobe Premiere Pro:

- Add as much RAM as your computer is capable of taking.
- Keep your media on a separate drive from the hard drive that your operating system (OS) and applications are on. A RAID (redundant array of independent disks) is recommended if you are editing a media format that has a high data rate. Hard drives with fast read/write speeds are recommended, whether they're

7200 RPM (revolutions per minute) hard drives, solid-state hard drives, or Fusion Drives (available on Apple computers).

- Keep your project files separate from your media files, preferably on another physical hard drive, for safety's sake. Although losing either your project files or your media to a hard drive crash would be bad, losing both to the same hard drive crash would be tragic. You might consider storing your project files in the folder that you use for the 20 gigabytes of storage that comes with your Creative Cloud subscription. For added redundancy, consider setting the location of your Adobe Premiere Pro auto-save folder to a different drive than where you manually save your project files.

● **Note:** For more information on recommended graphics cards for use with Adobe Premiere Pro, go to www.adobe.com/products/premiere/tech-specs.html.

- Add an Adobe-certified graphics card for GPU acceleration.

What is a RAID?

A redundant array of independent disks (RAID) is a combination of multiple hard drives that are recognized by a RAID hardware controller or by the operating system as a single hard drive. RAID configurations were originally developed for the purpose of security and redundancy where multiple disks would store redundant data. Because hard drives tend to fail over time due to physical friction and heat, redundancy of data decreases the probability of data loss.

Today, RAID configurations are signified by a number from 0 to 6. Common RAID configurations include the following:

RAID 0. Two or more hard drives configured to alternate in reading and writing of data in small blocks. A RAID 0 offers no redundancy but can achieve exponentially higher speeds with the inclusion of more physical hard drives. RAID 0 configurations are ideal for media storage in video post-production. It's important to accompany RAID 0 configurations with some external means of redundancy, because a RAID 0 has no inherent redundancy.

RAID 1. Two or more hard drives configured to mirror each other for maximum redundancy and security. A RAID 1 is ideal for archiving media, because it provides inherent redundancy that a RAID 0 does not.

RAID 5. Three or more hard drives configured for speed and redundancy. A RAID 5 is capable of operating even if one hard drive in the array has failed.

● **Note:** For in-depth coverage on Adobe Premiere Pro, it's recommended that you read *Adobe Premiere Pro CC Classroom in a Book* (Adobe Press, 2013).

Creating a new project in Adobe Premiere Pro

Let's start by exploring how to create a new project in Adobe Premiere Pro!

1 Launch Adobe Premiere Pro.

   The Welcome screen appears.

2 Click the New Project button to open the New Project window.

3 Click the Browse button. Navigate to the Assets/Lessons/Lesson 03 folder on your hard drive and click Choose.

4 Double-click the Name field to select the default name; type **Poolside Edit 01**.

● **Note:** If you have not already down-loaded the project files for this lesson to your computer from your Account page, make sure to do so now. See "Getting Started" at the beginning of the book.

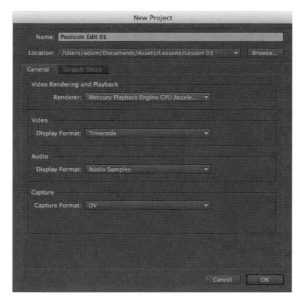

5 Click the Scratch Disks tab. For each of the settings here—Captured Video, Captured Audio, etc.—click the Browse button and set a location on your computer, preferably on a separate physical hard drive than your Assets root folder.

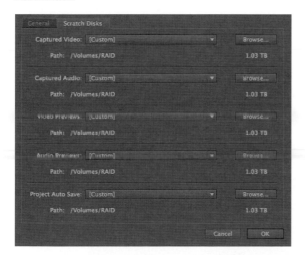

6 Click OK.

Your new project is now open in Adobe Premiere Pro.

Understanding the Adobe Premiere Pro user interface

Now that you have a project open in Adobe Premiere Pro, let's take a look at the interface.

When you launch Adobe Premiere Pro for the first time, you're presented with the default Editing workspace. This workspace puts the most commonly used panels at your fingertips. Adobe Premiere Pro allows you to configure the layout panels in multiple ways, to suit your particular way of working, and those configurations are saved on a file-by-file basis.

Let's reset the Editing workspace to its default setting.

1   Choose Window > Workspace > Editing.

2   Choose Window > Workspace > Reset Current Workspace.

3   In the dialog that appears, click Yes.

Six panels are visible on the surface of the Editing workspace:

* The Source Monitor is where you preview your footage, audio, and graphics clips and set In and Out points for editing them into your sequence.

- The Program Monitor is where you view the edit that you assemble on your Timeline.

- The Project panel is where you organize your media files, sequences, and other components of your project, as well as create bins.

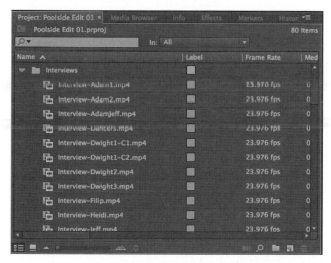

- The Tools panel is where you select different tools used in the editing process.

- The Timeline is where you compose and adjust your edit. You work on sequences within the Timeline.

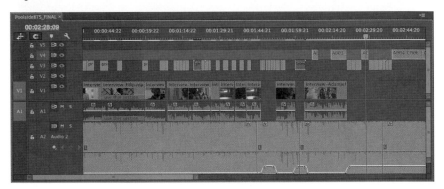

- The Audio Meters display the master audio level of your edit.

Importing footage and other media using the Media Browser

The Media Browser is where you browse the contents of any of the drives or cards connected to your computer, and it provides one way to add those files to your project.

1 Click the Media Browser tab.

2 Navigate to your Assets folder, click the disclosure triangle next to Assets to expand the list of folders (also referred to as *twirling down* or *twirling open*), and then choose your Footage folder.

The contents of the Footage folder appear in the Media Browser.

You can display the contents of a folder in List view or Thumbnail view.

3 If this is not your current setting, click the Thumbnail View icon at the bottom of the Media Browser.

You can preview the content of the footage by hovering your mouse pointer over any clip's thumbnail and scrubbing left to right.

4 Drag your mouse pointer so it's over the pre_adam_crew_whiteboard.m4v clip and park it there.

5 Move your mouse pointer left and right to preview the contents of the clip. This is called a *hover scrub*. By doing this, you can scrub through the frames of this clip for faster previewing.

6 You can import individual clips or entire folders full of clips. In this case, import the entire contents of the Footage folder, including clips and subfolders.

7 Press Command+A (Ctrl+A) to select everything in it, including all the clips as well as the Interview and R3D subfolders.

8 Right-click and choose Import.

9 You may see a File Import Failure window appear. Disregard this by clicking OK.

10 Choose the Project panel tab.

You will notice that all of the clips and subfolders in the Footage folder are imported into your project.

11 Press Command+S (Ctrl+S) to save your project.

Capturing from tape

The workflow you're learning in this *Classroom in a Book* uses media that was captured in a file-based format. Most modern video cameras record video to a memory card or other type of solid-state media. Older cameras record to a tape-based format.

If you're editing media from a videotape, you need to capture that media with Adobe Premiere Pro to create files that you can edit on your computer.

The standard workflow is to connect your camcorder or tape deck to your computer via FireWire and then open the Capture tool in Adobe Premiere Pro by choosing File > Capture.

In this workflow, you use the Capture tool to control your camcorder/tape deck and tell Adobe Premiere Pro which section of the tape to capture and what you want to name the resulting files.

You can find more detailed instruction on capturing media from tape in *Adobe Premiere Pro CC Classroom in a Book* (Adobe Press, 2013).

Understanding the Project panel

The Project panel is where you organize all the assets in your project. By default, it displays all the items in Icon view, which can be useful because this view displays thumbnails, giving you a visual representation of what is contained within each file.

Viewing your Project panel in List view is also useful, because it gives you an overview of information about each clip and also makes it easy to organize your clips.

Let's explore the Project panel.

1   In the Project panel, click the List View button at the bottom left.

The items in the Project panel now display as an alphabetized list. You can click the column headings to sort your Project panel in a variety of ways.

2   With your mouse pointer hovering over the Project panel, press the tilde (~) key to maximize the panel to fill the screen.

> ▶ **Tip:** By hovering your mouse pointer over a panel and pressing the tilde (~) key, you can toggle maximizing the panel to fill your screen.

3   Click the Media Duration heading.

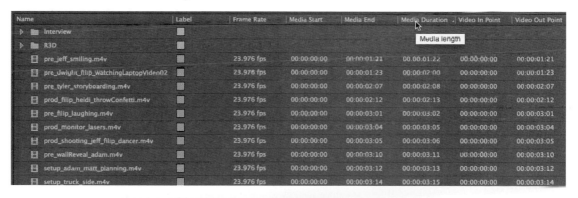

The clips are now sorted based on their duration, from shortest to longest.

4   Click the Name heading.

The clips are once again sorted alphabetically.

If you read Chapter 2, you know that any metadata you add to a video clip in Adobe Bridge or Prelude stays attached to that clip and can be used in Adobe Premiere Pro CC as well as the other components of Production Premium. The Log Notes entered on these clips can be viewed in the Log Note column of the Project panel.

5 Using the scroll bar at the bottom of the Project panel, scroll to the right until the Log Note column heading is visible.

● **Note:** These Log Notes won't be visible if you did not complete Chapter 2.

6 Twirl down the Interview bin to reveal its contents.

Note that the Log Notes entered on the Interview-Dwight-C1.mp4 and Interview-Dwight1-C2.mp4 clips are visible.

You can reorder the columns of information in the Project panel so you can easily access the information most important to you.

7 Click the Log Note column heading and drag it to the left.

8 Drop the Log Note column heading to the left of the Label column.

The Log Note column now displays next to the filename, making it easy to view your Log Notes.

9 Twirl the Interview bin shut.

10 Press the tilde (~) key again to toggle the size of the Project panel back down to its previous size.

Interpreting footage

Most of the video clips that you imported were shot at a frame rate of 23.976 fps. Your final movie will be set to play back at that same frame rate; therefore, the clips that were originally shot at 23.976 fps will play back at that same speed, and the motion in the clips will appear to be at a normal speed.

About seconds and frames

When a camera records video, it captures a series of still images of the action. If enough images are captured each second, the result looks like moving video when played back. Each picture is called a *frame*, and the number of frames each second is usually called *frames per second (fps)*. The fps will vary depending on your camera format and settings. It could be 23.976, 24, 25, 29.97, 50, or 59.94 fps. Some cameras let you choose between more than one frame rate, with different options for accompanying frame sizes. Adobe Premiere Pro plays back video at all common frame rates.

However, you have a video clip that was shot at 59.94 fps. If this clip were played back at 59.94 fps, the playback speed of the clip would appear normal as well (although very smooth, due to the high frame rate). But if this clip were played back at 23.976 fps, the motion in the clip would appear slower than normal.

Adobe Premiere Pro can interpret the native frame rate of a video clip as a different frame rate. Interpreting this 59.94 fps clip as 23.976 fps can turn it into a slow-motion clip in your sequence and give your final movie added production value.

In this exercise, you'll interpret the footage and set the frame rate to 23.976.

1   Deselect all clips that may currently be selected in your Project panel by pressing Command+Shift+A (Ctrl+Shift+A).

2   In the Project panel, select the prod_sweepingConfetti_60fps.m4v clip.

3   Choose Clip > Modify > Interpret Footage. The Modify Clip window appears. This is where you'll set the clip's interpreted frame rate.

4   Select "Assume this frame rate" and type **23.976** in the fps field. Click OK.

5   Double-click prod_sweepingConfetti_60fps.m4v to open it in the Source Monitor. Press the spacebar to play the clip to verify that it is now in slow motion.

Creating bins

As mentioned in Chapter 2, bins are folders you create to sort and contain your media files. It's essential for an efficient workflow that you sort your media into bins in a way that will make it easy to find the clip you need when you need it.

Importing assets as a bin

In some cases, you may already have your media sorted into folders on your hard drive. We've provided a folder called Audio with your assets that you'll now import into your project as a bin.

1   Click the Media Browser tab.

2   Navigate to your Assets folder and then click the Audio folder to select it.

3   Choose File > Import from Media Browser.

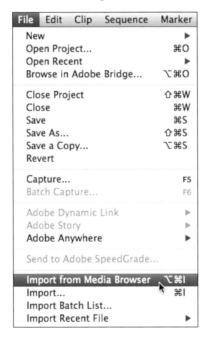

Tip: Use the keyboard shortcut Command+Option+I (Ctrl+Alt+I) to import the selected item from the Media Browser.

4   Click the Project tab.

You'll see that the Audio folder has been imported into your project as a bin.

5 Double-click the Audio bin.

The Audio bin opens in a new floating panel. You'll see three audio files contained within, which you'll use later on.

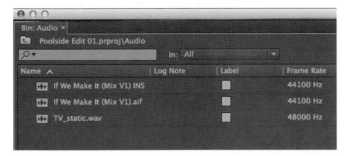

6 Press Command+W (Ctrl+W) to close the Audio bin panel. Choose the Project panel and press Command+Shift+A (Ctrl+Shift+A) to deselect all.

Creating a new bin

Now you'll create a new bin from scratch.

1 In the Project panel, click the New Bin icon.

A new bin appears in the Project panel.

2 Type **B-Roll** to name the bin, and then press Return (Enter).

You now have a new bin called **B-Roll**. You'll put the clips of pre-production, setup, and production into this bin. These clips are named with the prefixes *pre_*, *setup_*, and *prod_* for easy reference.

● **Note:** After naming a bin, if you press Return (Enter), Adobe Premiere Pro will highlight the next bin. To prevent this, click a blank area in the Project panel to register the bin name.

3 Scroll down until all the pre_ clips are visible (you may need to make your Project panel bigger to see them all).

4 Place your mouse pointer to the left of the first pre_ clip, drag down and to the right until all pre_ clips are selected, and release the mouse button. This is called *marquee-selecting*.

5 Drag your selected clips into the B-Roll bin. Press Command+Shift+A (Ctrl+Shift+A) to deselect all.

● **Note:** Be sure not to have a bin or any items in that bin selected when you click the New Bin icon, or the new bin will appear in the selected bin.

Continue by selecting and dragging all of the prod_ clips into the B-Roll bin, and then do the same with the setup_ clips.

You can also select items in your Project panel and then drag to the New Bin button, and a new bin will be created with the selected items contained within.

6 Twirl all open bins shut.

7 Marquee-select the B-Roll, Interview, and R3D bins.

8 Drag these three bins onto the New Bin icon and release. A new bin will be created with these bins placed inside of it.

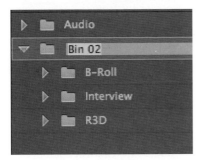

9 Name this new bin **Footage**. Press Return (Enter).

10 Press Command+S (Ctrl+S) to save your project.

Viewing your footage

A good work practice as an editor is to take some time to look at all of your clips. Familiarize yourself with all of the well-composed moments that will help tell your story. Also become familiar with the mistakes and flubbed takes that you'll want to avoid using.

The video that you will be editing shows the behind-the-scenes activities of the making of a music video by the band Poolside. The clips that you have in your Footage bin include interviews with the video director, producers, and the band members themselves, where they talk about their process of planning, setting up a sound stage, and shooting video footage.

The B-Roll bin includes lots of secondary but essential footage that shows the making of the music video in some detail. These clips do not have audio.

The R3D bin includes a few clips of raw footage from the music video itself. Since there are only a few of these clips, you can conclude that you can't construct very much of your edit with these. However, since these are clips from the actual music video and are high-quality 4K resolution, they should definitely be included in your edit where they will serve a climactic purpose.

For this exercise, you'll review the raw footage in the Interview bin and look at various features that might help you tell your story.

You can view your clips in the Source Monitor.

1 In the Project panel, double-click your Interview bin to open it.

2 In your Interview bin, double-click Interview-Adam1.mp4. It will open in the Source Monitor.

3 Press the spacebar or click the Play icon to play the clip.

Listening to your footage

As you view your clips, look and listen for moments that stand out in terms of usable sound bites. View all of the Interview clips, one at a time, to become familiar with them.

The Interview clips will make up the framework of the entire edit. As you will notice, several key segments of audio—sound bites—are obvious choices for moving your story forward.

▶ **Tip:** Depending on how much screen space you have, you may need to move the Bin panel on your screen so that the Source Monitor is not obstructed. To move it, click the top of the panel interface and drag it elsewhere.

1   Listen to the audio in Interview-Adam1.mp4. Notice that it starts with the interviewer off-camera, prompting Adam (the person being interviewed) for what to talk about. You will probably not want to include the off-camera interviewer speaking, because it will be distracting for the viewer to hear an unidentified voice. You will want to isolate one or more sound bites of what Adam is saying. Even with that content, you may not want to use all of what Adam says in this clip, so listen carefully for a short sound bite that you can use later.

2   Double-click Interview-Adam2.mp4 to open it in the Source Monitor. Press the spacebar to play the entire clip, and listen to the audio. This clip was apparently recorded well into the process of setting up the sound stage for the music video shoot. Listen closely to the audio and you will notice a few usable sound bites.

The first sound bite in this clip occurs at timecode 00:00:15:16, when Adam says "Just kinda getting everything together..." ending with "Wow! This is just moving so fast!" You can use this sound bite in your edit as a cue to show a lot of visual activity on the set.

Another sound bite in this clip occurs at timecode 00:00:22:20, when Adam says "We've got a projection going..." ending with "I can't wait! This is gonna be awesome." This is another example of a sound bite that can serve as a cue for a lot of visual activity.

3   Double-click Interview-Dwight1-C1.mp4 to open it in the Source Monitor, and press the spacebar to play the clip. At the beginning of the clip, a few seconds go by before Dwight, one of the producers of the music video, begins speaking. Obviously, you do not want to include this bit of silence in your edit, as it will

slow down the pace of your story. However, the sound bite of Dwight speaking could serve as an introduction to what is about to happen in the video that you are going to edit.

4   Now double-click Interview-Dwight1-C2.mp4 to open it in the Source Monitor, and press the spacebar to play the clip. This is another shot of the same interview bit, but recorded from another camera, from a different angle than the previous clip. Consider your options with this and the previous clip. You could decide to use one clip or the other, depending on your preference. From this angle, though, the lighting on Dwight's face is a bit dark, so you might prefer to use Interview-Dwight1-C1.mp4 in your edit instead.

5 Double-click Interview-Dwight3.mp4 to open it in the Source Monitor, and press the spacebar to play the clip. This shows Dwight during production as he talks about a video being projected onto a backdrop. Listen carefully and notice the low-frequency hum sound, which was probably the result of a microphone that wasn't grounded properly. This unwanted sound is something that you will want to fix later.

6 Double-click Interview-Filip.mp4 to open it in the Source Monitor. If you are continuing from Lesson 2, you will notice the "use this section" markers that were applied in Prelude; if you began at Lesson 3, you won't see this, but don't worry about it. Play the whole clip, and you will notice that it is a bit long. Also, there is a segment of time when Filip, the singer and bass player for Poolside, isn't talking; instead he is listening to an off-camera interviewer. You probably won't want to include this in your edit.

Filip does give a good sound bite between timecodes 00:00:10:17 and 00:00:29:00, in which he talks about how the tone of the song can correlate to the look of the music video.

7 Another way to open clips in the Source Monitor is by choosing and dragging them. Choose and drag Interview-Jeff.mp4 into the Source Monitor. This is Jeff, one of the members of Poolside. Notice that there is no audio until about five seconds into the clip. But because of this, the sound bite will serve as a good way to introduce him in the edit; it can also serve as a good start to the edit itself.

8   Choose and drag the clip Interview-Tyler1.mp4 into the Source Monitor, and press the spacebar to play it. You will notice a good sound bite between 00:00:02:04 and 00:00:11:06, in which Tyler describes what the production will entail. This clip will play nicely with other footage of the sound stage, the band performing on-camera, and the backup dancers.

9   Choose and drag Interview-Dancers.mp4 into the Source Monitor and play the clip. This is an obvious clip to use in the edit after Tyler's sound bite in Interview-Tyler1.mp4. Tyler mentions the backup dancers, and in this clip, the dancers introduce themselves. At this stage of the editing process, you should always be thinking about ways to match your clips together.

10 Choose and drag Interview-Tyler2.mp4 into the Source Monitor. Play the clip. Listen carefully and notice there is a momentary pop sound right after Tyler says "when that fog first came out." This is another unwanted sound that you will fix later.

View and listen to the rest of the clips in the Interview bin. Become familiar with them. Other clips not noted in this exercise will be called out in later lessons.

What is B-roll?

It would be rather difficult to watch a documentary or video that only consisted of shots of a person talking. Not only would you feel bored from looking at their face for a long period of time, but if we never cut away from an interview shot, we lose an opportunity to illustrate or add depth to what they are saying. This is why, whenever a videographer is getting coverage of an event or subject, they are always sure to capture plenty of B-roll. The term *B-roll* refers to any footage that is intended to accompany the main footage, or *A-roll*, most often interview footage or dialogue. When you have a handful of interview clips as well as plenty of B-roll to work with, you can create an audio-visual experience that goes far beyond the words that are being said by the interviewee. There are many reasons, both technical and creative, to make use of B-roll. You can use it to mask an edit or mistake in the interview, to add context or credibility to what they are saying, or simply to offer visual variety.

For example, if we are interviewing an expert on solar panels, by simply inserting a clip of that person installing a solar panel, we not only provide visual variety, but we establish credibility so that the audience can believe what the expert is saying on the subject. If the person made a mistake in the interview that requires an edit or says something really great later on in the clip, by using a clip of B-roll, we can hide a break in the A-roll, allowing the audio to flow smoothly throughout. B-roll can be used to further the experience of the video, but when too many unnecessary clips are used, it takes away from what the person is saying and can leave the audience unsure what to focus their attention on.

Viewing your B-roll footage

► **Tip:** When viewing your footage, keep your eyes open for quick camera pans or movements, obstructions, and other unintended abstract moments in your clips. You can intersperse these moments throughout your edit to give a stylistic dimension to your story.

Now let's look at the B-roll clips.

1 Choose the Interview bin window, and press Command+W (Ctrl+W) to close it.

2 In the Project Panel, double-click the B-Roll bin to open it.

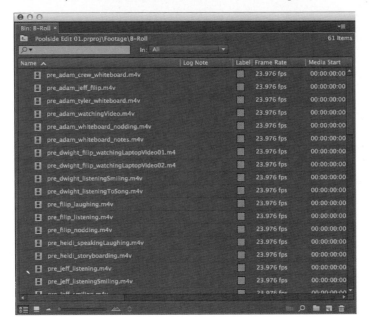

Scroll down through the list of video clips in this bin. As noted earlier, these clips have been named based on whether they show pre-production activity, setup, or production/shooting activity. An essential practice in editing is keeping all of your media as organized as possible, including how you name your raw clips.

You will also notice that there are several dozen clips in this bin. It is easier to sift through lots of video media if you can see the video rather than looking at a list of filenames. And since these clips don't have any audio, you don't need to play them back in real time to become at least vaguely familiar with them.

3 Press the Icon View icon at the bottom left of the B-Roll bin window.

You should now see all of the clips in the B-Roll bin as video thumbnails that you can hover scrub through.

There are a couple of clips that should be noted in this exercise for future reference.

4   Choose and drag prod_watchingMonitors.m4v into the Source Monitor and
    press the spacebar to play it. First, incidentally, this clip shows Adam wiping his
    nose. Note this for later as something not to include in your edit. Also notice
    that at 00:00:04:12, right after the camera zooms in, Adam steps into frame and
    obstructs the camera. This kind of random accident can be used as an edit point
    to cut to another shot that starts out obstructed.

5 Choose and drag pre_wallReveal_adam.m4v to the Source Monitor. This clip starts out with the shot obstructed by a wall. The camera tracks left to reveal Adam standing in a room in front of a whiteboard. Between this shot and the one noted in the previous step, you can create an edit that transitions from the production in progress to the pre-production phase. This is what makes editing magical—you can transport your viewer to another moment in time in the blink of an eye.

Note that there are several B-roll clips of various people that we also see in the Interview clips. These B-roll clips can be shown as the particular individual is talking, to visually reinforce what they're talking about or move the story forward, and also so that the viewer doesn't have to look at talking heads for very long.

Take the time to view all of these clips and become familiar with them.

6 Click the List View icon at the bottom left of the B-Roll bin window.

What motivates an edit?

Although the process of editing a video can often feel like an entirely technical endeavor, it is important not to lose sight of the process as an art form in itself. Choosing to cut from one image to another forces the audience to tie different ideas together and draw connections. There are several different reasons to cut from one image to another.

Cutting for emotion. The main reason we may cut from one shot to another pertains to how it will affect the audience emotionally. This is true for narrative editing as well as documentary, because in both forms of storytelling, the purpose is to deliver some kind of message to the viewers, and this is most often accomplished through emotions. Cutting from an image of a deer drinking from a stream to a shot of a tree being cut down delivers a strong message that is greater than either shot on its own.

Cutting on action. One of the most common reasons for placing an edit is for continuity of action. Movements on screen grab viewers' attention, like a person putting a cup down on the table or a person swinging a baseball bat. To cut on action is to move the viewer to a different angle at the time that a noteworthy action takes place, like when the cup hits the table or when the ball hits the bat. Cutting on action helps to provide rhythm and spatial and temporal continuity, and it keeps the viewer engaged.

Cutting for content. We can throw a bunch of different random clips together on the Timeline, but without a unifying subject, they do not deliver much of an impact when strung together in sequence. Making a cut on the basis of content keeps the flow of information logical and consistent. Adding a series of relevant shots that pertain to what an interviewee is saying is a great way to keep the video piece on topic.

Viewing your RED footage

Finally, let's look at the clips in the R3D bin. These .R3D clips are raw clips from the music video.

1   Choose the B-Roll bin window and press Command+W (Ctrl+W) to close it.

2   Double-click the R3D bin to open it.

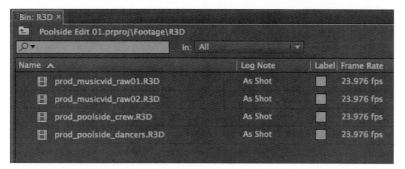

3   Choose and drag prod_musicvid_raw02.R3D into the Source Monitor. Press the spacebar to play it.

    Depending on the speed of your computer, you may need to reduce the Playback Resolution (the menu at the bottom right of the Source Monitor) in order to play these clips in real time.

    Notice that this clip is playing in slow motion. These .R3D clips were shot at 48 fps. Adobe Premiere Pro has natively interpreted them at 23.976 fps. You will want to interpret these clips to play back at their native 48 fps.

4   Marquee-select all four .R3D clips.

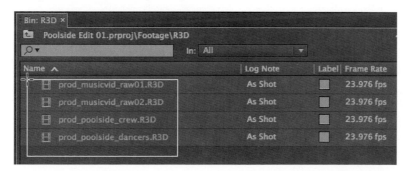

5 Choose Clip > Modify > Interpret Footage.

6 In the Modify Clip window, select "Assume this frame rate:" and enter an fps value of **48**. Click OK.

7 Now play prod_musicvid_raw02.R3D in the Source Monitor again and you will see it playing at normal speed. This clip—which has no audio—shows Filip lip-synching to playback audio on set, as the song is ending. Notice that at timecode 16:02:48:10, Jeff does a dramatic flip of his hair.

8 Select the R3D bin window and press Command+Shift+A (Ctrl+Shift+A) to deselect all.

Watch the rest of these .R3D clips to become familiar with them.

Music and sound effects

You've imported a couple of clips that are just audio with no video. Let's become familiar with these clips.

1 Select the R3D bin window and press Command+W (Ctrl+W) to close it.

2 In the Project panel, double-click the Audio bin to open it.

Notice that there are only two audio clips in this bin. If We Make It (Mix V1).aif is the song that was used in the music video. If We Make It (Mix V1) INSTRUMENTAL.aif is the instrumental version of the same song.

3 Choose and drag If We Make It (Mix V1) INSTRUMENTAL.aif into the Source Monitor.

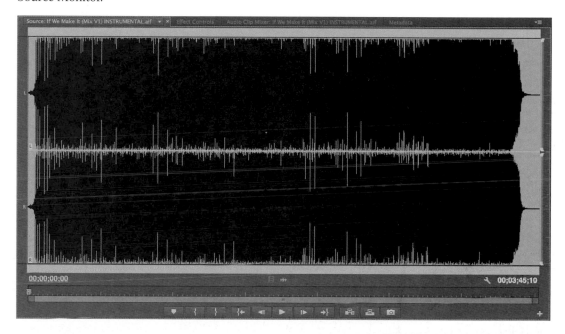

Notice that, since there is no accompanying video with this clip, you will not see any. Instead you will see two audio waveforms for this clip, one for the left stereo channel and one for the right.

4 Press the spacebar to play this audio clip. This would be an obvious choice to use as an underscore for your edit. You could also transition between the instrumental version and the vocal version of the song, since you have both and they are otherwise identical and thus easy to sync.

5 Select the Audio bin window and press Command+W (Ctrl+W) to close it.

6 Press Command+S (Ctrl+S) to save your project.

Now that you've become familiar with all of your clips, think about how you'd create a compelling story with them.

About subclips

Sometimes you may have a very long clip in your bin that has two or more segments in it that can serve as stand-alone clips. You can extract these segments as *subclips.* Although a subclip is a reference to a segment of the master clip, Adobe Premiere Pro shows a subclip in a bin as a self-contained clip.

You can use a subclip in your project much like a master clip but with a few exceptions. For instance, you can trim a subclip only within its initial start and end frames. You can set new In and Out points for a subclip but only if they fall between the In and Out points you set when you first created the subclip.

● **Warning:** If you relink a subclip that has been taken offline, it becomes a master clip and all connections to the original master clip are broken.

A subclip is a reference to the master clip's media file. If the master clip is taken offline or deleted from the project, any subclips derived from it will remain online. However, if you remove the master clip's media file from your system, its subclips will go offline.

Creating a subclip

Especially with longer takes, creating a subclip is an efficient method of breaking down a piece of footage to just the components you want to use in your edit.

In this exercise, you will open a long clip in the Source Monitor and create two subclips from it.

First you will need to perform an edit to the clip.

1   Double-click the Interview bin to open it.

2   Double-click Interview-Adam2.mp4 to open it in the Source Monitor.

This is one of the clips from an earlier exercise. It has two sound bites that merit their own subclips.

3 Scrub the playhead in the Source Monitor to timecode 00:00:15:15. This is where we want the first subclip to start.

One of the advantages of a nonlinear video editing tool like Adobe Premiere Pro is the ability to edit clips nondestructively. Frames that you trim from a clip can always be recalled later. By trimming frames from the beginning of a clip, you are effectively creating a new starting frame. This starting frame is referred to as an *In point*. And as you might expect, trimming frames from the end of a clip creates a new ending frame, or *Out point*.

Let's set the current frame as the In point of this clip.

4 With the Source Monitor active, press the I key to Mark In, or set the clip's In point to the current frame.

5 Now let's set the Out point. Scrub the playhead to 00:00:21:13.

6 Press the O key to Mark Out, or set the clip's Out point to the current frame.

7 Now let's create a subclip with this trimmed portion. Choose Clip > Make Subclip.

8 The Make Subclip window will appear. Call your new subclip **Interview-Adam2.mp4.movingSoFast**. Click OK.

This new subclip will appear in your Interview bin.

9 Double-click Interview-Adam2.mp4.movingSoFast to open it in the Source Monitor. Press the spacebar to play the clip. Notice that only the trimmed portion from the source clip is in this subclip.

10 Now let's make another subclip from the longer source clip. In the Interview bin, double-click Interview-Adam2.mp4 to open it in the Source Monitor.

11 Scrub your playhead to 00:00:22:17.

12 Press the I key to Mark In, or set the clip's In point to the current frame.

12 Scrub your playhead to 00:00:30:04.

13 Mark Out at this frame by pressing the O key.

14 Now create a new subclip by choosing Clip > Make Subclip.

15 The Make Subclip window will appear. Call your new subclip
Interview-Adam2.mp4.gonnaBeAwesome. Click OK.

16 When this appears in the Interview bin, double-click it to open it in the Source
Monitor. Press the spacebar to play the clip.

Editing Interview clips

The remaining Interview clips need to be trimmed, but they don't need to be split
into subclips. Let's do some editing to these clips by opening them individually in
the Source Monitor and setting new In and Out points for them.

1 Open Interview-Adam1.mp4 in the Source Monitor. Mark In at 00:00:07:06.
Mark Out at 00:00:15:19.

2 Open Interview-Dancers.mp4 in the Source Monitor. Mark In at 00:00:02:17.
Mark Out at 00:00:06:06.

3 Open Interview-Dwight1-C1.mp4 in the Source Monitor. Mark In at
00:00:03:23. Mark Out at 00:00:12:05.

4 Open Interview-Dwight2.mp4 in the Source Monitor. Mark In at 00:00:00:19.
Mark Out at 00:00:08:23.

5 Open Interview-Dwight3.mp4 in the Source Monitor. Mark In at 00:00:02:06.
Mark Out at 00:00:06:17.

6 Open Interview-Heidi.mp4 in the Source Monitor. Mark In at 00:00:04:03. Mark
Out at 00:00:18:12.

7 Open Interview-Jeff.mp4 in the Source Monitor. Mark In at 00:00:05:00. Mark
Out at 00:00:09:04.

8 Open Interview-Tyler1.mp4 in the Source Monitor. Mark In at 00:00:02:05.
Mark Out at 00:00:11:04.

9 Open Interview-Tyler2.mp4 in the Source Monitor. Mark In at 00:00:04:11.
Mark Out at 00:00:12:06.

10 Press Command+S (Ctrl+S) to save your project.

Speech to Text workflow

If you are editing interview footage, you may want to try the Speech to Text feature in Adobe Premiere Pro. This feature analyzes the audio and attempts to create a text transcript.

Simply right-click any clip containing audio in the Project panel and choose Analyze Content.

Make sure the Speech check box is selected, as well as the language your audio is in. When you click OK, Adobe Media Encoder will launch, analyze the clip, and then put the Analysis Text into the Metadata panel in Adobe Premiere Pro. Selecting the clip in the Project panel and then opening the Metadata panel will reveal the analyzed text.

Of course, in the event that the Speech to Text feature makes a few errors, they can be edited manually or improved with a script text file.

Relinking media with Link & Locate

One inescapable occurrence when editing video from multiple source clips is that sometimes your media goes offline. Sometimes this happens if a file gets accidentally moved or deleted. Other times, it happens if you move a project to another computer and, while all of your files are in the same relative location to each other, Adobe Premiere Pro may need a little reminder of where things are.

New in Adobe Premiere Pro is Link & Locate, which gives you a streamlined interface for finding offline media.

Let's pretend that one of your source clips is offline. Then we will link this media using Link & Locate.

1   In the Interview bin window, currently open, select all clips by pressing Command + A (Ctrl + A).

2 Choose Clip > Make Offline.

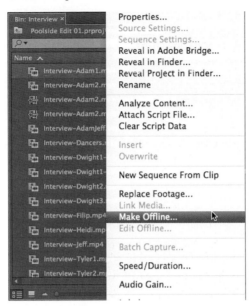

3 The Make Offline window will appear. Select the option (if it isn't already selected by default) Media Files Remain on Disk. Then click OK.

All of the Interview clips now show with a question mark icon in the Interview bin window, indicating that Adobe Premiere Pro doesn't know where they are.

Although we are deliberately taking media offline for the purpose of this exercise, this process is sometimes handy. There are times when you want to refresh a clip with any updates made to it in another application, and you want to force that to happen. Although this may not be the most elegant way to do that, deliberately taking media offline in order to relink it is sometimes the necessary brute-force way of getting it done.

Now that these clips are offline, we can use Link & Locate to bring them back online.

1   With all clips selected in the Interview bin, choose Clip > Link Media.

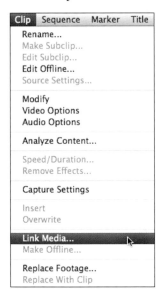

The Link window will appear.

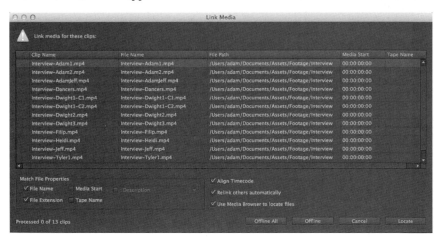

This shows you any media that is currently offline in your open Adobe Premiere Pro project, plus the last known folders for each missing clip. At the bottom, you can toggle a checkbox to determine if Link & Locate will find other missing clips if they are located in the same folder as the one you are currently searching for.

There is another checkbox to toggle whether Link & Locate uses the Media Browser interface. If this is off, then Adobe Premiere Pro will use your operating system's folder navigation interface. Leave both of these checked.

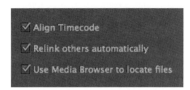

2   Click Locate. This will open the Locate File window, which resembles the Media Browser that you used earlier in this lesson. This shows an icon view of all of the clips in the same folder as the clip you are currently looking for. Click OK.

If there are any other missing clips, you would be sent back to the Link window to continue searching. However, since the only missing clips in our exercise are in the same folder, Link & Locate finds them all and the interface disappears. All clips in the Interview bin should now be back online.

3   Select the Interview bin. Press Command+Shift+A (Ctrl+Shift+A) to de-select all clips. Press Command+W (Ctrl+W) to close it.

With Link & Locate, relinking your offline clips is easier than ever.

Link & Locate

At some point, unfortunately, you may run into a case where some or all of your media goes offline due to a hard drive being disconnected, or to a root folder being renamed or relocated. Adobe Premiere Pro will not see the source video files where it expects to see them, which would, until now, require you to locate offline clips in the Project panel, and reconnect them through a file navigation window. However, with the new Link & Locate feature, you can make easy work of relocating offline media. The Link & Locate window provides an index of all the offline clips, with options to help you search for your offline media and get back on track with your edit.

Creating the first sequence

In terms of editing in Adobe Premiere Pro, a *sequence* is a series of edits arranged in the Timeline, that, when played from beginning to end, shows the order of your chosen clips and transitions. Clips can easily be added, removed, trimmed, and rearranged in a sequence. Because clips are merely instances of project media, any edits performed on clips in a sequence are nondestructive to the raw media on your system.

The easiest way to create a new sequence in Adobe Premiere Pro is to drag a clip to the New Item button. This will create a new sequence in the same video format, frame size, and frame rate as the clip.

1   In the Project panel, twirl open the Interview bin.

2   Choose and drag the Interview-Jeff.mp4 clip onto the New Item icon at the bottom right of the Project panel.

Doing so will make a new sequence in your project. This shows as an item called Interview-Jeff.mp4, the same as the clip used to create it. A new sequence will appear in the same bin as its clip of origin when created this way.

This new sequence also opens automatically in the Timeline, with the Interview-Jeff.mp4 clip placed at its first frame.

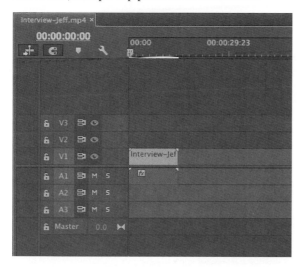

The first frame of this sequence shows rendered in the Program Monitor.

Management of project media is a constant process. Let's change the name of this new sequence to something more appropriate.

1 In the Project panel, choose the Interview-Jeff.mp4 sequence (not the raw clip!) and its name will become highlighted.

2 Type in a new name for this sequence, **Poolside_BTS_01**, and press Enter.

Now let's make a new bin, this one for sequences.

▶ **Tip:** To make a new bin, you can also press Command+/ (Ctrl+/)

1 Choose the New Bin icon at the bottom right of the Project panel.

▶ **Tip:** By hovering your mouse pointer over a panel and pressing the tilde (~) key, you can toggle maximizing the panel to fill your screen.

A new Bin will appear in the Interview bin, because the Poolside_BTS_01 sequence was selected when the new bin was made.

2 Rename this new bin **Sequences** and press Enter.

▶ **Tip:** Drag any number of selected items onto the New Bin button. This creates a new bin, with the dragged items placed inside of it.

3 Select the Poolside_BTS_01 sequence and drag it into the Sequences bin.

4 Now select and drag the Sequences bin all the way outside of the Footage bin.

5 Twirl your Footage bin shut in the Project panel to see the Sequences bin listed with the Audio and Footage bins.

6 Press Command+S (Ctrl+S) to save your project.

Using markers

There are times when you'll want to mark specific frames for future reference, either to indicate when something happens in a clip or when you want something to happen in your sequence.

Adobe Premiere Pro lets you add markers to clips as well as to your sequence.

Adding a marker to a clip

The instrumental music track will serve as the audio bed for your edit. You can use various audio cues in the music—a change in tone or tempo, an instrumental moment, and so on—to motivate visual edits.

1 In the Project Panel, twirl open the Audio bin.

▶ **Tip:** You can adjust the width of a column in the Project panel or a Bin in list view by clicking a dividing line between its name and that of an adjacent column and then dragging to the left or right.

2 Double-click If We Make It (Mix V1) INSTRUMENTAL.aif to open it in the Source Monitor. Press the spacebar to play the clip.

Listen carefully for moments in the music that could serve as audio cues. For example, at timecode 00;00;04;16, the drumbeat starts. Let's add a clip marker to this frame.

3　To do this, scrub your Source Monitor playhead to 00;00;04;16. Make a new clip marker at this frame by clicking the Add Marker icon at the bottom left of the Source Monitor. Or, you could use the M keyboard shortcut.

Notice the marker icon that now appears in the Source Monitor timeline.

4　Scrub your Source Monitor playhead ahead to timecode 00;00;20;20. This is when a synthesizer comes into the soundscape and the tone of the song changes slightly. This could serve as a cue for a visual transition. Add a new marker here by pressing the M key.

However, if the synthesizer marks a first transition in the music, which in turn would logically serve as a cue for a visual transition, you probably don't want to have an intro to your music that is just over sixteen seconds. That seems a bit long for a video that will probably end up being less than three and a half minutes. You could probably afford to trim off some of the beginning of the music track.

5　Scrub your playhead to timecode 00;00;12;08. Press the I key to Mark In.

6　Scrub your playhead ahead to timecode 00;02;00;04. This is when a cymbal enters the soundscape. This could serve as a cue for a visual. Add a new marker here by pressing the M key.

Now let's add this audio clip to your sequence.

7 Select If We Make It (Mix V1) INSTRUMENTAL.aif in the Project panel and drag it into the Timeline on the track, Audio 2, as shown in the next figure. Make sure that the In point of the music clip comes right after the Out point of Interview-Jeff.mp4 in the sequence.

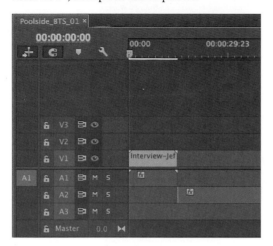

8 You won't see the clip markers on your music clip in the Timeline unless your make a slight adjustment to the interface. Click the Timeline Display Settings icon at the top right of the Timeline. It resembles a wrench.

9 Doing this will reveal a menu. From this menu, choose Expand All Tracks.

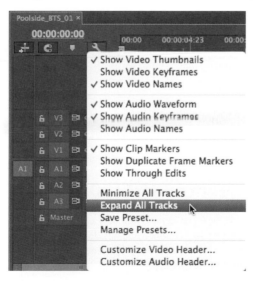

Tracks will be explained in some detail later. For now, you should see the clip markers you added to your music clip.

▶ **Tip:** You can expand all tracks with the keyboard shortcut Shift+=. You can also expand selected video tracks with Command+= (Ctrl+=) and audio tracks with Option+= (Alt+=). Use the minus key (–) instead of the equal key (=),along with the appropriate modifier key, to minimize selected tracks.

▶ **Tip:** You can press the equal key (=) to zoom in on your Timeline and the minus key (–) to zoom out.

Note: Snapping is covered in more detail later in this lesson.

10 Hold down the Shift key and scrub your Timeline playhead to where the first visible clip marker is on the music clip. You will see your playhead snap to the marker.

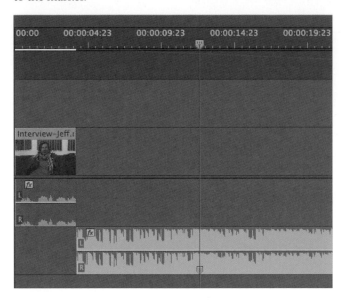

Adding a marker to a sequence

Just as you can add markers to a clip, you can also add markers to a sequence, because sometimes you want to mark when you want certain things to happen in your edit.

1 Create a sequence marker at the current time by pressing the M key.

This sequence marker correlates with the clip marker at the corresponding time in your sequence, which marks a slight shift in tone in the music and would serve as a logical point of transition in the narrative.

2 Press Command+S (Ctrl+S) to save your project.

Clip markers vs. sequence markers

A sequence marker is attached to a specific frame in the sequence, whereas a clip marker is attached to a specific frame on a clip. Sequence markers do not move as clips move in the sequence. However, if a clip with a marker on it is moved in the sequence, its marker will move in time with it.

Working in the Timeline

The Timeline is where you'll do most of the work when you are editing. It's where you assemble and arrange your footage, add transitions and effects, and do most of the creative work involved in editing film and video.

Preparing to edit in the Timeline

The sequence you just created contains only a single video clip at this point. To fully understand the Timeline, you need to add more clips to your sequence.

1   In your Project panel, twirl open the Footage bin to reveal the Interview bin, which should already be twirled open.

2   Adjust your Timeline playhead to timecode 00:00:18:17. From the Interview bin, choose and drag Interview-Dwight1-C1.mp4 into the Timeline on track Video 1, so that its In point is at the current time.

3   Choose and drag Interview-Filip.mp4 from the Project panel into the Timeline directly after Interview-Dwight1-C1.mp4.

4   Choose and drag Interview-Dwight2.mp4 from the Project panel into the Timeline directly after Interview-Filip.mp4.

5   Choose and drag Interview-Heidi.mp4 from the Project panel into the Timeline directly after Interview-Dwight2.mp4.

6   Choose and drag Interview-Adam1.mp4 from the Project panel into the Timeline directly after Interview-Heidi.mp4.

7   Choose and drag Interview-Tyler1.mp4 from the Project panel into the Timeline directly after Interview-Adam1.mp4.

8   Choose and drag Interview-Adam2.mp4.movingSoFast from the Project panel into the Timeline directly after Interview-Tyler1.mp4.

9   Choose and drag Interview-Dwight3.mp4 from the Project panel into the Timeline directly after Interview-Adam2.mp4.movingSoFast.

10   Choose and drag Interview-Adam2.mp4.gonnaBeAwesome from the Project panel into the Timeline directly after Interview-Dwight3.mp4.

11   Choose and drag Interview-Tyler2.mp4 from the Project panel into the Timeline directly after Interview-Adam2.mp4.gonnaBeAwesome.

12 Choose and drag Interview-AdamJeff.mp4 from the Project panel into the Timeline directly after Interview-Tyler2.mp4.

Now you have a sequence with multiple clips.

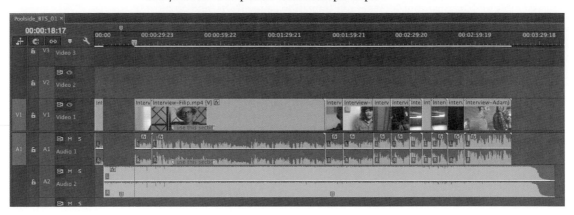

13 Press Command+S (Ctrl+S) to save your project.

The components of the Timeline

Here are the main components of the Timeline that you'll be working with in Adobe Premiere Pro:

Video tracks. Contain your visual elements, such as video, titles, and graphics.

Audio tracks. Contain your audio, such as dialogue, soundtrack, and sound effects.

Playhead. Indicates which frame in your sequence you are viewing in the Program Monitor. You can drag the playhead around to change your position in time.

Muting and locking tracks

The Timeline interface in Adobe Premiere Pro can have multiple layers, or tracks, of video, audio, graphics, titles, and other elements. Certain properties of tracks can be toggled on and off.

1 Scrub your playhead to the beginning of the sequence. You may notice that currently the music clip overpowers the volume of the Interview clips.

   For the time being, let's mute the Audio 2 track, where the music clip is.

2 Click the M (or "mute") button at the left of the Timeline, on track Audio 2. Doing this will mute the audio in Audio 2.

Since the music clip is trimmed and placed in the sequence where it needs to go for now, let's lock the track that it's in so that further changes cannot be applied to anything in that track.

3 Click the Toggle Track Lock icon at the left of the Timeline, on Audio 2. Doing this will lock the track.

Notice that the music clip now has a diagonal striped pattern on it, indicating that its track is locked.

4 Now press the spacebar to play back your sequence to review the Interview clips you have placed there.

5 Press Command+S (Ctrl+S) to save your project.

Editing on the Timeline

Now that you have your Interview clips in place in your edit, you'll perform some edits in the Timeline.

Ripple edit

A *ripple edit* allows you to trim frames from the In or Out point of clips in your Timeline, and any clips in all unlocked tracks after the edit will move to the left, back in time, to fill in the gap that would be left behind.

Let's perform a ripple edit to Interview-Filip.mp4.

1   Adjust your Timeline playhead to 00:00:38:21. At this frame, Filip begins to say "With this particular song...."

2   Choose the Ripple Edit tool from the Tools panel.

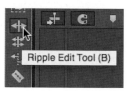

3   With the Ripple Edit tool active, choose the In point of Interview-Filip.mp4, and drag to the right, until the In point snaps to the playhead.

Notice that the tool tip shows, in real time as you make the adjustment, how much time is being trimmed from the clip as well as the clip's new duration.

Notice that the ripple edit left no gap in the Timeline when you trimmed these frames.

4   Scrub the playhead to the In point of Interview-Filip.mp4 and press the spacebar to play the edit. Notice how the clip has been trimmed.

5   Adjust your playhead to timecode 00:00:44:02 in the Timeline.

6   With the Ripple Edit tool still active, choose the Out point of Interview-Filip.mp4 and drag it to the left, until the Out point snaps to the playhead.

Once you complete this edit, notice how all clips in the Timeline on tracks Video 1 and Audio 1 have automatically moved to the left, to fill in the time gap.

Ripple delete

A *ripple delete* is an edit in which the selected clip in the Timeline is removed, and all clips after it in unlocked tracks move to the left to fill in the time gap.

Let's perform a ripple delete, this time to Interview-AdamJeff.mp4.

1   Adjust your Timeline playhead to timecode 00:01:52:01, at the point when Adam begins speaking.

2   Choose the Razor tool from the Tools panel.

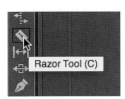

● **Note:** There is a clip marker on the music clip in track Audio 2 near the current time. Make sure you are not snapping the Razor tool on this clip marker.

The Razor tool will automatically snap to the playhead.

3   With the Razor Tool, click Interview-AdamJeff.mp4 once at the current time.

4   Adjust the playhead so that it is over the first bit of Interview-AdamJeff.mp4 in the Timeline.

5   Press the D key. This will select the clip (or clips) that are under the playhead.

6 Choose Edit > Ripple Delete. Notice that the remaining segment of Interview-AdamJeff.mp4 has automatically moved to the left to fill in the time gap.

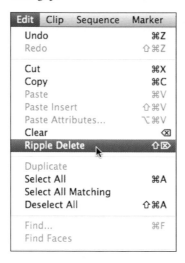

7 Now adjust your playhead to 00:02:06:20, as Adam and Jeff finish sharing a laugh.

Since there are no clips after this one in the Timeline, a simple trim edit will suffice.

8 Choose the Selection tool, then choose and drag the Out point of Interview-AdamJeff.mp4 to the left until it meets the playhead.

▶ **Tip:** You can perform a ripple delete by selecting a clip or a gap and pressing Shift+Delete. If you have a shortened keyboard, press Fn+Shift+Delete.

Extract

Adobe Premiere Pro allows you to define a range of time in your sequence, and perform what is essentially a ripple delete (or *extract*, as it's called) to segments of clips in all unlocked tracks that fall within this time range.

1 Scrub your playhead to the In point of Interview-Tyler1.mp4. Press the spacebar to play the sequence from this frame. Listen to the audio, and you'll notice that Tyler says "We've got..." with a brief pause, and then he begins speaking quickly about the sound stage.

Let's edit out the beginning of this sound bite by setting an In point and Out point in your sequence and then using the extract function to remove any segment of media that falls within that time range.

2 Adjust your playhead to the In point of Interview-Tyler1.mp4. Press the I key to Mark In.

3   Adjust your playhead to 00:01:16:19, right as Tyler says "a sound stage." Press O
    to Mark Out at this frame.

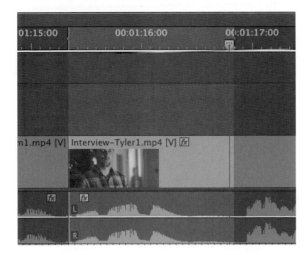

Now let's remove this pause in the sound bite by using the Extract feature.

4   At the bottom of the Program Monitor is a row
    of icons. The second one from the right is the
    Extract icon.

5   Click this icon. Scrub your playhead back a few
    seconds, then press the spacebar to play your
    sequence from there. You will notice that the first
    bit in Tyler's sound bite is gone.

Note that the extract removes all media from within the In and Out points in a
sequence and then automatically scoots everything after the resulting gap to the
left in the Timeline, in order to fill the gap. Also note that if the Audio 2 track
was not locked, the same segment of time would have been extracted from the
music clip, as well.

6   Press the Home key to adjust your playhead to the beginning of your sequence.
    Press the spacebar to play your sequence. If you want to zoom out your view of
    the Timeline panel interface, use the minus (–) and equal (=) keys to zoom out
    and in, respectively, your view of the Timeline. You can also press the backslash
    key (\) to show a full view of all clips in the Timeline panel interface.

7   Press Command+S (Ctrl+S) to save your project.

▶ **Tip:** If you are using a reduced size keyboard on an Apple iMac or MacBook, press Fn+left arrow
to adjust your playhead to the beginning of your sequence and Fn+right arrow to adjust your
playhead to the end of your sequence.

▶ **Tip:** To adjust your
playhead to a specific
frame in your sequence,
click once on the
Playhead Position at the
top left of the Timeline
panel, type in the
desired timecode, and
press Return (Enter).

Adding B-roll

Now let's add some B-roll clips to your edited sequence. These clips will go on track V2. Any clip that is on V2 will cover up what is on V1 at the same frame, as long as the clip on V2 is at least as large in pixel dimensions as the sequence's frame size, and so long as the clip on V2 is not semitransparent. Adding B-roll clips to a separate video track ensures that any edits made on V1 will still be preserved, just obscured by what's in V2.

1 Adjust your playhead to the beginning of the sequence, right after the first clip, Interview-Jeff.mp4. Notice the several-second gap in the sequence here, before Interview-Dwight1-C1.mp4. Let's fill that gap with B-roll.

2 In the Project panel, within the Footage bin, find the B-Roll bin. Double-click it to open it in its own window.

3 Find the clip prod_ladder.m4v. This clip shows the inside of the sound stage while production on the music video is in progress.

4 Choose and drag this clip into the Timeline panel on track Video 2, so that its In point is adjacent to the Out point of Interview-Jeff.mp4. This clip is a wide shot that helps establish the location. It could also serve as a background clip for an opening title graphic.

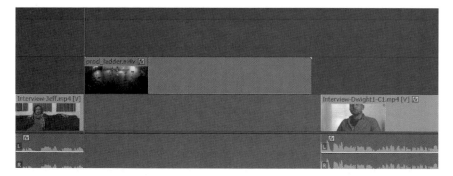

Basic trim edits

1 In the Timeline, adjust your playhead to the In point of Interview-Dwight2.mp4. Here you will add a couple of clips that reinforce what Dwight is talking about.

2 In the B-Roll bin, find the clip pre_dwight_filip_ watchingLaptopVideo02.m4v. Choose and drag this clip into the Timeline in track Video 2, so that its In point is at the current frame.

3 In the B-Roll bin, find the clip pre_dwight_filip_ watchingLaptopVideo01.m4v. Choose and drag this clip into the Timeline in Video 2 so that its In point is directly after the Out point of pre_dwight_filip_ watchingLaptopVideo02.m4v.

4 Using the Selection tool currently active, select the Out point of pre_dwight_ filip_watchingLaptopVideo01.m4v and drag it to the left, until the duration of this clip is three seconds.

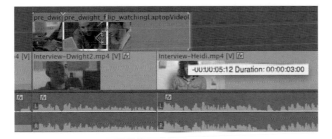

Using the Razor tool

1 Adjust your playhead to timecode 00:01:18:18 in your Timeline. This is when Tyler is describing the overall action that will be shown in the music video.

2 In the B-Roll bin, find the clip prod_monitor_adam_filip.m4v. Choose and drag this into the Timeline so that its In point is at the current time.

3 Choose the Razor tool from the Tools panel.

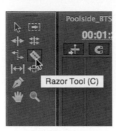

4 Adjust your playhead to timecode 00:01:20:06, or one and a half seconds into the prod_monitor_adam_filip.mp4 clip in the Timeline.

5 Using the Razor tool, click once this clip once at the current time. The clip is now split into two pieces.

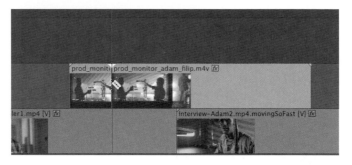

6 Press the V key to choose the Selection tool.

7 Select the segment of this clip that is after the current time. Press Delete to remove it from the Timeline.

8 In the B-Roll bin, find the clip prod_shooting_jeff_filip_dancer.m4v. Choose and drag it into the Timeline so that its In point is at the current time, 00:01:20:06.

9 Scrub ahead to 00:01:21:16 in the Timeline, at which point Tyler is saying "some backup dancers."

10 Activate the Razor tool with the C keyboard shortcut. With the Razor tool, click prod_shooting_jeff_filip_dancer.m4v once at the current time.

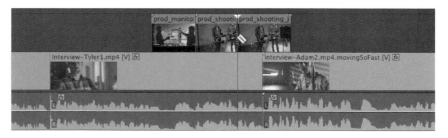

11 Activate the Selection tool by pressing the V key. Select the segment of this clip that shows after the current time, and press Delete to remove it.

12 In the B-Roll bin, find the clip prod_monitor_dancer.m4v.

13 Choose and drag this clip into the Timeline on Video 2, so that its In point is at the current time.

14 Adjust your playhead so it is at 00:01:22:18, which should be an edit point between two Interview clips.

15 Activate the Razor tool with the C keyboard shortcut. Click prod_monitor_dancer.m4v once at the current time.

16 Activate the Selection tool again by pressing V. Select the latter part of prod_monitor_dancer.m4v and press Delete to remove it.

Using the Slip tool

The Slip tool allows you to move a clip's frames forward or backward in the Timeline while maintaining that clip's In and Out points in the Timeline.

1   Scrub through the prod_monitor_dancer.m4v clip. You will notice that the portion of the raw footage that is in the clip doesn't show very much or look very interesting.

2   Choose the Slip tool from the Tools panel.

3   Drag over the clip with the Slip tool.

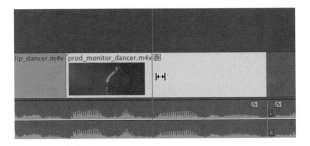

Notice in the Program Monitor the interface changes to show four frames. At top left is the Out point frame of the previous clip in the track. The bottom two frames are the In point and Out points of this clip, updating in real time as you drag with the Slip tool.

4   Adjust the clip with the tool so that the In point shows as 00:00:02:10 and the Out point shows as 00:00:03:11.

5 In the Timeline, scrub the playhead back several frames, then press the spacebar to play through the edit. Notice that the clip now starts wide on a video monitor and then zooms in.

Let's apply a slip edit to another shot.

1 Adjust your playhead to timecode 00:01:24:11 as Adam is about to say "We're about to roll some camera." This would be a good point to show B-roll of the crew setting up the video camera.

2 In the B-Roll bin, find the clip prod_matt_movingCamera.m4v. Choose this clip and drag it into the Timeline on Video 2 so that its In point lands at the current time.

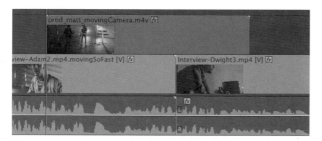

3 Adjust your playhead to 00:01:25:22, just as Adam finishes saying "roll some camera." Using the Selection tool, trim the Out point of this clip to the current time.

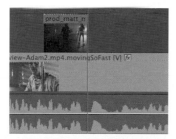

4 Choose the Slip tool from the Tools panel.

5 Click prod_matt_movingCamera.m4v and drag to the left and right. You will notice the Program Monitor shows the In and Out points of this clip in real time as you made Slip adjustments to it. Adjust this clip at your discretion.

6 Adjust your playhead to 00:01:34:15. Here, Adam is talking about the "laser thing" for creating background visuals.

7 Activate the Selection tool again by pressing V. In the B-Roll bin, find the clip prod_monitor_lasers.m4v. Choose and drag this into the Timeline panel on track Video 2 so that its In point is at the current time.

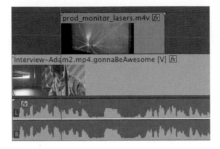

8 Adjust your playhead to 00:01:35:18, just as Adam finishes saying "laser thing." Using the Selection tool, trim the Out point of prod_monitor_lasers.m4v to the current time.

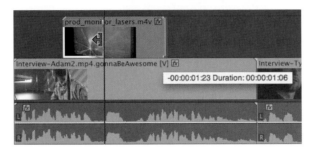

9 Activate the Slip tool by pressing the Y key. Adjust this clip so that the first frame shows Adam's hand in front of the monitor, pointing at the lasers.

10 Press Command+S (Ctrl+S) to save your project. Press the V key to activate the Selection Tool.

Reordering clips on the Timeline

You added Interview clips to your sequence, along with some B-roll clips. Now you'll rearrange some of the clips on the Timeline so they play in the desired order.

Creating an overwrite edit

To begin with, you'll move a clip to replace another clip on the Timeline.

1 In your Timeline panel, scrub your playhead to 00:00:46:02, the edit point between the two clips that shows Dwight and Filip looking at videos on a laptop.

Let's get rid of the first of these two clips by performing what's called an *overwrite edit*. This basically means moving a video clip onto the same place in the Timeline as another video clip, thus overwriting it and removing it from the Timeline.

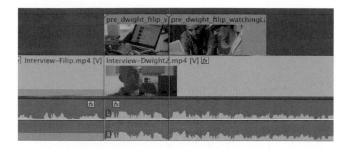

2   Select the second of these two clips, pre_dwight_filip_watchingLaptopVideo01.
    m4v. Drag it to the left while holding down Shift so that its In point covers the
    In point of pre_dwight_filip_watchingLaptopVideo02.m4v.

3   Once completed, you will notice that
    pre_dwight_filip_watchingLaptopVideo02.m4v has been removed.

Creating an Insert edit

Now you'll learn a technique that allows you to insert a clip between other clips
without overwriting.

1   Select the B-Roll bin and press Command+W (Ctrl+W) to close it.

2   In your Timeline panel, scrub the playhead to the edit point between
    Interview-Tyler1.mp4 and Interview-Adam2.mp4.movingSoFast.

    Here you will insert a shot of the dancers. All clips in the Timeline—in unlocked
    tracks—after the edit point will automatically scoot to the right in the Timeline,
    just enough for the inserted clip to fit.

3   In the Project panel, look in the Interview bin and find the clip Interview-Dancers.mp4.

4   Choose this clip and drag it into the Source Monitor.

You will recall that this is one of the clips that you trimmed in an earlier exercise.

5   Click the Insert button at the bottom of the Source Monitor interface.

6   Notice that in the Timeline panel, the Interview-Dancers.mp4 clip is now placed between Interview-Tyler1.mp4 and Interview-Adam2.mp4.movingSoFast, which maintained its current duration.

Reorder an additional clip

You've successfully rearranged the clips on Video 2 without overwriting existing content on the Timeline or rearranging the other video and audio tracks. Now you'll reorder an additional clip.

Let's move Interview-Heidi.mp4 from after Interview-Dwight2.mp4 to before Interview-Filip.mp4 in the Timeline.

▶ **Tip:** You can zoom in on your Timeline using the equal (=) key. Zoom out by using the minus (–) key.

1   Scrub your playhead to the edit point between Interview-Dwight2.mp4 and Interview-Heidi.mp4. Select the Interview-Heidi.mp4 clip.

2   While holding down the Command (Ctrl) key, drag Interview-Heidi.mp4 to the left so that its In point lines up with the In point of Interview-Filip.mp4, then release.

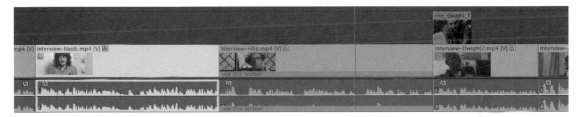

3   Press Command+S (Ctrl+S) to save your project.

Notice how easy it is to reorder clips in your Adobe Premiere Pro Timeline.

Using new audio enhancements

Adobe Premiere Pro has new features that make working with and editing your audio much easier. You have already noticed one of these, which is the improved audio waveforms in the Timeline interface. These allow you to see the peaks and valleys of your audio so you can determine when the loud and quiet parts happen just by looking at the waveforms.

Another new audio enhancement is the new Audio Clip Mixer, which allows you to adjust the volume for individual clips using the sliders. In earlier versions of Adobe Premiere Pro, the mixer slider interface was only used to adjust volume of entire audio tracks in a timeline.

● **Note:** Audio editing is covered in more detail in Chapter 7.

Using Snap

Adobe Premiere Pro has a handy Snap feature, which makes it easy to move your playhead between edit points in your sequence as well as add clips to your sequence and move clips in your sequence.

Snapping between edit points

The Snap feature is turned on by default and can be toggled on and off by pressing the Snap icon at the top left of the Timeline.

Snap Preferences

In the General preferences of Adobe Premiere Pro, there is a setting that allows you to toggle whether the playhead snaps to any Timeline object—edit points, markers, and so on —when the playhead is scrubbed.

> ☐ Set focus on the Timeline when performing Insert/Overlay edits
> ☐ Snap playhead in Timeline when Snap is enabled
> ☑ At playback end, return to beginning when restarting playback

This setting is deactivated by default, but you may find it useful.

1   Scrub your playhead through your Timeline with the Shift key held down. You'll notice that the playhead "snaps" between edit points and markers automatically. Edit points and marker locations appear as white triangles when the playhead is snapped to them.

2   Click the Snap icon to deactivate it. Now scrub through your Timeline. Notice how the playhead no longer snaps to edit points and markers.

3   Click the Snap icon to reactivate it.

Snapping clips into a sequence

The Snap feature also simplifies adding clips to your sequence. You'll use the Snap feature as you place clips in Video 2.

1   In your Timeline panel, adjust the playhead to 00:00:16:00.

2   In your Project panel, double-click the B-Roll bin to open it. Find the clip pre_wallReveal_adam.m4v.

3 Choose this clip and drag it into your Timeline on Video 2 so that its In point snaps to the playhead.

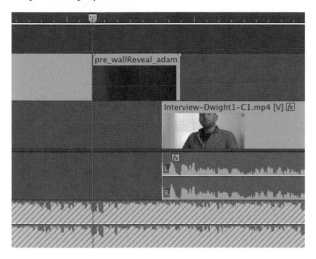

4 Hold down the Shift key and scrub the playhead to the right until it snaps to the In point of Interview-Dwight1-C1.mp4.

5 With the Selection tool active, grab the Out point of pre_wallReveal_adam.m4v, and drag it to the left until it snaps to the playhead.

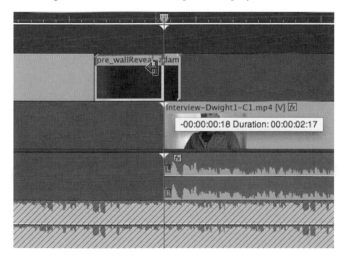

6 Hold down Shift and scrub the playhead to the left so that it snaps to the In point of pre_wallReveal_adam.m4v. Recall that this is one of the shots that we looked at earlier.

7 Go into the B-Roll bin again, and find the clip prod_watchingMonitors.m4v.

8 Choose this clip and drag it into the Source Monitor. Scrub the Source Monitor playhead to 00:00:04:11, when the camera becomes obscured.

9 Press O for Mark Out at the current frame.

10 Now choose the video frame in the Source Monitor and drag down into the Timeline panel on Video 2, so that its Out point snaps to the playhead, currently at 00:00:16:00.

Let's add a B-roll clip of Dwight over the first shot of Dwight speaking.

1 In your Timeline, go to timecode 00:00:18:17.

2 In the B-Roll bin, find the clip pre_dwight_listeningSmiling.m4v. Choose and drag it into the Source Monitor.

3 Adjust the Source Monitor playhead to 00:00:02:00. Press I for Mark In.

4 Adjust the Source Monitor playhead to 00:00:03:01. Press O for Mark Out.

5 Choose the Drag Video Only icon and drag the clip into the Timeline on Video 2 so its In point snaps to the playhead.

6 Scrub the Timeline playhead back several seconds, before the In point of prod_watchingMonitors.m4v. Press the spacebar to play the sequence. You will notice the cool transition from the production crew on set to the production crew in the planning stages.

However, this opening foreshadowing sequence could use one more shot. We don't see the band very clearly in the wide shot. We will take care of this in the next exercise.

Snapping clips within a sequence

If Snap is enabled, when you move clips within a sequence, the clip's head or tail will snap to markers or edit points.

1 Set your Timeline playhead to 00:00:13:13.

2 Go into the B-Roll bin and find the clip prod_productionMonitor.m4v. Choose and drag this clip into the Timeline on track Video 3, near where the playhead is, but this time, don't snap the clip to the current time.

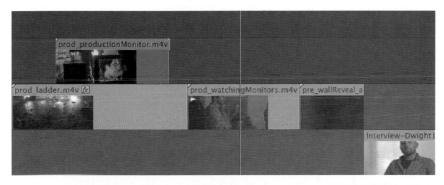

3 Using the Selection tool, grab the prod_productionMonitor.m4v clip and drag it to the right so that its Out point snaps to the playhead.

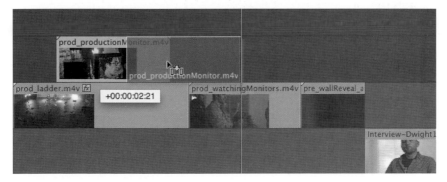

4 Scrub your playhead back in time a few seconds, to 00:00:10:00, to the frame that shows Filip beginning to tilt his head.

5 Grab the In point of prod_productionMonitor.m4v with the Selection tool, and drag it to the right until it snaps to the playhead.

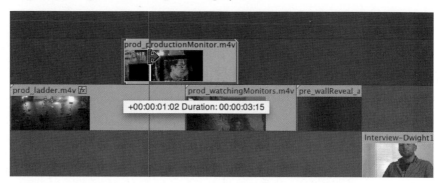

6 Now grab the entire prod_productionMonitor.m4v clip and drag it down one track to Video 2, where it should snap into place.

7 Press the Home key and then the spacebar to play back the opening sequence of your edit.

8 Press Command+S (Ctrl+S) to save your project.

Let's continue using the Snap feature to lay down a few more B-roll clips in your edit. In this exercise, you are going to use a clip marker as a snapping point.

1   Hold down the Shift key as you scrub your Timeline playhead to the Out point of Interview-Dancers.mp4 so that your playhead snaps to this frame.

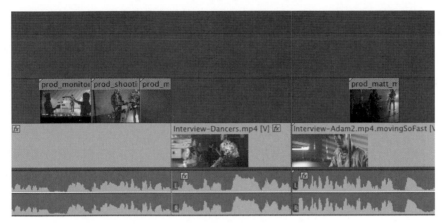

2   Go into the B-Roll bin and find the clip prod_dancers_highFive.m4v. Choose this clip and drag it into the Timeline on track Video 2 so that the In point of this clip snaps to the In point of Interview-Dancers.mp4.

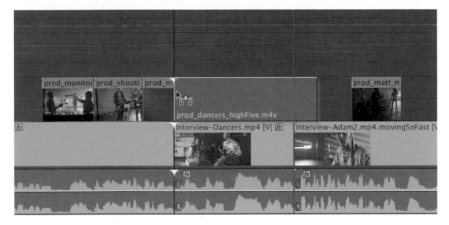

3   Double-click the prod_dancers_highFive.m4v clip in the Timeline, and it will open in the Source Monitor.

4   Scrub the playhead in the Source Monitor to 00:00:02:15, when the dancers high-five each other.

5 Press the M key to add a clip marker to this frame.

6 Now go back to your Timeline panel. Because you have chosen Expand All Tracks in your Timeline Display Properties, you should plainly see the clip marker that is on the prod_dancers_higFive.m4v clip in your Timeline.

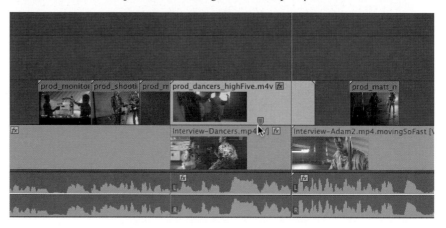

7 Select this clip and drag it to the right so that the clip marker snaps to the playhead.

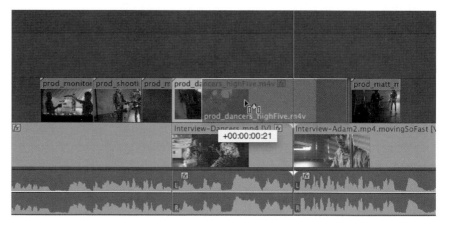

8 With the audio waveform of Audio 1 visible, you can see roughly when the two dancers say "hey!" in unison (at approximately 00:01:25:00). Using the Selection tool, grab the In point of prod_dancers_higFive.m4v and drag it to that frame.

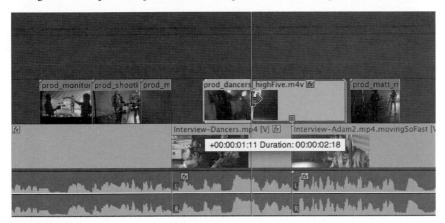

9 Grab the Out point of prod_dancers_higFive.m4v and drag it to the left until it snaps to the edit point between Interview-Dancers.mp4 and Interview-Adam2.mp4.movingSoFast.

Just as clip markers will snap to the Timeline playhead, the reverse is true: The playhead can snap to clip markers on clips that are in the Timeline.

1 Scrub your Timeline playhead to 00:01:51:23, where there is a clip marker on the music clip in Audio 2. Hold down Shift and your playhead will snap to this marker.

This clip marker on the music clip marks the point in the song when the cymbals crash, which can serve as a cue for something visual to occur. If Adam's sound bite at approximately 00:01:42:00 says "I can't wait, this is gonna be awesome," then that could serve as a cue for the start of a short montage of production B-roll. The clip Interview-Tyler2.mp4 could coincide with the cymbal crash and serve as the end point for this montage.

2 Activate the Track Select tool in the Tools panel. This tool is for selecting all clips in all tracks or just one track in the Timeline. Any clips that are not in a selected track but are linked to a clip in a selected track will become selected.

3 Choose the Interview-Tyler2.mp4 clip in the Timeline. Doing so will also select the Interview-AdamJeff.mp4 clip in the same track.

4 Activate the Selection tool, and drag Interview-Tyler2.mp4 (and consequently Interview-AdamJeff.mp4) to the right until its In point snaps to the playhead.

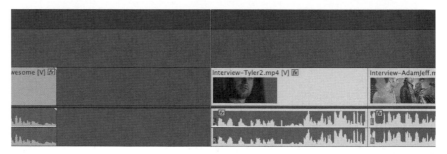

Now let's put some B-roll over this interview clip of the fog machine "blasting" Jeff and Filip.

5 Go into the B-Roll bin again, and find the clip prod_shooting_jeff_filip.m4v. Choose and drag this into the Source Monitor. With the Source Monitor playhead, scrub to 00:00:03:08.

6 Press the I key to Mark In.

7 Choose the Drag Video Only icon and drag the clip from the Source Monitor into the Timeline on Video 2, snapping its In point to the In point of Interview-Tyler2.mp4.

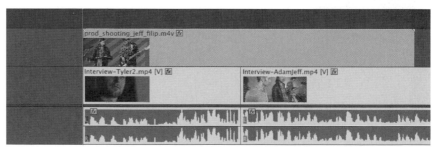

8 Grab the Out point of prod_shooting_jeff_filip.m4v and drag it to the left, lining it up with the brief pause in dialogue, visible in the audio waveform on Audio 1 at 00:01:55:11.

Let's put some clips in the Timeline that you will need for the next lesson.

1 Adjust your Timeline playhead to 00:01:39:12.

2 Go to the B-Roll bin and find the clip prod_adam_onSet.m4v.

3 Choose and drag it into the Source Monitor. Press the spacebar to play the clip. It shows Adam giving a bit of direction to the dancers, off-camera.

4 Adjust the Source Monitor playhead to 00:00:01:05, and press I to Mark In.

5 Adjust the Source Monitor playhead to 00:00:04:16, and press O to Mark Out.

6 Choose the Drag Video Only icon and drag it to the Timeline playhead so that the In point of the clip snaps to the playhead on Video 2.

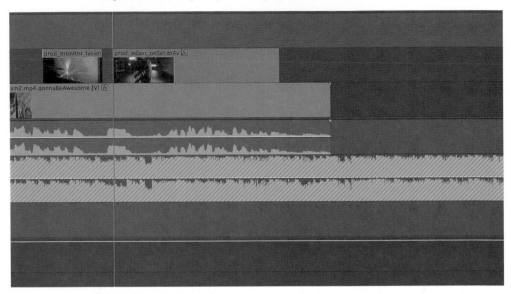

7 Adjust your Timeline playhead so that it snaps to the Out point of this clip.

8 Go to the B-Roll bin and find the clip prod_matt_jeff.m4v.

9 Choose and drag it into the Source Monitor. Press the spacebar to play the clip. It shows the cameraman, Matt Rome, shooting video of Jeff.

10 Adjust the Source Monitor playhead to 00:00:00:13, and press I to Mark In.

11 Adjust the Source Monitor playhead to 00:00:04:06, and press O to Mark Out.

12 Choose the Drag Video Only icon and drag it to the Timeline playhead so that the In point of the clip snaps to the playhead on Video 2.

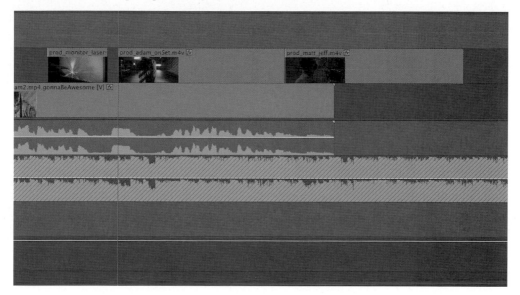

Just a few more.... These show how hard the production crew worked to make an electric fan blow confetti everywhere.

1 Adjust your Timeline playhead to 00:02:30:10.

2 Go to the B-Roll bin and find the clip prod_shooting_heidi_fan_confetti.m4v.

3 Choose and drag it into the Timeline so that its Out point snaps to the playhead on Video 2.

4 Adjust the playhead to 00:02:26:04.

5 With the Selection tool, grab the In point of the clip and snap it to the playhead on Video 2.

6 Snap the playhead to the Out point of this clip.

7 Go to the B-Roll bin and find the clip prod_shooting_crew_confetti_fog.m4v.

8 Choose and drag it to the Timeline on track Video 2 so that its In point snaps to the playhead.

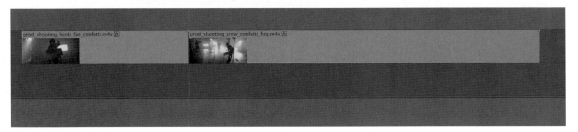

Yes, it took hours to clean up all that confetti.

1 Adjust the playhead to 00:02:34:11.

2 Use the Selection tool to grab the Out point of the clip and snap it to the playhead on Video 2.

3 Go the to B-Roll bin and find the clip prod_filip_heidi_throwConfetti.m4v.

4 Drag it into the playhead so that its In point snaps to the playhead on Video 2.

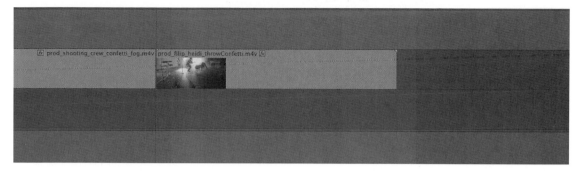

5 Adjust the playhead to 00:02:35:10.

6 Snap the Out point of this clip to the playhead on Video 2.

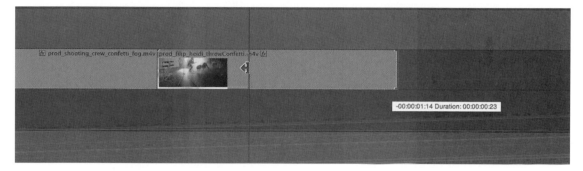

7 Go the to B-Roll bin and find the clip prod_confetti_lyrics.m4v.

8 Drag it into the playhead so that its In point snaps to the playhead on Video 2.

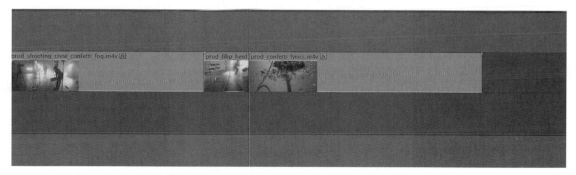

9 Adjust the playhead to 00:02:37:00.

10 Snap the Out point of this clip to the playhead on Video 2.

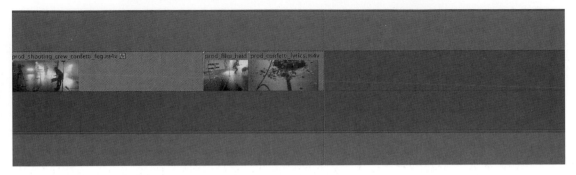

11 Press Command+S (Ctrl+S) to save your project.

In the next lesson, you will use these clips in some trimming exercises. Leave them untouched for now.

As you can see, the Snap feature allows you to make precise edits to your sequence, and you are encouraged to use it.

Refining your story

There are still a few tasks left to perform on this rough edit. Many of them are small and subtle, but there is one significant edit to make.

Shorten the music clips

The music clip can be shortened significantly and still not lose any of its emotional impact on the viewer.

Although this book covers audio editing in more detail in Chapter 7, this task is necessary before you proceed.

You will need to make edits to not only the instrumental version of the song but also the vocal, since, in a later lesson, you will create a mix between the two so that the edit starts out using the instrumental and transitions to the vocal version in order to make full use of the RED clips.

1 Select the B-Roll bin and press Command+W (Ctrl+W) to close it.

2 In the Project panel, twirl open the Audio bin, if it isn't already open. Inside, double-click If We Make It (Mix V1) INSTRUMENTAL.aif to open it in the Source Monitor.

3 Adjust your Source Monitor playhead to 00;02;42;14. This is the beginning of the segment that will be removed later. Press the M key to create a clip marker at this frame. Then adjust your playhead to 00;03;15;28 and press M to create another clip marker. This marks the end of the segment to be removed.

4 Now that you have created these clip markers on the instrumental clip, you will see these markers on this clip in the Timeline panel.

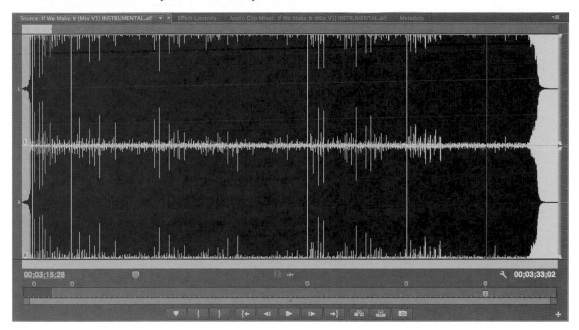

5 Go back in the Audio bin, and double-click If We Make It (Mix V1).aif to open it in the Source Monitor.

You will apply an edit to its In point.

1 Adjust the Source Monitor playhead to 00;02;42;14, and press the I key to Mark In.

2 Adjust your Timeline playhead to 00:02:34:07, snapping the playhead to the clip marker on the instrumental music clip in track Audio 2.

3 Now drag the If We Make It (Mix V1).aif clip from the Audio bin to Audio 3 in the Timeline, snapping its In point to the playhead.

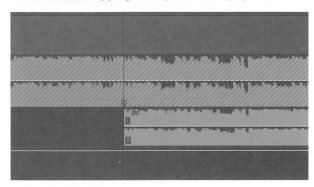

Before you go any further, verify that these two clips are playing in sync.

At the far left of the Timeline panel, you will see the Lock Track and Mute icons. Note that they are still active for Audio 2.

1   Click the Lock Track icon for Audio 2 to unlock the track.

● **Note:** Yes, it has to be done in this order. You must first unlock the track before you can do anything to it, including un-mute it.

2   Click the green M icon to un-mute the track.

3   Now play the sequence audio by pressing the spacebar. The two music clips should be playing in sync.

4   Snap your playhead back to the In point of If We Make It (Mix V1).aif in Audio 3.

Now you will use the Razor tool to make a cut to the instrumental clip on Audio 2.

1   Choose the Razor tool from the Tools panel.

2   Use the Razor tool to cut the instrumental clip in Audio 2.

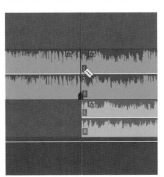

3   Now hold down Shift again and scrub the playhead to the right, snapping to the clip marker that corresponds to the sequence timecode of 00:03:07:16.

You can use the Razor tool to cut multiple clips in multiple tracks, as long as they aren't locked, and you hold down Shift while cutting.

4 Press Shift+C as you snap the Razor tool to the playhead; then make a cut to the clips in Audio 2 and Audio 3.

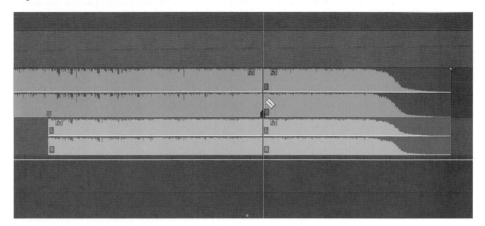

5 Press the V key to activate the Selection tool. Do a marquee-select of the first portion of the vocal track in Audio 3 and the corresponding portion of the instrumental clip in Audio 2.

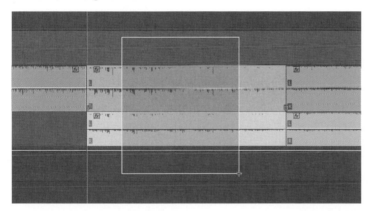

Next, you will want to do a ripple delete of the selected two clips. However, because there is unselected media in Video 2 after the In points of both audio clips, Adobe Premiere Pro won't permit it.

A way around this is to lock the Video 2 track so that nothing you do will affect it, even a ripple delete on other tracks.

1 Press the Toggle Track Lock icon for Video 2, to lock the track.

2 Now choose Edit > Ripple Delete. The selected portions of both songs are now removed, and the endings to both songs automatically scoot to the left to fill the time gap.

3 Press the Toggle Track Lock icon for Video 2, to unlock the track.

4 Adjust your playhead back a few seconds and then press the spacebar to play. You have successfully edited out a portion of the song, and the edit is barely noticeable.

For the time being, we are going to keep these tracks muted and locked.

5 Press the Mute icon for both Audio 2 and Audio 3.

6 Press the Toggle Track Lock icon for both Audio 2 and Audio 3.

7 Twirl your Audio bin shut in your Project panel.

8 Press Command+S (Ctrl+S) to save your project.

Making an audio gap

Whenever you are mixing dialogue and music in the same edit, especially when you have a lot of interesting B-roll, it's a good approach to not have dialogue playing for the entire duration. Instead, add a bit of variety by allowing the music to come forward in the soundscape, even if only for a few seconds at a time. It breaks the monotony for the viewer and allows for interesting editing of footage that has no person speaking.

Your edit already includes a couple such audio gaps. Let's create a third.

1 In your Timeline, select the Interview-AdamJeff.mp4 clip. You will nudge it to the right in the Timeline approximately two seconds.

2 Adjust your Timeline playhead to 00:02:03:00.

3 With the Selection tool, drag Interview-AdamJeff.mp4 to the right until its In point snaps to the playhead.

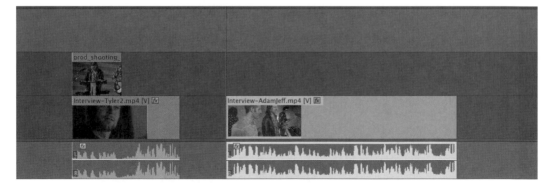

4 Scrub the playhead back to before Interview-Tyler2.mp4, then press the spacebar to play the sequence from here.

5 Press Command+S (Ctrl+S) to save your project.

Adding a reaction shot

Let's add a shot of Tyler reacting enthusiastically to the fog machine. By cutting from action to a shot of people reacting, you can reinforce the emotion that you're trying to evoke in your scene.

1   Snap the Timeline playhead to the Out point of prod_shooting_jeff_filip.m4v.

2   Double-click the B-Roll bin in the Project panel and find the clip prod_tyler_dwight_reaction.m4v. Choose and drag this into the Source Monitor.

3   Adjust the Source Monitor playhead to 00:00:02:03 and press I to Mark In.

4   Adjust the playhead to 00:00:03:07 and press O to Mark Out.

5   Choose the Drag Video Only icon and drag the clip into the Timeline on Video 2 so its In point snaps to the playhead.

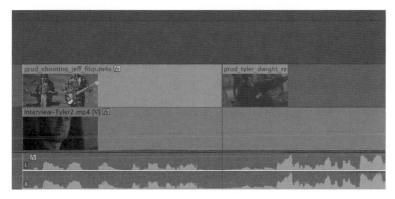

6   Move your playhead back a few seconds, then press the spacebar to play through the edit.

Adding the last clip

The last shot in the edit will be a slow-motion shot of a push broom sweeping confetti off the soundstage floor, providing a "You were here and it was real" feel to the piece.

1   Find the clip prod_sweepingConfetti_60fps.m4v in the B-Roll bin.

2   Choose and drag this into the Source Monitor.

3   Adjust the Source Monitor playhead to 00:00:07:15, and press I to Mark In.

4   Adjust the playhead to 00:00:12:08, and press O to Mark Out.

5 Choose the Drag Video Only icon and drag the clip into the Timeline on Video 2 so its In point snaps to the Out point of the clip in Audio 2.

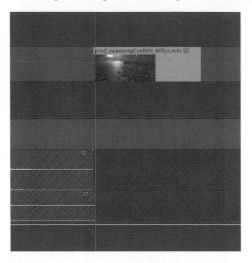

6 Scrub through this clip in the Timeline with your playhead. There is one small problem to solve: This clip is natively 1280×720 pixels, while the sequence has dimensions of 1920×1080 pixels. No problem. Adobe Premiere Pro gives you a way to easily deal with frame size mismatches amongst your footage.

7 In the Timeline, choose the prod_sweepingConfetti_60fps.m4v clip. Right-click it to get a context menu, and from that, choose Scale to Frame Size.

There! Problem solved!

8 Select the B-Roll bin. Press Command + W (Ctrl + W) to close it.

Final marker

Last but not least, we want to add a marker to the sequence, in order to indicate where the final RED clips will go in the edit.

1 In your Timeline, adjust your playhead to timecode 00:02:37:00. This is where the final RED clip will start.

2 With your Timeline panel as the active window, click the Add Marker button. A new Sequence Marker appears on the Timeline.

3 Press Command+S (Ctrl+S) to save your project.

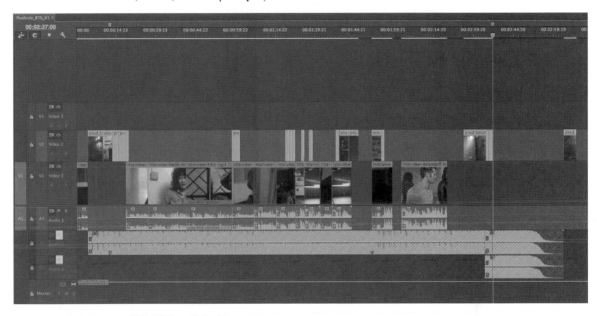

No additional B-roll or Interview clips are to be put in the sequence after this marker.

Multicam editing

If you are editing a project shot with multiple cameras, the Multicam editing features of Adobe Premiere Pro will help you cut between your cameras in real time, similar to editing a live TV show.

In Adobe Premiere Pro, the process of creating a multicamera sequence has been improved, with the ability to automatically sync audio and video, from sources with different audio sample rates and different video frame rates, as well as the ability to view video thumbnails of those sources in the Program Monitor. For more information, we recommend *Adobe Premiere Pro CC Classroom in a Book* (Adobe Press, 2013).

Finishing your rough edit

Okay, now that you've gotten some practice with basic editing techniques, your final exercise is to fill in the edit with B-roll clips at your discretion. As before, put the B-roll clips on track Video 2. Be sure to cover any time gaps. Use layer markers when needed. Snapping is a handy feature, but remember that you can turn it off if you don't want everything to snap to everything else. Set In and Out points in the Source Monitor if you prefer trimming clips before placing them in the Timeline.

In a later lesson, you will be adding lower third graphics to the edit to identify the people speaking on camera. For all of the initial shots of on-camera speakers, leave three to four seconds of unobstructed talking heads.

And most important of all: Save your work often!

Have fun.

Review questions

1 How is the Slip tool useful?

2 What is a subclip, and how can it be useful?

3 Why would you lock an audio or video track?

4 What are clip markers, and how are they useful?

5 What is a ripple delete?

6 What are the advantages of using the Snap feature?

Review answers

1 The Slip tool allows you to move a clip's frames forward or backward in the Timeline while maintaining that clip's In and Out points in the Timeline.

2 A subclip is a portion of an existing clip. Making subclips allows you to extract sound bites from a long interview clip.

3 You would lock an audio or video track to prevent any accidental edits to clips in those tracks, or when the presence of clips in unlocked tracks would prevent edits in other tracks.

4 Clip markers are indicators you place on specific frames of a clip so that those frames can be easily found or referenced later in your edit.

5 A ripple delete removes a clip from a track and automatically moves all clips after the deleted clip in all unlocked tracks to the left in the Timeline to fill in the gap created by the deleted clip.

6 The Snap feature allows the playhead to easily adjust to edit points in the Timeline. It also allows easy adjustment of the playhead to clip markers and sequence markers.

4 ADVANCED EDITING TECHNIQUES

Lesson overview

In the previous lesson, you created a basic edit with Adobe Premiere Pro. In this lesson, you'll use more advanced editing techniques and learn how to

- Apply various clip-trimming techniques in your Timeline

- Apply and modify an effect to clips in your Timeline

- Incorporate RED footage into your Timeline

- Create simple dissolve transitions between clips in your Timeline

- Create a static title with the Abobe Premiere Pro Title tool

- Edit closed captions

- Use the Warp Stabilizer effect to smooth unsteady camera movement in a clip

- Generate a preview render of your Timeline

- Upload a file and sync your settings to Creative Cloud

 This lesson will take approximately 120 minutes to complete.

Download this lesson and its project files from the Lesson & Update Files tab on your Account page at www.peachpit.com and store them on your computer in a convenient location, as described in the Getting Started section of this book.

Your Account page is also where you'll find any updates to the chapters or to the lesson files. Look on the Lesson & Update Files tab to access the most current content.

Applying the Warp Stabilizer effect to a clip in
Adobe Premiere Pro

5 CREATING BASIC MOTION GRAPHICS AND VISUAL EFFECTS

Lesson overview

Creative Cloud gives you the power to create a wide range of motion graphics and visual effects—from simple animated titles to effects shots for motion pictures. In this lesson, you'll learn how to

- Use Dynamic Link to integrate work between Adobe Premiere Pro and After Effects

- Manage your media in After Effects

- Create and modify compositions and layers in After Effects

- Use text animation presets in After Effects

- Import and manipulate layered Illustrator images in After Effects

- Understand the fundamentals of keyframe-based animation in After Effects

 This lesson will take approximately 160 minutes to complete.

Download the project files for this lesson from the Lesson & Update Files tab on your Account page at www.peachpit.com and store them on your computer in a convenient location, as described in the Getting Started section of this book.

Your Account page is also where you'll find any updates to the chapters or to the lesson files. Look on the Lesson & Update Files tab to access the most current content.

Keyframing a layer's position in After Effects

Beginning this lesson

If you are continuing from the previous lesson, feel free to continue with the Adobe Premiere Pro project you already have open. Skip ahead to "Preserving your rough edit in Adobe Premiere Pro."

If you are starting here

If you are starting at this lesson, generate your own Adobe Premiere Pro project file from a copy of one provided for you.

Note: Important! Currently, Adobe Premiere Pro CC does not retain interpret-footage settings on clips even though those clips don't need relinking. Refer to the Getting Started section "Interpret frame rate of linked files" for steps on fixing this issue so you can follow this lesson.

1 Navigate to the Assets > Lessons > Lesson 05 folder on your hard drive.

2 Double-click to open the Adobe Premiere Pro project, Lesson05_Start.prproj.

3 In Adobe Premiere Pro, choose File > Save As.

4 Navigate to the Lesson 05 folder on your hard drive. Name your Adobe Premiere Pro project file **Poolside Edit 03**. Click Save.

Preserving your rough edit in Adobe Premiere Pro

Because you are continuing with a previous version of this edit, you'll first save a new version of your sequence. This allows you to go back to the previous version if need be and is a recommended best practice in the video editing workflow.

1 In the Project panel, twirl open the Sequences bin.

Tip: Press Command+C (Ctrl+C) to copy. Press Command+V (Ctrl+V) to paste. This will make a duplicate of this sequence outside of the Sequences folder.

2 Click the Poolside_BTS_02 sequence to select it. Choose Edit > Copy to copy it to your clipboard. Then choose Edit > Paste.

3 To modify the name of the sequence, click the name of the sequence to select it.

Potential Error Messages

When opening an Adobe Premiere Pro project file that was last saved on a different computer, you may encounter a couple of error messages. Don't panic!

One such error message will tell you that the local scratch disk is not in the same place.

● **Note:** This sidebar also appeared in Chapter 1 and is repeated here for your convenience if you have not followed these chapter lessons in order.

If this happens, choose File > Project Settings > Scratch Disks, then, for all settings in the Scratch Disks window, click the Browse button and navigate to a local folder on your hard drive where you want Adobe Premiere Pro to save your Captured Video and Audio, your Video and Audio Previews, and your Project Auto Saves.

Another error message you may encounter is one that tells you that there is a missing renderer.

This just means that the project file was last saved on a machine that was using a graphics processing unit (GPU) that is not present on the current machine. Again, don't panic. Just click OK and carry on.

4 Change the name of the sequence to **Poolside_BTS_03**, press Return (Enter), and then drag it into the Sequences folder.

5 Double-click the Poolside_BTS_03 sequence to load it in your Timeline.

Note that the sequence appears in a new tabbed Timeline in front of your original sequence.

Having multiple Timelines open simultaneously can be useful in certain situations, but it can also be confusing. For the time being, you'll close the first Timeline to eliminate the possibility of accidentally modifying the wrong sequence.

6 In the Timeline, click the Poolside_BTS_02 tab to select it.

7 Press Command+W (Ctrl+W) to close this sequence.

The new sequence is now the only one visible in the Timeline, which will ensure that you are working on the most recent iteration.

8 Press Command+S (Ctrl+S) to save your Adobe Premiere Pro project.

About After Effects

After Effects is the Swiss army knife of motion graphics and effects tools. It has a wide range of uses, from creating simple animated text to creating elaborate title sequences for motion pictures. After Effects is the industry-standard tool for creating motion graphics and compositing visual effects.

In this lesson, you'll learn some of the basic skills you'll need to create basic graphics and effects for your video production projects. This lesson only scratches the surface of the capabilities of After Effects. If motion graphics and/or visual effects are a significant part of your workflow, we strongly recommend obtaining *Adobe After Effects CC Classroom in a Book.*

The "link" between motion graphic artists and video editors

Note that as a video editor, it is possible to launch After Effects directly from your Adobe Premiere Pro Timeline by replacing a clip in your sequence with an After Effects composition. As a motion graphics artist, you generally spend more time working in After Effects than in an Adobe Premiere Pro project, and as a result, you would likely begin many projects in After Effects than in Adobe Premiere Pro. The Dynamic Link workflow between these two applications has allowed motion graphic artists, who are usually more familiar with After Effects than Adobe Premiere Pro, to become better video editors and, on the flip side, video editors to become better motion graphic artists.

The concepts of compositing and animation

When you're working in After Effects, you'll be spending most of your time assembling visual elements into a composition and animating them. Put simply, the crafts of compositing and animation can be defined as follows:

Compositing is the merging of multiple images from different sources. For example, your After Effects composition may include video clips, photographs, vector graphics, and text, each with their own unique settings. Sometimes it's necessary to composite layers in a composition so there is a seamless blend between them to create the illusion that multiple layers are a single visible element.

Animation is the rapid display of images to create the illusion of motion. After Effects allows you to animate both the motion and the properties of visible layers. For example, you could have a text object moving across the frame while a blur effect animates the text object simultaneously.

Creating a new project in After Effects

● **Note:** If you encounter the After Effects Welcome screen at startup, uncheck "Show Welcome Screen at startup," and then click Close.

Let's get started in After Effects!

1 Launch After Effects and click File > Save As > Save As.

2 Navigate to the Lesson 05 folder (Assets > Lessons > Lesson 05), type in the project name, **Poolside AE 01**, and click Save.

Optimizing performance

After Effects is extremely flexible in the ways it can render and display your compositions. The more powerful your hardware, the better After Effects will perform. You can do all the basic tasks in After Effects on modest hardware, but the processing required for more advanced tasks generally means you'll have a better experience using more powerful hardware.

One important fact about After Effects is that it does not play back your compositions instantly, in real time, like Adobe Premiere Pro can. It needs to render the frames first before playing them back.

After Effects has made significant strides in making the best use of the hardware you have to render and cache frames in the background while you work.

The main components of your hardware that will affect performance in After Effects are

RAM. After Effects *loves* RAM, and you simply cannot have enough. The performance of the software, in general, as well as the number of frames you can cache in RAM for previews and playback, greatly depends on having a good amount of RAM in your system.

OpenGL. After Effects takes advantage of the OpenGL graphics language to offload certain rendering tasks to the GPU.

● **Note:** For more information on graphics cards that support GPU acceleration in Digital Video, go to www. adobe.com/products/ premiere/tech-specs. html.

Graphics card. A graphics card with a powerful, Adobe-approved GPU can handle multiple rendering tasks in After Effects, freeing up your CPU to handle other tasks, which results in better performance.

Hard drive. A fast hard drive is especially important if you work with high-resolution, high-bitrate, video formats. The faster your drives can read and write data, the faster your system can render and display frames. Although After Effects can run on a laptop with a single hard drive, for optimum performance, we recommend that you run After Effects on a workstation that has a separate hard drive for your system drive (with your operating system and applications), another hard drive or a RAID for your media and renders, and a third hard drive for your cache. Ideally, the cache drive would be a solid state drive to achieve the fastest render that would utilize the Global Performance Cache (see the next section, "The Global Performance Cache"). Any standard hard disk drive (HDD) in your configuration should operate at 7200 rpm (revolutions per minute) or faster.

Solid-state drives (SSDs)

Thanks to advances in solid-state memory technologies, it is now possible to obtain a computer or external storage device with an SSD. These have their advantages and disadvantages when compared to standard HDDs of similar storage capacity.

Pros of SSDs:

- Faster performance
- Lighter weight
- Smaller form factor
- Silent operation

Cons of SSDs:

- More expensive
- Smaller capacity

The Global Performance Cache

Essential to understanding the After Effects rendering pipeline is the Global Performance Cache. This feature greatly speeds up your workflow by taking full advantage of your computer's 64-bit CPU cores, RAM, and hard drive(s). For instance, if you have made a preview render of an animation in After Effects and you then make a change to that animation, you can revert to the previous state of the animation without having to make another preview render of it. Also, the Global Performance Cache will save RAM Previews of your After Effects compositions so you can access them the next time you reopen your project. The Global Performance Cache makes your workflow more efficient and allows you more time to be creative.

In order to make the most of the Global Performance Cache, your system needs a supported GPU installed. You can find a list of supported graphics cards at www.adobe.com/products/premiere/tech-specs.html.

Setting preferences for the Global Performance Cache

If you have a supported graphics processor, you should optimize some of your After Effects preferences.

1 To view and set your Media & Disk Cache preferences, on Mac OS, choose
   After Effects > Preferences > Media & Disk Cache. On Windows, choose
   Edit > Preferences > Media & Disk Cache.

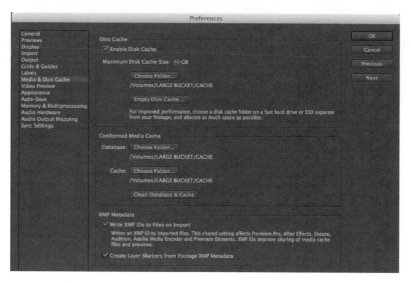

2 Select Enable Disk Cache, and click the Choose Folder button. Navigate to a
   folder on your system that is on a fast hard drive, preferably an SSD that is
   separate from your system and your media.

3 Set the Maximum Disk Cache size to as high as your cache drive will allow. If
   you only have one hard drive for your system and your media, we recommend
   that you allow at least 20 megabytes for your disk cache.

4 Select the Memory & Multiprocessing preferences.

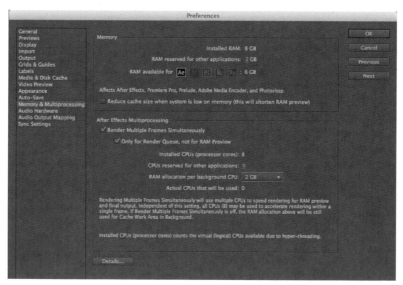

5 Based on your Installed RAM, allocate at least 2GB for each CPU core on your system.

6 Select Render Multiple Frames Simultaneously. With this feature activated, After Effects will devote the allotted amount of RAM, divided among each CPU core, to dramatically speed up your render times.

7 The Installed CPUs (Processor Cores) accounts for actual CPU cores as well as virtual CPUs that are available due to hyper-threading. Without getting too technical, ideally you want After Effects to render your frames with actual CPUs, so set "CPUs reserved for other applications" to the number of actual CPUs on your system.

8 Click OK.

Understanding the After Effects user interface

When you launch After Effects for the first time, you'll be presented with the default Standard workspace. This workspace is a combination of the most commonly used panels.

To reset the Standard workspace to its default settings, follow these steps.

1 Choose Window > Workspace > Standard.

2 Choose Window > Workspace > Reset "Standard."

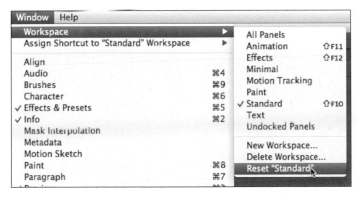

3 In the dialog that appears, click OK.

On the surface of the Standard workspace, seven panels are visible:

- The Project panel is where you store and organize all of your assets, such as footage and compositions.

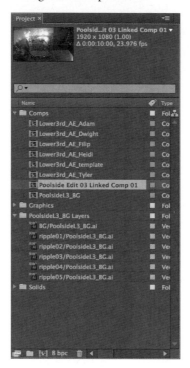

- The Composition panel is where you view your graphics and make spatial manipulations to layers.

- The Timeline is where you adjust your layer order, layer properties, and time-based animations.

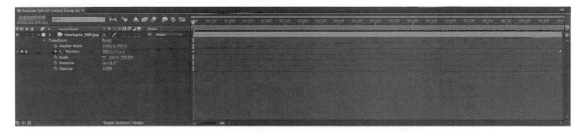

- The Tools panel is where you select different tools to use in the animation process.

- The Info panel is where you view data about an action, such as spatial coordinates, color values, and numerical changes in layer properties.

- The Preview panel is where you manipulate playback and preview settings for the active composition.

- The Effects & Presets panel is where you access and apply effects and presets to the selected layer or layers.

Notwithstanding the obvious differences, you may notice some similarities between the user interfaces of Adobe Premiere Pro and After Effects. For instance, both applications have a Project panel, a Timeline, and a Tools panel, all of which serve the same basic respective functions. The Composition panel in After Effects works much like the Program Monitor in Adobe Premiere Pro.

Creating folders in After Effects

Let's make some folders in your After Effects Project panel. These are analogous to bins in Adobe Premiere Pro. They provide a way to organize all your project media.

At the bottom left of the Project panel, there is a row of icons.

1 Click the New Folder icon.

This will create a new folder in your Project panel, with its name highlighted.

2 Change the name to **Comps** and press Return (Enter).

3 Deselect this by pressing Command+Shift+A (Ctrl+Shift+A).

4 Click the new folder icon again, and this will make another new unnamed folder.

5 Change the name to **Graphics** and press Return (Enter).

6 Press Command+S (Ctrl+S) to save your After Effects project.

7 Switch back to Adobe Premiere Pro by pressing Command+Tab (Alt+Tab).

Using Dynamic Link: from Adobe Premiere Pro to After Effects

Adobe Premiere Pro and After Effects are designed to work seamlessly together so that you can bring an element from one to the other without having to do a full render beforehand. For instance, you can bring a clip from Adobe Premiere Pro into After Effects and apply changes to it, and those changes will dynamically update in Adobe Premiere Pro.

For more information about Dynamic Link, refer to Lesson 1.

In this exercise, you'll bring an image sequence clip from your Timeline in Adobe Premiere Pro into After Effects and then apply an effect to it.

First, you must import this clip to your Adobe Premiere Pro project and add it to your Timeline. Then you will snap the Timeline playhead to the tail of Interview-Tyler2.mp4, at 00:01:59:19. When you do, notice the gap in time here between your clip and Interview-AdamJeff.mp4.

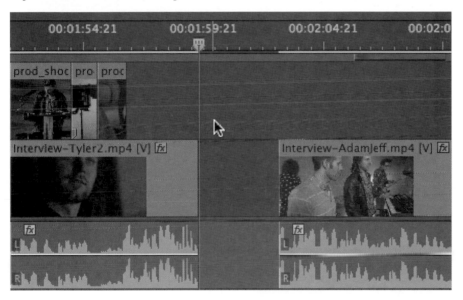

You will then create a timelapse clip out of images taken by a camera that was pointed at the set and that took a picture once every few seconds. These images, if played in sequence at 24 fps, show the frenetic activity on set at a very quick speed.

Importing an image sequence

▶ **Tip:** To import a file to Adobe Premiere Pro, press Command+I (Ctrl+I).

First, you need to import these images as an image sequence.

1 Choose File > Import.

2 Navigate to Assets > Graphics > Timelapse.

3 Select the first image, timelapse_000.

4 Select the check box for Image Sequence so that it is checked.

5 Click Import. Because you had the sequence Poolside_BTS_03 selected in the Sequences bin, the timelapse clip is imported to the Sequences bin.

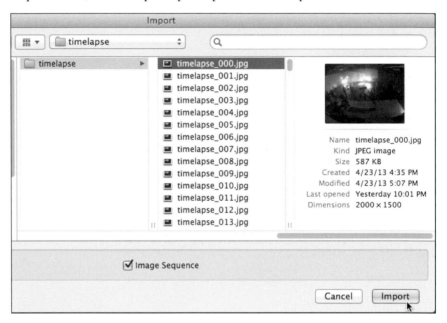

6 Choose and drag timelapse_000.jpg into the Graphics bin, then twirl open the Graphics bin to reveal it.

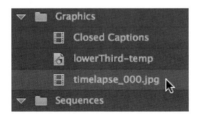

An image sequence is a series of separate image files that, if named with chrono-logical numbers, Adobe Premiere Pro, After Effects, or other video editing applica-tions can import as a single footage item. Essentially, this new unit is treated as a video clip, with a certain frame resolution and frame rate.

Since the timelapse images are all sequenced according to the order in which they were shot, and the image files are numbered chronologically, the timelapse images are a good example of an image sequence.

Let's compare some of the properties of this image sequence with the DSLR clips in the Footage bin.

● **Note:** DSLR stands for digital single-lens reflex, generally referring to a high-end digital camera. Some DSLR cameras, like the Canon 5D Mark III or the Nikon D7000, shoot high-definition video. The .mp4 and .m4v clips included with this book's assets were shot with a DSLR camera.

1 Twirl open the Footage bin, and then twirl open the Interview bin.

2 In the Project panel, scroll to the right to reveal the Video Info column.

Notice that this has a slightly larger frame size than the DSLR footage.

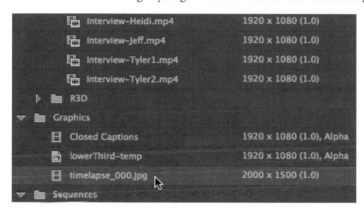

▶ **Tip:** You can maximize a panel to fill the screen if you hover your mouse pointer over the panel and press the apostrophe (`) key.

3 Twirl the Interview bin and the Footage bin shut.

Interpreting the timelapse

Before you do anything else, you must tell Adobe Premiere Pro to re-interpret this clip's frame rate.

1 Scroll to the left in your Project panel. Notice the timelapse clip's frame rate of 29.97 fps. Ideally, you would want your footage to use the same frame rate as your sequence.

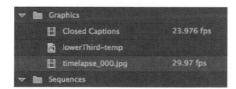

2 Select timelapse_000.jpg, and choose Clip > Modify > Interpret Footage.

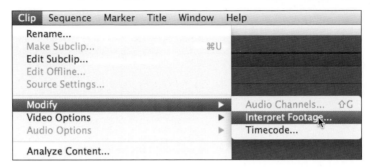

3 Select Assume This Frame Rate, and change its value to 23.976. Click OK.

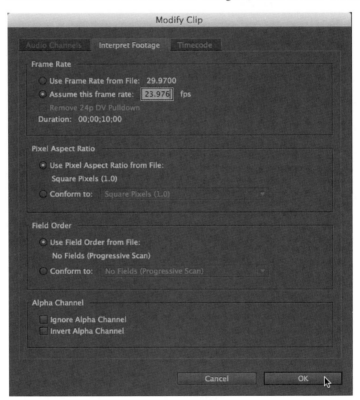

4 Verify that the frame rate now shows in the Project panel as 23.976.

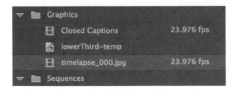

Adding the timelapse clip to the sequence

First, let's look at the timelapse clip.

1 Choose and drag timelapse_000.jpg to the Source Monitor.

2 Press the spacebar to play the clip.

3 Choose the Drag Video Only icon and drag the clip to the Timeline on track Video 2 so its head snaps to the playhead at 00:01:59:19.

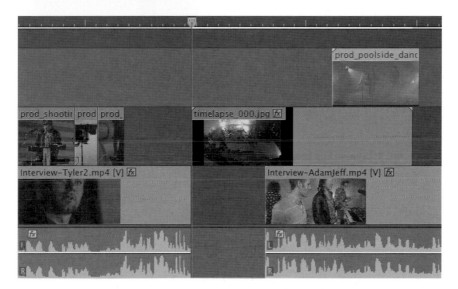

4 Press the spacebar to play the clip in your sequence.

Notice that the timelapse would look better if it had some movement, as if the shot was taken by a very slowly tilting timelapse camera.

You can do simple motion like this with Adobe Premiere Pro, but let's take this opportunity to see how to do it with After Effects.

1 Right-click timelapse_000.jpg in the Timeline.

2 A menu appears next to the clip. Choose Replace With After Effects Composition.

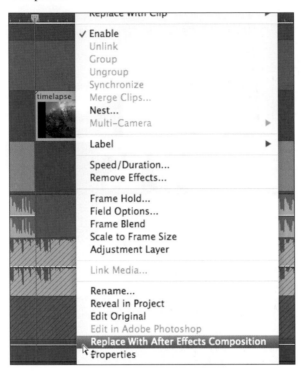

Doing this brings After Effects into focus.

Notice the presence of a Poolside Edit 03 Linked Comp 01 composition in the Project panel, as well as the timelapse_000.jpg image sequence. Because you had the Graphics folder selected, these imported into that folder.

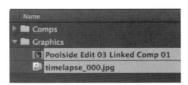

3 Press Command+Shift+A (Ctrl+Shift+A) to deselect all.

4 Choose and drag the Poolside Edit 03 Linked Comp 01 composition into the Comps folder.

5 Double-click the Comps folder to reveal the composition.

6 Press Command+S (Ctrl+S) to save your project.

Creating a motion graphic with After Effects

A motion graphic is, simply, an animated graphic design. It can incorporate abstract graphics, photographs, vector logos, video clips, and text, all of which can be animated separately to convey an overall message.

Motion graphics are used for a variety of purposes, most commonly for titles in motion pictures and television programs; animated graphics in advertisements and corporate presentations; photographic slide shows; and user interfaces for mobile applications.

After Effects has been available since 1993—yes, 20 years ago!—and has established itself as the industry-standard application for creating motion graphics, largely due to its tight integration with Photoshop and Illustrator.

Working with layers

Layers can be still images, video, vector graphics, and text. A layer can be an imported graphic created in another program, such as Photoshop Extended or Illustrator, or it can be created natively in After Effects. Most layers contain visual content. However, in some cases, as with adjustment layers or null objects, they can be used to affect other layers.

As in Photoshop or Illustrator, layers in an After Effects composition can be stacked on top of one another. The top-to-bottom stacking order of layers in a composition generally corresponds to its front-to-back visibility. In other words, if a layer is stacked above another, it will generally appear in front of the other. If you want to change the front-to-back visibility of layers in your composition, you can adjust the stacking order of layers by dragging them up or down in the layer order.

With layers in After Effects, you not only have spatial visibility to consider, but also temporal visibility, or duration. Each layer has its own duration within the time of the composition that it's in. All layers in a composition don't need to have the same duration within the composition's duration.

1 If it didn't open automatically, double-click to open the Poolside Edit 03 Linked Comp 01 composition, brought in from Adobe Premiere Pro.

2 Scrub through it with the playhead.

▶ **Tip:** You can zoom out your view of the Composition panel by pressing the comma (,), and you can zoom in by pressing the period (.).

3 Use the Selection tool to select and move the layer around in the Composition panel. Notice that because the layer is taller than the composition's frame height, the timelapse image sequence can animate its vertical position for a bit without showing its top or bottom edges and always be filling the frame.

4 While dragging the layer, hold down Command+Shift (Ctrl+Shift) and snap the layer's center to the center of the composition's frame.

5 Twirl open the timelapse_000.jpg layer, then twirl open Transform. Notice the Position property and its values.

You're now going to animate the position of this layer, from one vertical position to a different vertical position, using what are called keyframes.

Understanding keyframes

In traditional hand-drawn animation, the term keyframe refers to a single frame (or drawing) that illustrates key points in an animation. After the keyframes are drawn by a senior animator, the junior animators draw all of the in-between frames.

In After Effects, keyframes work similarly to their traditional counterparts: A keyframe refers to a fixed property value at any given moment in time. After Effects automatically calculates all of the values in between two or more keyframes.

In After Effects, you will use keyframes to animate Position, Scale, Opacity, and other properties.

Animating your layers

To create keyframes for a property, you must first activate the stopwatch icon next to the property's name in the Timeline or in the Effect Controls panel.

The stopwatch icon acts as a switch to toggle whether the property is animated or not. When a property's stopwatch is activated, After Effects makes a keyframe at the current time. This keyframe will have the property's current value. Changing the property's value while the playhead is on a frame without a keyframe will create a new keyframe at the current time, giving the keyframe the property's current value.

You may change any property's value at any given frame in your composition. Making these changes will automatically add or modify a keyframe for that property at the current time. To put it plain and simple, you click a property's stopwatch to begin animating it.

If you are more familiar working with clips in a timeline and not keyframes, this general workflow may not feel intuitive. However, the more you practice with it, the more you will become familiar with this process.

Some properties have only one value, like Opacity. Other properties, like Position or Scale, are arrays of multiple values. Position has separate values for horizontal and vertical.

1   Select the second Position value, the vertical value. Change it to **330** and press Return (Enter).

2   Set the first Position keyframe by clicking its stopwatch icon.

▶ Tip: Do not deactivate a property's stopwatch once you have created keyframes. Doing so will automatically delete all of that property's keyframes!

The diamond-shaped icon that you see is a Keyframe icon. They are not always diamond-shaped, as you will discover.

In order for a property to animate with keyframes, it needs at least two keyframes with different values at different times.

3 Scrub the playhead all the way to the end of the Timeline, or press Command+Option+Right Arrow (Ctrl+Alt+Right Arrow).

4 Select the vertical position value, change it to **750**, and press Return (Enter).

5 Notice that this automatically makes a new keyframe at the current time.

6 Press Command+Option+Left Arrow (Ctrl+Alt+Left Arrow) to go to the beginning of the Timeline.

Using RAM Preview

Whenever you create an animation in After Effects, you should preview your work to make sure it looks the way you intended. In most cases, what you apply in After Effects will not instantly play back in real time unless you render it first. After Effects allows you to render your composition frames and store them in your computer's RAM so you can preview the composition—hence, the term RAM Preview.

Let's do a RAM Preview of your composition so that we can preview the timelapse.

RAM Previewing your timelapse

You can activate a RAM Preview in After Effects in a couple of ways: You can either press the 0 key on your numeric keypad, or (if you are using a laptop that doesn't have a numeric keypad) you can press Control+0 (Ctrl+0) or go to the Preview panel and click the RAM Preview button.

1 Do a RAM Preview of your composition.

Depending on the speed of your computer, how much RAM your computer has, and a multitude of other factors, the time required for this RAM Preview will vary. Eventually, you should see a green line along the top of the Timeline, underneath the gray Work Area bar, indicating the frames that are rendered and stored in RAM.

▶ Tip: To navigate in your After Effects Timeline by single frames, click the Next Frame or Previous Frame button in the Preview panel. You can also press Page Down to move your playhead to the next frame, and press Page Up to move to the previous frame.

2 Press Command+S (Ctrl+S) to save your After Effects project.

3 Switch to Adobe Premiere Pro by pressing Command+Tab (Alt+Tab).

Final changes to timelapse

Notice that in your Adobe Premiere Pro Timeline, the original timelapse image sequence has been replaced by an imported After Effects composition.

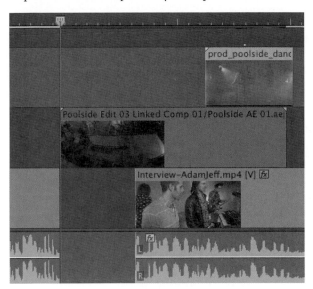

Let's trim the Out point of the Timelapse clip in your sequence.

1 Adjust your Timeline playhead to right after Adam, in Interview-AdamJeff.mp4, says "approaching."

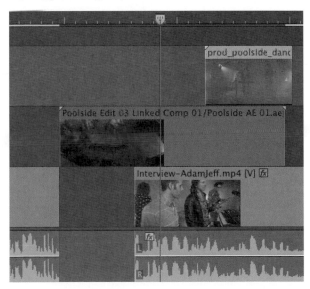

The clip needs to be shortened, but you'll do this by speeding it up.

2 From the Tools panel, choose the Rate Stretch tool.

3 Grab the tail of the timelapse clip with the Rate Stretch tool, then snap it to the playhead. Even though this is an imported After Effects composition, it can be rate-stretched like any other clip in Adobe Premiere Pro.

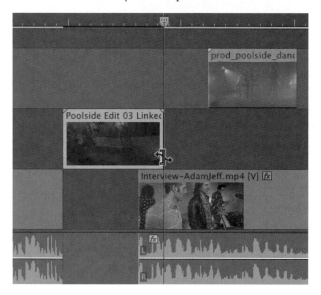

4 Adjust the Timeline playhead to the In point of the timelapse clip.

5 Press the spacebar to play through the clip. Notice that the timelapse plays back a bit faster.

6 Press the V key to activate the default Selection tool.

Updating a dynamically linked composition

Notice that at the beginning of the clip, we see too much of the area below the camera where a lot of equipment is stacked but where nothing is actually happening in frame.

Because this clip is dynamically linked to a composition in After Effects, you can switch to After Effects and edit the composition, and the change will automatically update on the corresponding clip in your Adobe Premiere Pro sequence.

1 Switch to After Effects by pressing Command+Tab (Alt+Tab).

You should see the timelapse composition in the After Effects interface.

2 Press the Home key. Select the vertical Position value for the layer and change it to **575**. Press Return (Enter).

▶ **Tip:** If your keyboard doesn't have Home or End keys, press Command+Option+Left Arrow (Ctrl+Alt+Left Arrow) to move the playhead to the beginning of the Timeline. Press Command+Option+Right Arrow (Ctrl+Alt+Right Arrow) to move the playhead to the end of the Timeline.

3 Save your project by pressing Command+S (Ctrl+S).

4 Switch to Adobe Premiere Pro by pressing Command+Tab (Alt+Tab).

5 Adjust the Timeline playhead to the In point of the timelapse clip.

6 Press the spacebar to play the sequence. Notice that after making a change to this raw clip in After Effects, the change automatically updates to the clip in your Adobe Premiere Pro sequence.

7 In your Project panel, choose the Poolside Edit 03 Linked Comp 01/Poolside AE 01.aep clip (the imported timelapse composition) and drag it into the Graphics bin.

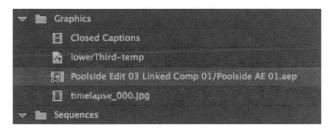

8 Save your project by pressing Command+S (Ctrl+S).

Reducing resolution for RAM Previews

In some cases, After Effects will not make a RAM Preview of all of the frames in your composition. This is not a bug. You need to consider a couple of factors when doing a RAM Preview. First, because After Effects stores frames in your computer's RAM, you need to determine how much RAM your computer has. Second, you need to determine how much of this RAM is being allocated to other applications currently open.

Although this composition is fairly short, you may end up working with compositions that are longer, and no reasonable amount of RAM on your computer will be enough to preview all of the frames. In such a scenario, you might consider reducing your composition's resolution from Full to Half (or even Third or Quarter) so that, at the expense of RAM Preview image quality, After Effects can render more frames with greater speed.

About Illustrator

Illustrator is the industry standard application for creating static vector graphics for print, video, and the Web. With it, you can create layered images that can be integrated with other layers in Photoshop, Flash, and After Effects.

Raster images versus vector images

It's important to know the difference between raster images and vector images. Here is a brief explanation of the differences and what each is typically used for.

A *raster image* is made up of a finite grid of pixels. Typically, this would be a digitized photograph, but it could also be a frame from a video clip or a scanned drawing. A raster image can be saved in a variety of different file formats, such as a .jpg, .png, .tiff, or in the native Photoshop Extended .psd format. Raster images can offer high-resolution photorealistic detail but are limited by their native image size. If a raster image is scaled larger than its native size, then the edges in the image look jagged and pixelated.

A *vector image* is made up of paths; each is defined by an underlying mathematical formula that determines how the path is shaped. The paths are assigned colors as strokes on the paths or fills within the paths. A vector image would typically be a logo graphic saved as a .eps file or in the native Illustrator .ai format. The advantage of vector graphics is that they can be scaled without showing pixelated edges and thus retain their image quality.

Making a new image in Illustrator

Let's make a lower third background graphic in Illustrator.

1   Open Illustrator.

2   Choose File > New.

3   In the New Document window, enter a Name: **PoolsideL3_BG**.

4   From the Profile menu, choose Video and Film.

5   From the Size menu, choose HDTV 1080.

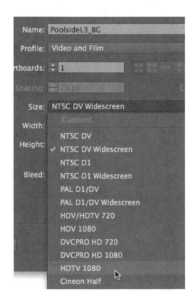

6 Click the triangle next to Advanced to reveal more properties.

7 In the Color Mode menu, choose RGB.

8 In the Raster Effects menu, choose Screen (72 ppi).

9 In the Transparency Grid menu, choose Medium.

10 Click OK.

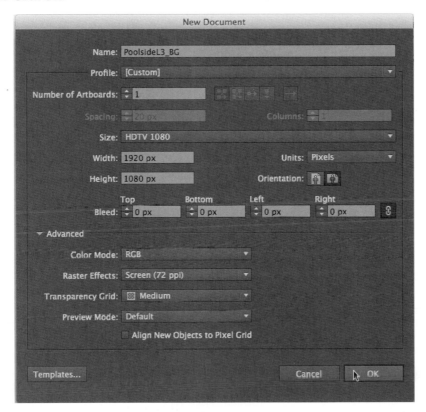

You will see a blank image with a transparency grid.

Before you proceed any further, save your image.

1 Choose File > Save As.

2 Navigate to Assets > Graphics.

3 Make sure the Format is set to Adobe Illustrator (ai).

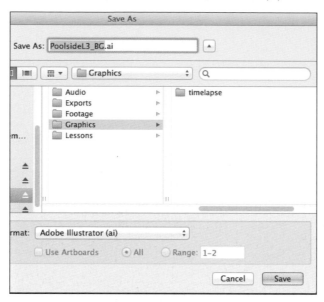

4 Click Save.

5 In the Illustrator Options window, set Version to Illustrator CC (17.0), then click OK.

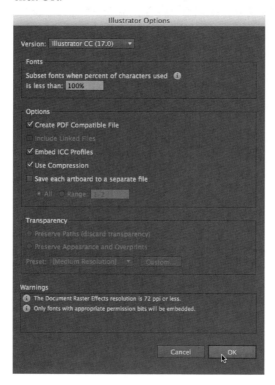

Overview of the Illustrator interface

The Illustrator user interface (UI) is similar to the UI in other Adobe applications. You will notice many familiar objects and discover that some of the tools work in a familiar way.

- The main window is the Document window. This shows the graphic that you are making, along with visual guides that help you measure and place objects where you want them to go.

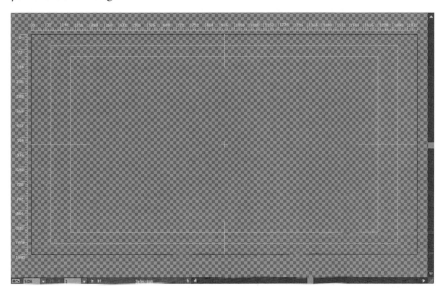

Tools panel

- At the left of the interface is the Tools panel. As the name suggests, this is where you find all of the tools you work with in Illustrator.

- The primary tool you will be using is the Selection tool.

- At the top of the interface is the Control panel; it shows various properties and values for the object that is currently selected.

Control panel

- And at the far right of the interface is a row of icons, each of which brings up a specific panel where you can adjust properties for your Layers, Brushes, Stroke, Gradients, and so on.

Making the lower third background

You will create a static lower third background vector graphic in Illustrator, use that to create animated lower third graphics in After Effects, import those into Adobe Premiere Pro, and replace the temporary lower third title clips with them.

Let's quickly tour Illustrator and then make the lower third background graphic.

The Poolside lower third background graphic will have two main components: a rectangle with a gradient fill that will be the background of everything in the lower third, and a group of five concentric circles, designed to resemble ripples in a pool of water. There will be five copies of this ripple group, varying in size and position in the canvas.

Making the background shape

Let's start by making the background shape. This will be a rectangle with a gradient fill.

1 Choose the Rectangle tool from the Tools panel.

2 Hover your cursor over the center of your image until the Intersect smart guide appears. Click once here.

3 The Rectangle window appears. Here, enter dimensions for the rectangle you want to make.

4 Change the value for Width to **1480 px**, and the value for Height to **280**.

5 Make sure that the Constrain Proportions switch is not activated.

6 Click OK.

A white rectangle appears in the canvas.

At the top of the interface, you will see values for X and Y, or horizontal position and vertical position, in the canvas.

▶ **Tip.** You can also access the Transform window by choosing Window>Transform.

7 Select the value for X and change it to **960**. Press Tab to select the Y value. Change it to **540** and press Return (Enter).

Applying a gradient fill

Now you will need to apply a gradient fill color. You will use a linear gradient, with three colors.

1   For the purpose of this exercise, press the D key to reset your default colors to white fill and black stroke.

    First, you will deactivate the stroke color so that the lower third background doesn't have an outline.

2   Select the stroke color swatch at the bottom of the Tools panel.

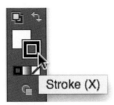

3   Press the None button to deactivate the stroke color.

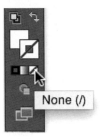

4   Select the fill color swatch at the bottom of the Tools panel.

5   Double-click the Gradient tool. This will open the Gradient panel.

6 In the Gradient panel, from the Type menu, choose Linear.

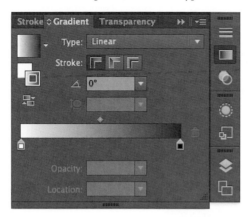

Doing this will draw a black and white gradient across the horizontal center of the rectangle.

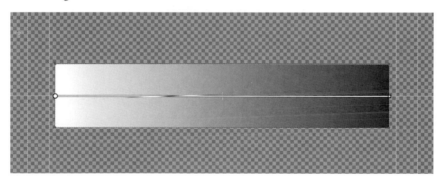

7 Redraw the axis of this gradient by clicking once at the bottom left of the rectangle, then by dragging the Gradient tool to the top right of the rectangle, then by releasing the tool.

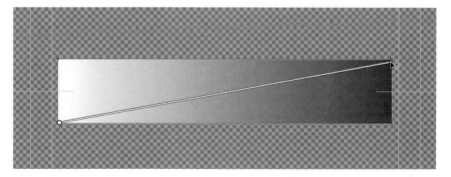

You don't want your gradient to be black and white, so let's change the gradient colors.

8 In the Gradient panel, you will see a Gradient Slider with two color swatches, one white and one black.

9 Double-click the white swatch.

This will open up a color properties panel, which is currently set to Grayscale.

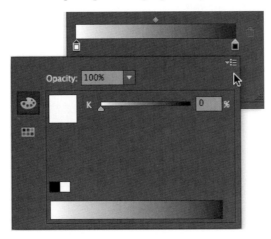

10 Click the options menu icon at the top right of this panel, and choose RGB from the menu.

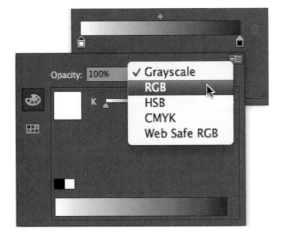

Now you can assign a specific RGB color value to your gradient.

11 Leave the R value at 255. Select the G value and change it to **161**. Select the B value and change it to **186**. Press Return (Enter).

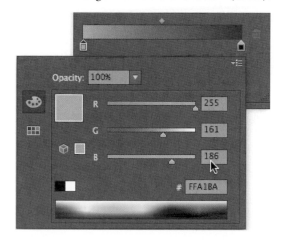

Your rectangle now has a pink and black gradient.

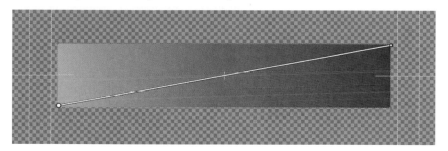

12 In the Gradient panel, double-click the black color swatch in the Gradient Slider.

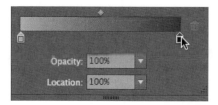

13 As before, click the options menu icon at the top right of this panel, and choose RGB from the menu. Enter RGB color values.

14 Select the R value and change it to **105**. Select the G value and change it to **225**. Select the B value and change it to **241**. Press Return (Enter).

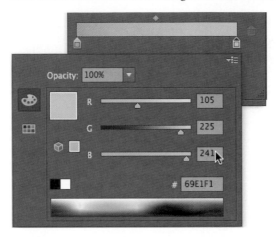

Now your rectangle has a pink and cyan gradient.

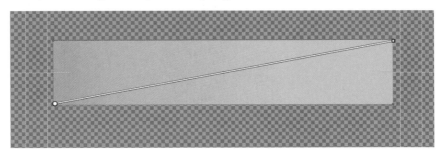

Let's add one more color to the gradient, a bright orange. It will be the middle color in the Gradient Slider.

15 In the Gradient panel, hover your cursor over the middle of the Gradient Slider. Your cursor changes so it has a "+" next to it.

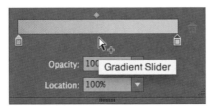

16 Click once in the middle of the Gradient Slider. A new color swatch appears on the Gradient Slider.

17 Choose this new middle color swatch. Select the value for Location and change it to **50%**. This ensures that this middle color is indeed in the exact middle.

18 Double-click the middle color swatch. This will already be an RGB color.

19 Select the R value and change it to **255**. Select the G value and change it to **167**. Select the B value and change it to **128**. Press Return (Enter).

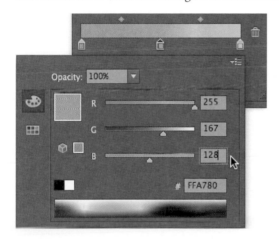

Your rectangle now has a pink, orange, and cyan gradient.

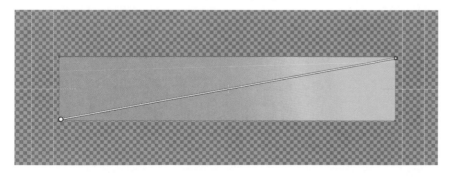

Layers in Illustrator

You can organize your vector objects in Illustrator on separate layers. To make organizing them easier, you can give your layers custom names.

1 Click the Layers icon to open the Layers panel.

Your rectangle is in Layer 1, currently the only layer.

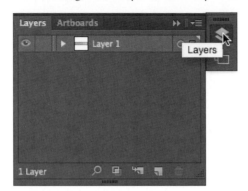

2 Double-click the name Layer 1 to highlight it. Change the name to **BG** and press Return (Enter).

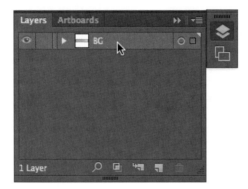

3 Lock this layer for now by clicking the Lock switch.

4 Press Command+S (Ctrl+S) to save your image.

Making a group of shapes

The next thing you will make in Illustrator is your initial ripple graphic. Again, this will be five concentric circles, of increasing diameter and diminishing opacity and stroke weight.

First make a new layer for your ripple.

1   Click the Create a New Layer icon at the bottom of the Layers panel. This makes a new layer, called Layer 2.

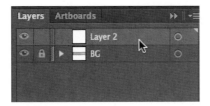

2   Double-click the name Layer 2. Change the name to **Ripple01** and press Return (Enter).

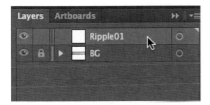

Choose a color

You want your ripple graphics to be white. However, the current fill color is set to the three-color gradient you just made.

Let's set the fill and stroke colors back to their defaults.

1   Press the D key to reset the default colors of white fill and black stroke.

2 You don't want your first ripple shape to have a stroke color, though. Select the black stroke color swatch to bring it forward.

3 Now set the stroke color to none by pressing the forward slash (/) key.

Any shape you draw from now on is going to have a white fill and no stroke color.

Draw the center circle

The center of the ripple graphic will have a white-filled circle.

1 Choose the Ellipse tool from the Tools panel by first choosing the Rectangle tool and then choosing the Ellipse tool from the menu that pops out from the Tools panel.

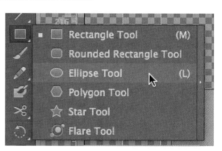

2 Hover your cursor over the center of the canvas until you see the Smart Guide for Center appear.

3 Click once in the center of the canvas and the Ellipse window will appear.

4 Change the values for Width and Height to **75 px**, then click OK.

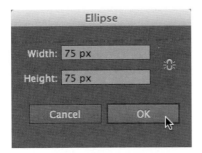

A new ellipse will appear off-center in your canvas.

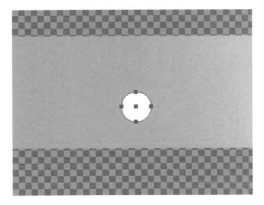

Move your circle to the center of the canvas by changing the X and Y position values at the top of the interface.

5 Select the value for X and change it to **960**. Press the Tab key to select the value for Y, and change it to **540**. Press Return (Enter).

6 Select the value for Opacity and change it to **50%**. Press Return (Enter).

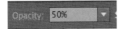

Duplicating shapes

To draw the remaining four circles, you will use duplicates of the first circle and make simple changes to the duplicates.

1 With the center circle selected, click Edit > Copy to copy it to your clipboard.

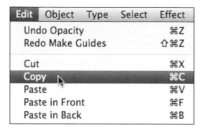

2 Then click Edit > Paste In Front. This pastes a copy so that it is stacked above the first shape on this layer.

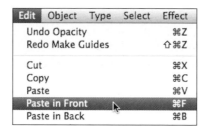

3 At the top of the interface, between the width and height values (or W and H) is an icon for Constrain Width and Height Proportions. Click this icon to activate it.

4 Select the value for W (or width), change it to **115 px**, and press Return (Enter).

The circle gets bigger, covering up the first circle. You want this circle and the rest of the circles that you draw for the ripple graphic to have a stroke but no fill.

5 Go to the Fill and Stroke colors at the bottom of the Tools panel. Click once on the Swap Fill and Stroke icon, or press Shift+X.

Your second circle now has a stroke but no fill.

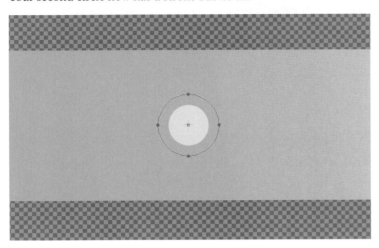

6 At the top of the interface, select the value for Stroke and change it to **10 pt**.

7 Verify that the value for Opacity is 50%.

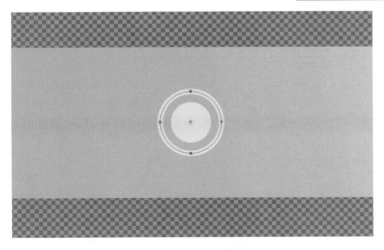

8 With this second circle selected, choose Edit > Copy. Then choose Edit > Paste in Front.

This makes a copy of the second circle that has the same dimensions and stroke weight.

9 Select the W (width) value and change it to **175**, then press Return (Enter).

10 Select the Stroke value and change it to **7**, then press Return (Enter).

11 Select the value for Opacity and change it to **25%**, then press Return (Enter).

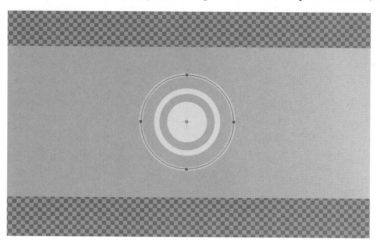

12 With this third circle selected, choose Edit > Copy. Then choose Edit > Paste in Front.

This makes a copy of the third circle that has the same dimensions and stroke weight.

13 Select the W (width) value and change it to **260**, then press Return (Enter).

14 Select the Stroke value and change it to **4**, then press Return (Enter).

15 Select the value for Opacity and change it to **20%**, then press Return (Enter).

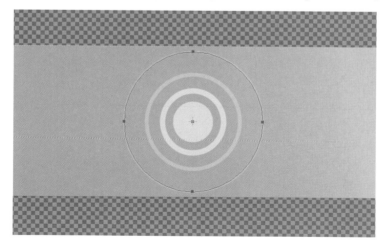

16 With this fourth circle selected, choose Edit > Copy. Then choose Edit > Paste in Front.

This makes a copy of the fourth circle, which has the same dimensions and stroke weight.

17 Select the W (width) value and change it to **400**, then press Return (Enter).

18 Select the Stroke value and change it to **2**, then press Return (Enter).

19 Select the value for Opacity and change it to **15%**, then press Return (Enter).

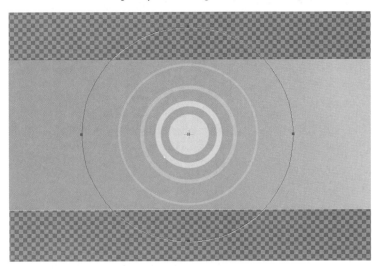

Grouping shapes

Now you have all of the component shapes for your initial ripple graphic. Let's group them so that they can be adjusted as a single object.

1 Press Command+A (Ctrl+A) to select all. Currently this would only select all of the circles on the Ripple01 layer.

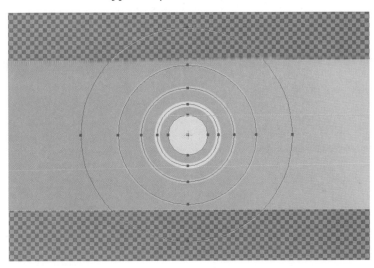

2 Now choose Object > Group. This creates a group with the selected objects.

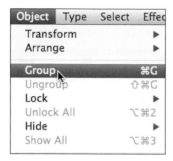

Grouping layers this way in Illustrator can make your workflow more efficient when you want to create and arrange duplicates of the same cluster of objects. Rather than forcing you to move objects individually, you can group them and move the group.

3 With this group selected, select the X (horizontal position) value and change it to **1385**. Press the Tab key to select the Y (vertical position) value, and change it to **415**.

4 Press the Tab key to select the W value and change it to **1025**, then press Return (Enter).

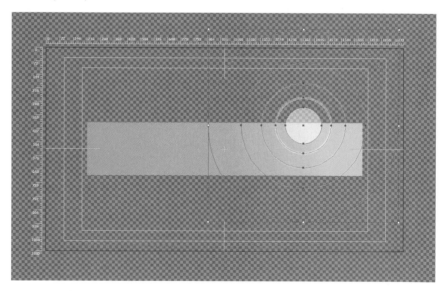

Duplicating layers in Illustrator

Now that you have one ripple layer with a group of shapes in it, all you have to do now is make duplicates of that.

1 In the Layers panel, select the Ripple01 layer.

2 Drag it onto the Create New Layer icon.

3 This results in a duplicate of the Ripple01 layer, called Ripple01 copy.

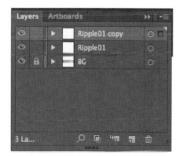

4 Double-click this layer name to highlight it. Change the name to **Ripple02**. Press Return (Enter).

Because the shape group in Ripple01 was selected when you duplicated Ripple01, the shape group in Ripple02 should be selected. Change its values for X, Y, and W at the top.

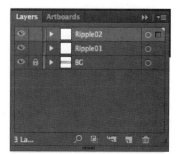

5 Select the value for X and change it to **311**. Press the Tab key to select Y and change it to **672**. Press the Tab key to select W and change it to **395**. Press Return (Enter).

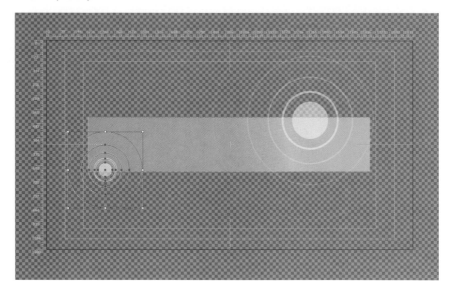

Let's do this a few more times.

1 In the Layers panel, select the Ripple02 layer.

2 Drag it onto the Create New Layer icon.

3 This a duplicate of Ripple02, called Ripple02 copy.

4 Double-click this layer name to highlight it. Change the name to **Ripple03**. Press Return (Enter).

The shape group in Ripple03 should be selected. Change its values for X, Y, and W at the top.

5 Select the value for X and change it to **369**. Press the Tab key to select Y and change it to **457**. Press the Tab key to select W and change it to **465**. Press Return (Enter).

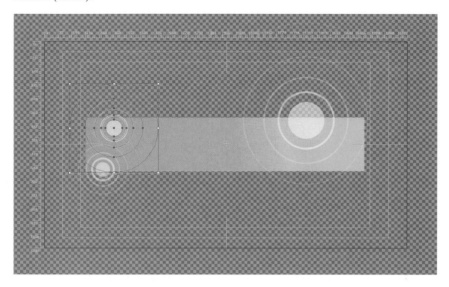

Let's duplicate Ripple03.

1 In the Layers panel, select the Ripple03 layer.

2 Drag it onto the Create New Layer icon.

This is a duplicate of Ripple03, called Ripple03 copy.

3 Double-click this layer name to highlight it. Change the name to **Ripple04**. Press Return (Enter).

The shape group in Ripple04 should be selected. Change its values for X, Y, and W at the top.

4 Select the value for X and change it to **935**. Press the Tab key to select Y and change it to **690**. Press the Tab key to select W and change it to **272**. Press Return (Enter).

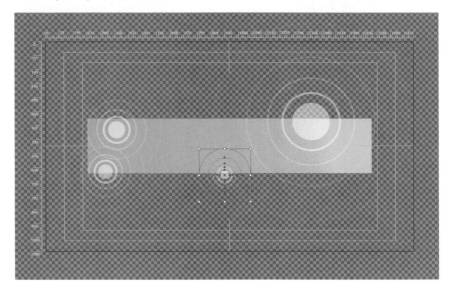

And the last one...

1 In the Layers panel, select the Ripple04 layer.

2 Drag it onto the Create New Layer icon.

This is a duplicate of Ripple04, called Ripple04 copy.

3 Double-click this layer name to highlight it. Change the name to **Ripple05**. Press Return (Enter).

The shape group in Ripple05 should be selected. Change its values for X, Y, and W at the top.

4 Select the value for X and change it to **1671**. Press the Tab key to select Y and change it to **672**. Press the Tab key to select W and change it to **305**. Press Return (Enter).

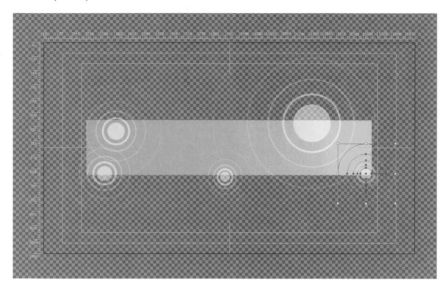

5 Finally, just so they are stacked in numerical order, in the Layers panel, select Ripple02 and drag it below Ripple01. Select Ripple03 and drag it below Ripple02. Select Ripple04 and stack it below Ripple03. And select Ripple05 and stack it below Ripple04. Make sure not to drag one layer *into* another.

6 Press Command+S (Ctrl+S) to save your image.

7 Press Command+Q (Ctrl+Q) to quit Illustrator.

8 Switch to After Effects by pressing Command+Tab (Alt+Tab).

9 Select the Project panel, then press Command+Shift+A (Ctrl+Shift+A) to deselect all.

Importing a lower third background to After Effects

In After Effects, let's import your lower third background graphic.

1 Choose File > Import > File.

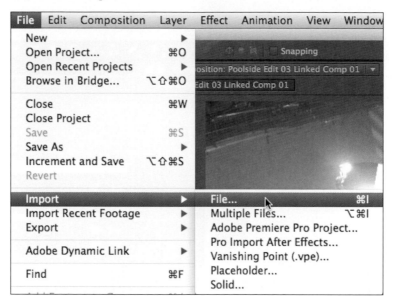

2 Navigate to Assets > Graphics.

3 Select PoolsideL3_BG.ai.

4 Click Open.

An import window will appear.

5 Set Import Kind: to Footage. Select Merged Layers.

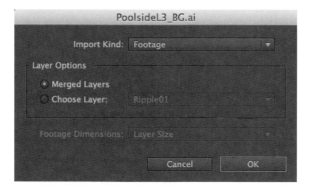

6 Click OK.

Next, you need to make a composition to put this in.

Creating a new composition

A composition in After Effects is analogous to a sequence in Adobe Premiere Pro in that it's your main work interface where you add layers (still images, video clips, vector graphics, text, etc.) and then manipulate the timing and properties of those layers to create an animation.

After Effects allows you to create multiple compositions within the same project.

The last time you made something in After Effects, a composition was made for you automatically when a clip in your Adobe Premiere Pro sequence was replaced with an After Effects composition. This time, you will be creating a composition from scratch.

Here's what you're going to do: You are going to make a composition that will have the lower third background graphic and some editable text. This composition will act as a template for all of the lower thirds. You will create this template composition, make duplicates of it for each lower third graphic needed, and edit the duplicates (change the text and composition name). Let's get started.

▶ **Tip:** Remember to keep your Project panel organized as you work. Making a habit of this early on will save you time and headaches in the long run.

Creating the lower third template composition

First, you will make a new composition for your lower third template.

1 Choose Composition > New Composition.

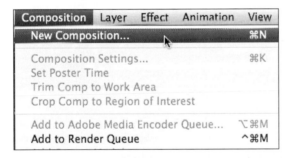

The Composition Settings window appears.

2 Change Composition Name to **Lower3rd_AE_template**.

3 Click the Preset drop-down menu and choose HDTV 1080 24. Change the frame rate to 23.976. Set the duration to 0:00:05:00 (zero hours, zero minutes, five seconds, zero frames). This is probably longer than you need, but it doesn't hurt to have a few extra frames just in case a final lower third graphic needs to be this long.

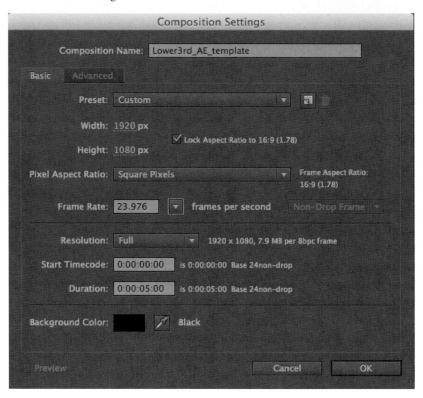

4 Click OK.

5 In the Project panel, choose and drag the PoolsideL3_BG.ai graphic into the Timeline, where it shows up as a layer in the composition.

6 Choose the layer's lock switch. We will come back to this layer shortly.

Creating a new text layer

Now you will create some template text layers that you will edit later.

1 Choose Layer > New > Text.

▶ **Tip:** To make a new text layer in After Effects, press Command+Opt+Shift+T (Ctrl+Alt+Shift+T).

2 Type **first last**, press Command+Return (Ctrl+Enter). Don't press Return (Enter), because that will make a line break and you don't want that now.

● **Note:** When editing a text layer in After Effects, the Return (Enter) key makes a line break, whereas Command+Return (Ctrl+Enter) registers your changes.

The text layer should be selected.

3 Go to the Character panel. For the font family, choose Arial. Set the font weight to Regular, the Font Size to **70**, and the Tracking to **150**.

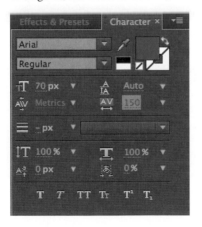

● **Note:** The Character panel will default to the settings that were used last.

4 Select the "Set To White" pure white color swatch in the Character panel to set the fill color to white.

5 Click the All Caps icon so that the text on the selected layer is all capital letters.

6 Choose the tab for the Paragraph panel. Click the Left Align Text icon.

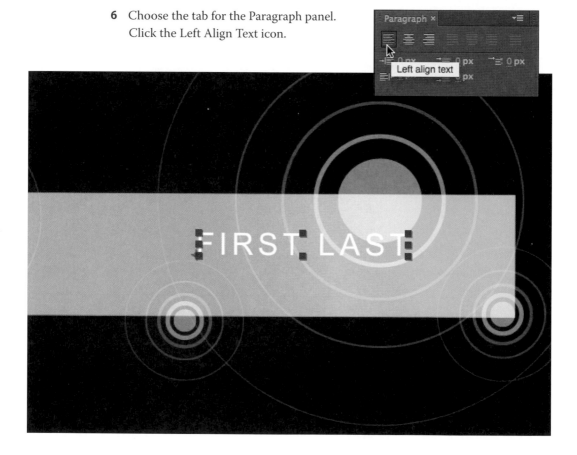

Now let's give this layer its own name, for easier reference.

1   Select this text layer in your Timeline. Press the
    Return (Enter) key to highlight the layer's name.

2   Type **Name** and press Return (Enter) again.

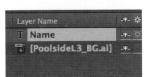

Applying the Drop Shadow effect

Because the text is white, and it's going to appear in front of a light background,
let's apply an effect that will apply a faint shadow behind the text in order to give it
some contrast with the background.

1   With the Name layer selected, choose Effect > Perspective > Drop Shadow.

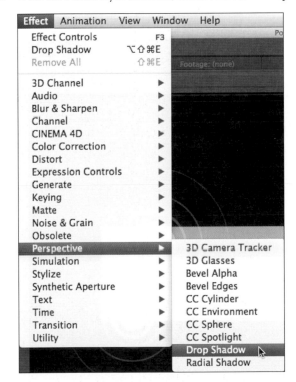

The Drop Shadow effect creates the illusion that the applied layer is casting a
shadow, even though the layer exists in two-dimensional space (there is no space
"behind" the layer for the shadow to be cast upon). This effect is very useful for

making text stand out against its background, while also giving control over subtle design elements.

An Effect Controls panel in the interface now shows all of the settings for effects on the selected layer. Here, you should see all of the settings for the Drop Shadow effect.

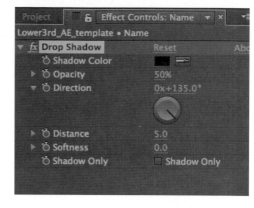

Let's adjust two of these settings from their defaults.

2 In the Effect Controls panel, select the value for Distance and change it to **3**. Press Return (Enter). This changes the distance away from the layer the shadow appears to be cast.

3 Select the value for Softness and change it to **10.0**. Press Return (Enter). This gives the shadow a bit of blur.

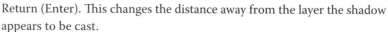

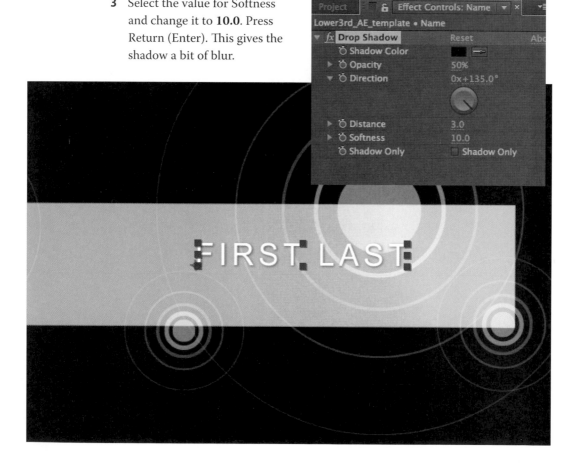

Duplicating a layer

In After Effects, any layer can be duplicated. A duplicate is then its own layer, with its own settings. However, a duplicate will have all the same settings as the layer you duplicated to create it, at the time that you duplicated it. This comes in handy when you need to have more than one layer in a composition that's a variation of the same design.

In this lower third design, you will have two text layers: one for the on-camera person's name, and another text layer for the person's title.

Rather than create a whole new layer from scratch for the title, especially if the two layers are going to be very similar anyway, you can simply duplicate the one you have and edit that.

1   Select the Name layer in the Timeline and choose Edit > Duplicate. Be careful not to duplicate the Drop Shadow effect!

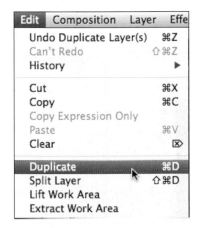

Tip: To duplicate a selected layer, press Command+D (Ctrl+D).

A new text layer called Name 2 will appear above the Name layer.

2   Select this duplicate layer. Press Return (Enter) to highlight its name. Change the name of the layer to **Title**, and press Return (Enter).

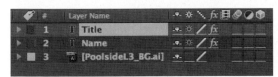

▶ **Tip:** Press Command+] (Ctrl+]) to move a selected layer in the Timeline stack up one layer. Press Command+[(Ctrl+[) to move a selected layer in the Timeline stack down one layer.

3 And simply so that there is some logical symmetry between the layer stacking order in the Timeline and how the text is going

to be arranged spatially in the Composition panel, choose and drag the Title layer below the Name layer in the Timeline.

In the Composition panel, it will appear as if there is still only one text layer. That's because the two layers are exact copies stacked on top of each other. To prove this, you will move the Title layer.

4 With the Title layer still selected, press the P key to show its position value.

5 Adjust the vertical position to **600**.

Now edit the text.

1 Double-click this layer in the Timeline. All of the text in the layer will become selected.

2 Change the text to **title**. Press Command+Return (Ctrl+Enter) to commit this change. Even if you typed in lowercase letters, the All-Caps option is on, automatically capitalizing any letters you type.

3 In the Character panel, set the Font Size to **48**, and the Tracking to **50**. You want the title subtext to be smaller so that the name text appears more dominant in frame.

Now you will want to move these two text layers to the left, to balance the design.

1 With the Title layer selected, hold down Command (Ctrl) and select the Name layer so that they are both selected.

2 Press the P key for position. This will shut both layers because Position was already visible on the Title layer. Press P again.

▶ **Tip:** For precision placement, move any selected layers with the arrow keys. If the Composition magnification is set to 100%, pressing any arrow key moves selected layers in the chosen direction by one pixel.

3 Choose and scrub only the horizontal position to 450.

Now that you have your template text layers in place where they need to be, relative to their background, let's shrink down everything and put it where it needs to go.

1 Click the lock switch on the PoolsideL3_BG.ai layer to unlock it.

2 Press Command+A (Ctrl+A) to select all layers.

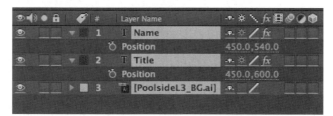

3 Press the S key to show the Scale property values on the layers.

4 Choose any of the scale values and change it from 100 to **50**.

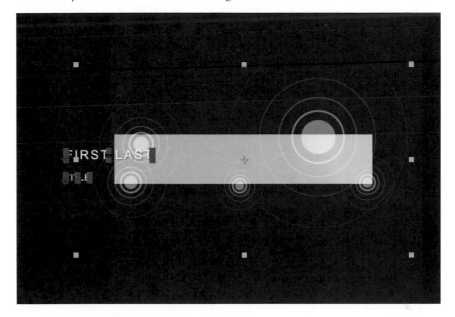

Notice how everything shrinks separately from each other. You don't want that.

5 Press Command+Z (Ctrl+Z) to undo.

You want everything to maintain relative scale to each other, to scale as a group.
One way to achieve that is by using null objects and parenting.

Optional exercise: parenting

For the sake of expediency, rather than make you build something only for the purpose of explanation, let's look at something pre-built that will explain some of the basics of parenting and null objects in After Effects. What you will be importing will have no consequence on the Poolside edit. If you want to skip this exercise, jump ahead to "Creating a null object."

▶ **Tip:** You can import an After Effects project file into an open After Effects project. The imported project's compositions and layers and folders remain intact and become part of the current project. Any changes made to the imported project's compositions do not affect the project file that was imported. This is a handy way of saving and re-using template animations.

1 Choose File > Import > File.

2 Navigate to Assets > Lessons > Lesson 05.

3 Select Parenting.aep. Click Open.

4 A new folder will appear in your Project panel. Double-click it to open it.

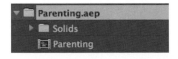

5 Double-click the composition Parenting to open it.

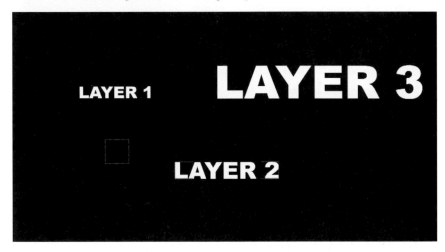

Look in the Timeline, and notice that there are four layers, all showing their Position and Scale and Rotation values.

There is a Null layer, stacked at the top. And there are three text layers, Layer 1, Layer 2, and Layer 3.

These layers are parented together, or linked so that the layer that is parented (or the child layer) will move and scale and rotate in relation to the parent layer.

Notice the Parent column in the Timeline. This shows which layer is parented to which. For example, Layer 3 is parented to Layer 2, therefore Layer 2 is the parent of Layer 3. When Layer 2 moves, Layer 3 moves with it.

Notice that Layer 2 is parented to Layer 1. If Layer 1 moves, Layer 2 would move with it. But since Layer 3 is parented to Layer 2 (which is parented to Layer 1), this would also move Layer 3.

Moving a child layer does not move its parent layer. If you move Layer 3, Layer 2 is not affected. Nothing is parented to Layer 3, therefore nothing else moves.

6 Adjust the Position, Scale, and Rotation of each text layer.

Notice that adjusting Layer 1 affects the other visible layers. What if you wanted to make adjustments to Layer 1 without affecting the other text layers, but you still wanted all the layers to be grouped?

Yes, you could create yet another layer, then parent multiple layers to it, but that layer may not serve a purpose in your visual design. Wouldn't it be nice if a layer could be a parent but not be visible? Meet your new friend, the null object.

Null objects

Among other uses, null objects are great for parent layers. Null objects don't render, hence they are already invisible and will not visually interfere with anything else in your composition frame.

1 Adjust the Position, Scale, and Rotation of the null. Notice that because Layer 2 and Layer 3 are parented to Layer 1 (because Layer 3 is parented to Layer 2 and Layer 2 is parented to Layer 1) all visible layers are affected. If you adjust Layer 1, then Layer 2 and Layer 3 are affected.

2 Marquee-select all but the Null layer.

Let's parent all of the text layers to the null.

3 Click the down-arrow icon on any of the selected layers' Parent columns, and choose Null as the parent. All selected layers will now be parented to the Null layer.

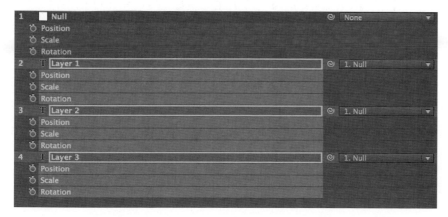

If you adjust the Position, Scale, or Rotation of each visible layer separately, no other layers are affected.

But if you adjust the Null layer, all text layers are affected, relative to the null.

So, to summarize: Parenting is an easy way to link layers together in a comp so they can be moved as a group. And null objects are useful as invisible parent layers.

1 Select the Parenting.aep folder in your Project panel, and press the Delete key. When After Effects prompts you whether or not you're sure you want to delete this, click the Delete button in the window that appears.

2 Select the Timeline tab for the Lower3rd_AE_template comp.

Creating a null object

Let's create a new null object. This will be the parent layer for all other layers in this composition, enabling you to move and scale everything as a group.

1 Choose Layer > New > Null Object.

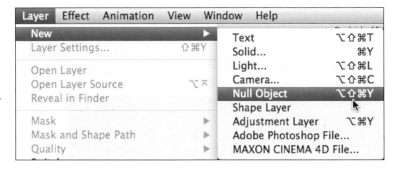

It appears in your Composition panel as a transparent square, and as a layer in the Timeline, above the Name layer.

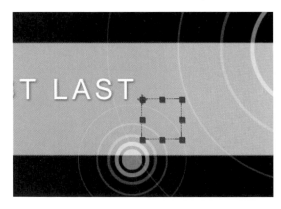
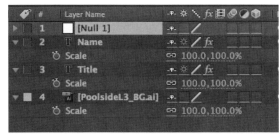

2 With this null selected, press Return (Enter) to highlight its name.

3 Type **Main Parent**, then press Return (Enter).

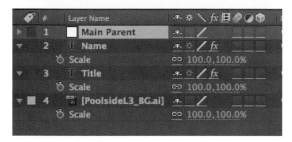

Moving the null into place

You will want to be able to not only move all of these layers as a group, but scale them all in relation to the bottom right corner of the gradient rectangle. Let's move the null there before you parent any other layers to it.

1 Press P to show the null's Position value.

2 Select the horizontal Position value and type **220**. Press the Tab key to select the vertical Position value and type **680**. Press Return (Enter).

3 Marquee-select all layers except for the Main Parent null.

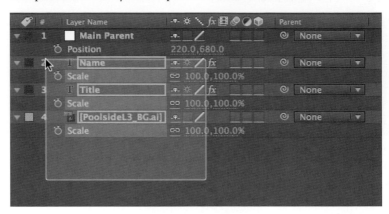

Using the Pick-Whip

One way to parent one layer to another is by using the Pick-Whip. Notice the spiral icons in the Parent column in the Timeline. When you click and drag one of these, the interface allows you to literally draw a line from that layer to another layer, thereby parenting it. If multiple layers are selected, then Pick-Whipping from one parents them all to the chosen layer.

1 Choose the parent Pick-Whip from the Name layer.

2 Drag this to the Main Parent null object.

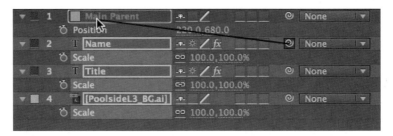

Notice that this parents the Name, Title, and PoolsideL3_BG.ai layers to the Main Parent null object.

Moving and scaling the group

Let's move the Main Parent layer's position again, but since all the other layers are parented to it, moving the Main Parent moves everything.

Let's place the Main Parent at the bottom left corner of the Action Safe area.

1 Activate the Title/Action Safe guides by clicking the Choose Grid and Guide Options icon and then choosing Title/Action Safe.

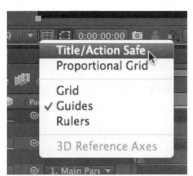

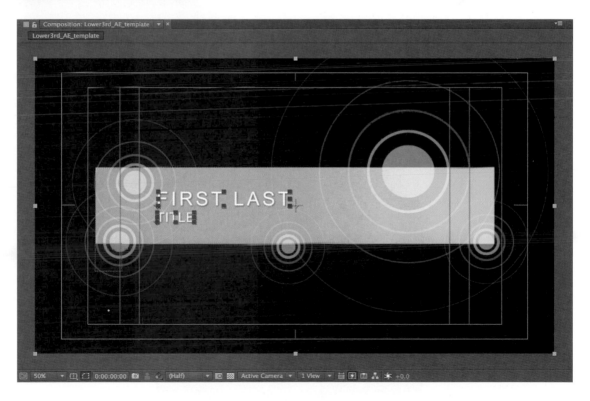

▶ **Tip:** Toggle the Title/Action Safe guides by pressing the apostrophe (') key.

2 Select the Main Parent layer. Press Shift+S to also show its Scale values.

3 Choose the horizontal Position value, and type **96**.

4 Press Tab to select the vertical Position value.

5 Change this to **1026**. Press Return (Enter).

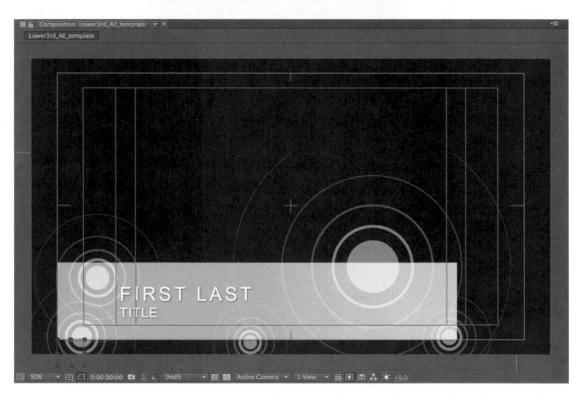

6 Now select either the horizontal or vertical Scale value of that Main Parent layer, and change it to **65**. Press Return (Enter). This scales down the whole group.

7 Press the apostrophe key (') to turn off the Title/Action Safe guides.

Nested compositions

Look closely at the top of the scaled-down PoolsideL3_BG.ai layer. Notice how it appears cropped? And where are all the separate layers that you made in Illustrator?

You need to tell After Effects to replace the merged-layers footage item with a layered composition.

1 In the Project panel, select the PoolsideL3_BG.ai footage item.

2 Choose File > Replace Footage > With Layered Comp.

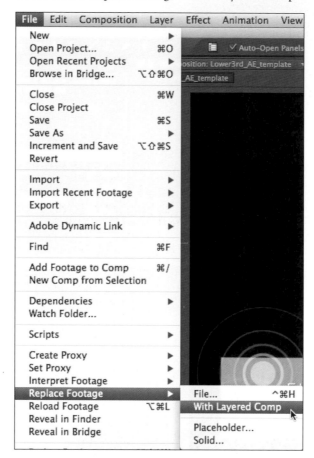

The .ai graphic has been replaced with a composition, and now there is a folder in the Project panel called Poolside L3_BG Layers.

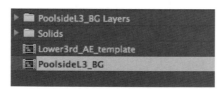

3 Double-click this new folder, and you should see a list of footage items, which are all of the original layers from the Illustrator graphic.

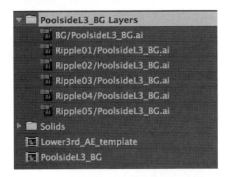

Look in the Lower3rd_AE_template composition, and you will see that the PoolsideL3_BG.ai layer has been replaced by a layer that, in the interface at least, appears to be something different.

A layer can be an imported footage item, and it can also be another composition! If you create an animation with several layers in one composition and then put that composition into a second composition, the layers of the first composition will be flattened into one layer in the second composition. This is called nesting a composition. Nesting compositions in After Effects is a way to group multiple layers, much like creating a folder of layers in Photoshop.

4 Double-click PoolsideL3_BG and it will open in its own Timeline. The Composition panel changes to show the layers in this composition.

Notice all the layers here, named and stacked just as they were in Illustrator.

Animating the background

You are going to animate the ripple layers with scale keyframes. You will also apply keyframe animation to their opacity so that they gradually fade away over time.

1 Click the lock switch on the BG layer to lock it. Since you won't be doing anything to this layer for now, it's a good idea to lock it so that you don't accidentally select it.

2 Press Command+A (Ctrl+A) to select all layers. Notice that because the BG layer is locked, it doesn't get selected.

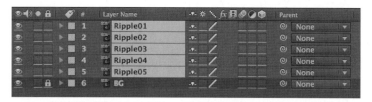

3 Press the S key to show the Scale of all the ripple layers.

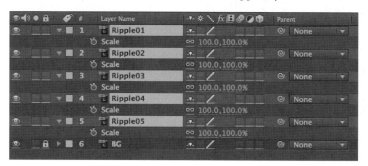

4 Click the stopwatch for Scale on one of them. Because multiple layers are selected, this affects all of them. Notice the Scale keyframes at the beginning of the Timeline.

5 Select the Scale value for one of them and change it to **75%**. Press Return (Enter). Again, because they're all selected, they all get changed.

6 Press Command+Option+Right Arrow (Ctrl+Alt+Right Arrow) to adjust your playhead to the last frame in the Timeline.

7 Select the Scale value for one of them and change it to **210%**. Press Return (Enter).

This automatically makes new Scale keyframes at the current time for all selected layers.

This also causes all of the ripple layers to get larger.

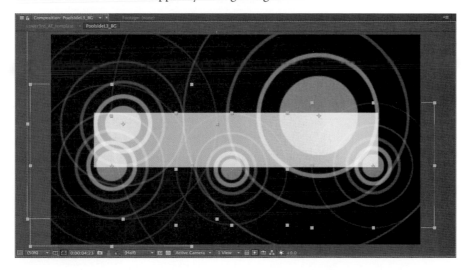

Continuous rasterization

Take a moment to notice that because the ripple layers have been scaled above their native 100%, they look pixelated.

Aren't these vector objects, and aren't vector graphics supposed to be resolution-independent? Yes, but by default, After Effects treats imported vector graphics as raster objects, or objects composed of a finite grid of pixels. In order to take advantage of the resolution-independent nature of vector graphics, you must turn on continuous rasterization.

This is a switch in the Timeline interface.

Basically, when this is activated on a vector layer, After Effects will re-rasterize (redraw the pixels for) the layer at any new scale it is given, and no blocky pixelization will occur.

1 Choose the box for Continuous Rasterization.

2 Look at the Composition panel. Notice how the edges look smooth again.

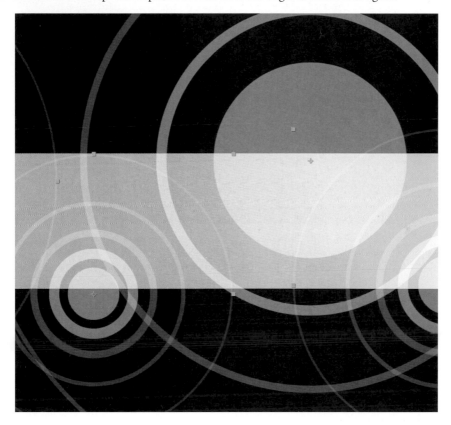

Collapse Transformations

Now take a moment to go back to the Lower3rd_AE_template composition.

1 Click the tab for the Lower3rd_AE_template to show it in the Timeline panel and Composition panel.

Notice how some of the layers still appear cropped. This is because by default, After Effects only renders what is in a nested composition's frame, but not any layer or part of a layer that is outside a composition's frame.

Because the background nested composition has some of its ripple layers scaling outside of the composition's frame, those layers appear cropped here.

Notice that this nested composition has a switch in the interface for Continuous Rasterization.

On a nested composition, however, this switch serves another purpose, which is referred to as Collapse Transformations. Basically, when this is activated for a nested composition, any layers that may have normally gotten cropped are fully visible, as if all of the nested composition's layers were in the current composition.

2 Choose the PoolsideL3_BG layer's collapse transformations switch.

3 Notice how the ripples are no longer cropped.

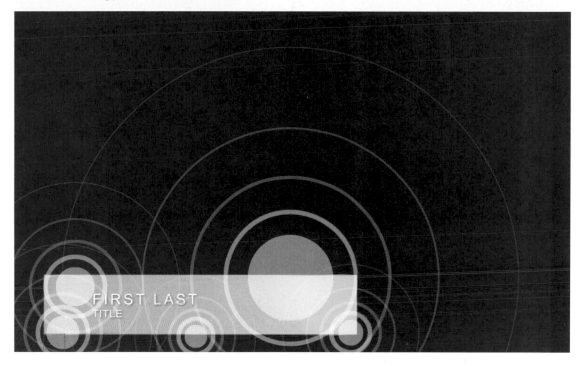

4 Select the Timeline tab for the PoolsideL3_BG composition to open it.

Animating opacity

Now let's animate the opacity of the ripple layers so that they gradually fade out.

1 With all ripple layers selected, press Shift+T. This shows any other visible property plus Opacity (the keyboard shortcut for Opacity is T).

2 With the playhead at the end of the Timeline, set the Opacity value to **20** for one of them. Because they're all selected, they all change.

3 Click the Opacity stopwatch for one of them. Again, this turns it on for all the ripple layers because they're all selected.

4 Press the Command+Option+Left Arrow (Ctrl+Alt+Left Arrow).

5 Adjust the Opacity value to **50** for one of them. They all change.

Let's add some variation, so that all of them don't fade out at the same rate.

1 Press Command+Shift+A (Ctrl+Shift+A) to deselect all layers.

2 Select the Opacity value for Ripple01. Change it to **25%** and press Return (Enter).

3 Select the Opacity value for Ripple05. Change it to **100%** and press Return (Enter).

4 RAM Preview your composition to see the animation.

5 Press Command+S (Ctrl+S) to save your project.

Verifying updates to a nested composition

Any change you make to a composition after it has been nested in another is automatically updated in all instances of that composition throughout the project. Let's verify the changes that you made to PoolsideL3_BG by viewing the Lower3rd_AE_ template composition.

1 Go back to the Lower3rd_AE_template composition by selecting its tab in the Timeline.

2 Scrub the playhead through the Timeline. Notice all the ripple layers are animating scale and opacity.

However, the text is still not animating. Let's fix that.

Animating text in After Effects

Let's give your text layers a bit of motion, using Position keyframes. You will also be applying some smoothness to the motion, as well as some blur. Finally, you will apply an animation preset to the text layers so that the letters appear one at a time.

Animating position

Let's animate the position of the text layers so that for the first 12 frames of the Lower3rd_template composition, they are sliding in from the left and then smoothly landing at their current position. You will create some variation between the two layers so that the Title layer doesn't move as far or as quickly.

1 Adjust the playhead to 0:00:00:12.

2 Select the Name layer, hold down Command (Ctrl), and select the Title layer.

3 Press the P key to show their Position properties.

4 Choose the Position stopwatch icon for either the Name or the Title layers to activate it on both (since they are both selected).

This makes new Position keyframes for these layers at the current time, using the current value.

5 Press Command+Option+Left Arrow (Ctrl+Alt+Left Arrow). to adjust the playhead to the beginning of the Timeline.

6 Press Command+Shift+A (Ctrl+Shift+A) to deselect all.

7 Select the horizontal Position value for the Name layer. Change it to **0** and press Return (Enter). Doing this makes a new keyframe at the current time. This moves the Name layer to the left edge of the background gradient.

8 Select the horizontal Position value for the Title layer. Change it to **100**, making a new Position keyframe at the current time. This moves the Title layer about halfway between the left edge of the gradient background and where it will stop moving.

Easy Ease interpolation

By default, when a property is animated with keyframes, After Effects will interpolate the property – gradually change the value over time – using linear interpolation. That is, immediately achieving and maintaining a maximum velocity with no acceleration or deceleration.

By applying Easy Ease interpolation to a keyframe, you automatically apply a gradual acceleration and/or deceleration to the speed of animation of that property.

There are three types of Easy Ease interpolation.

Easy Ease In: Gradually slowing down animation into a keyframe but not changing the outgoing animation speed.

Easy Ease Out: Not changing the incoming animation speed, but gradually speeding up animation out of a keyframe.

Easy Ease: Gradually slowing down the incoming animation speed as well as gradually speeding up the outgoing animation speed.

Easy Ease interpolation

Now you'll learn a simple trick for making your animations move more realistically.

1 Do a RAM Preview of your composition.

You will notice that both of the text layers slide in from the left and come to a sudden stop.

What if you wanted their motion to gradually slow down before it stops? A simple way to do that is by applying Easy Ease interpolation to their second Position keyframes.

When objects move in the real world, especially living organisms, they usually gradually accelerate and decelerate. Picture a bouncing ball. When the ball is dropped, it gradually builds up some speed before it hits the ground. When the ball bounces back up, it gradually slows down as it reaches a peak, then gradually speeds up as it falls, and so on.

Motion graphics can be more appealing to the human eye if the movements resemble, or at least evoke, motion in the real world. With Easy Ease interpolation, After Effects lets you apply gradual acceleration and deceleration to any property that is animated with keyframes.

2 Marquee-select the second Position keyframes on both text layers.

3 Choose Animation > Keyframe Assistant > Easy Ease, or right-click either of the selected keyframes, then choose from the menu Keyframe Assistant > Easy Ease.

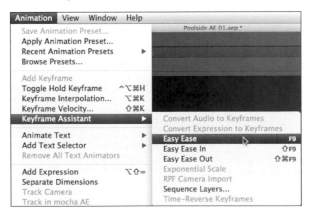

Notice how the keyframe icons are no longer diamond shaped.

Anytime a keyframe is not diamond shaped, it means that the speed of animation going into and/or out of that keyframe is not constant.

When Easy Ease is applied to a keyframe, the speed of animation going into the keyframe gradually slows down, and then the speed of animation going out of the keyframe gradually speeds up.

4   Do a RAM Preview of your composition.

Notice how the text layers start by moving quickly but gradually slow down before stopping.

Understanding and applying motion blur

Motion blur is a visual artifact that occurs in varying degrees based on the speed of a camera's shutter. Objects in motion will appear blurry, especially at lower shutter speeds.

After Effects can easily simulate this visual effect on a layer in motion.

Applying motion blur to text layers

Let's give the moving text layers some motion blur.

1   In the Lower3rd_AE_template composition, press Command+Right Arrow (Ctrl+Right Arrow) three times, so that the playhead is on frame 3.

Look at the text layers in the Composition panel. If you want these to look like they're moving fast, give them some motion blur to do the trick.

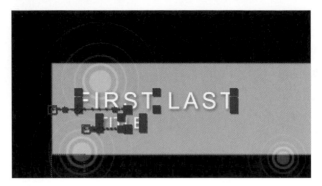

Look at the switches in the Timeline. If you are seeing the Modes and Track Matte columns, click the Toggle Switches/Modes button so that you see the switches.

The top of the Switches column shows icons that represent what the switches underneath them do. The third from the right icon (and respective switch on each layer) shows a ball moving very quickly.

This switch on each layer is for motion blur. When you activate this switch on your text layers, they will show motion blur when rendered.

2   Both text layers should be selected. If they are not, select the Name layer, hold down Command (Ctrl), and select the Title layer so that they are both selected.

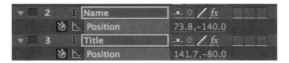

3   Choose the motion blur switch for either layer, activating the switch on both.

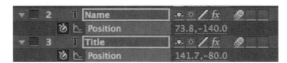

Now look at the Composition panel. Notice that there is no apparent motion blur. Did we do something wrong? No.

In order to see motion blur in your RAM Preview, you must activate the large motion blur switch at the top of the Timeline—"Enables Motion Blur for all layers with the Motion Blur switch set."

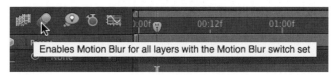

4 Choose this large icon, and you should see motion blur render on your text layers.

5 Press Command+S (Ctrl+S) to save your project.

Pixel motion blur

Motion blur is great for enhancing the look of layers that have their transform properties—position, scale, rotation—animated with keyframes. However, it cannot apply a motion blur to layers that are not animated in this way. For instance, if you have a layer that is a pre-rendered video clip that was shot with a high shutter speed, and you want to give it some smooth motion blur, but that layer isn't moving in your composition, After Effects will not render motion blur on it.

New in After Effects CC is the Pixel Motion Blur effect. This allows you to give motion blur to a prerendered video layer even though that layer is not keyframe animated.

Although there have been other effects that do this, such as Timewarp and various third-party effects, Pixel Motion Blur offers a solution when you want to smooth out the look of footage that otherwise appears too flickery or to compound motion blur that is already present.

Working with animation presets in After Effects

There are times when you don't have the time to go through all of the steps required to give your layers some animation. Even if the animation is extremely simple, sometimes several steps are involved in achieving it.

After Effects comes bundled with hundreds of what are called *Animation Presets.* These are collections of settings and/or keyframes that you can apply to a layer with a single action so that the layer is animated in a certain way. Several dozen such Animation Presets are designed for use on text layers.

In this exercise, you will animate all of the text so that each character fades up separately. You will do this by using an Animation Preset.

1 Both text layers should be selected. If not, select the Name layer, hold down Command (Ctrl), and select the Title layer, so that they are both selected.

2 Press the Home key or scrub the playhead all the way to the beginning of the Timeline.

3 Open the Effects & Presets panel by choosing Window > Effects & Presets.

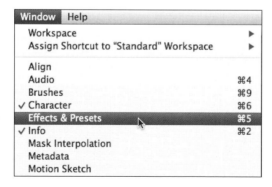

The Effects & Presets panel shows a list of not only all of the effects plug-ins currently installed, but also a list of all Animation Presets, grouped by category.

4 In the Effects & Presets panel, navigate to Animation Presets > Text > Animate In.

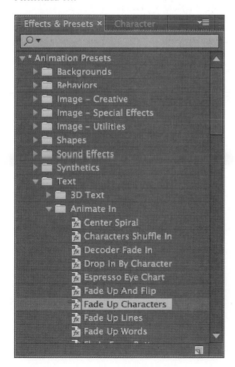

Browsing Animation Presets

If you want to get a better idea of what Animation Presets look like, you can see animated thumbnails of them by clicking the Effects & Presets options button and choosing Browse Presets from the drop-down menu.

This will open Adobe Bridge, showing you folders of presets to look at. Double-click any of these folders (some of these folders have folders in them) and you will find the presets themselves.

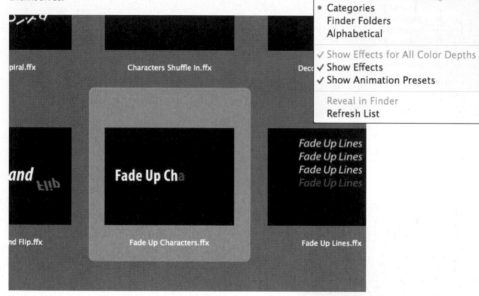

Select any one of these presets and you will see an animated preview of it in the Preview panel.

If you double-click an Animation Preset file, it will apply itself to the currently selected layer in After Effects. If the preset has keyframes built into it, they will be applied to the layer from the current composition frame onward.

5 Double-click Fade-Up Characters. This applies the preset to the selected text layers.

6 Select the Lower3rd_AE_template tab to make this panel active.

7 Press the U key to show all animated properties and their keyframes on the selected layers. Any keyframes built into the preset will apply themselves starting at the playhead.

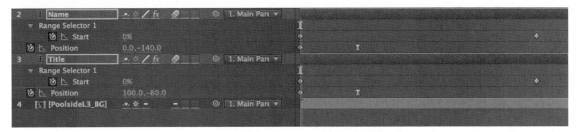

Notice the keyframes automatically applied with the Animation Preset.

Scrub through the animation with the playhead. Notice that each character fades up, in order from left to right, on each layer.

Currently, this is happening over two seconds. Let's make this happen faster.

8 The second keyframes are at two seconds into the animation. Select both of them.

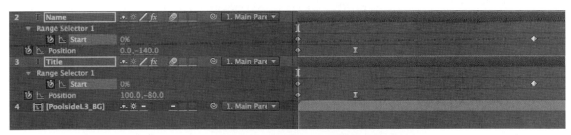

9 Adjust the playhead to frame 6 by pressing Command+Right Arrow (Ctrl+Right Arrow) six times.

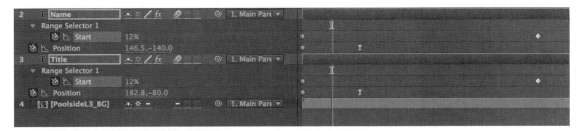

10 Hold down Shift and drag the selected keyframes to the left, snapping them to the playhead.

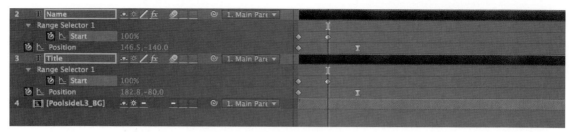

11 RAM Preview your animation.

12 Press Command+S (Ctrl+S) to save your project.

This completes the animation of the lower third template.

Finalizing lower third graphics

Now that you have a template composition, you will create the lower third graphics that you need by making duplicates of this template and editing the duplicates.

1 Select the tab for the Project panel to make it active. Here, select the Lower3rd_AE_template composition.

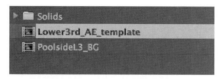

2 Press Command+D (Ctrl+D) to duplicate this composition.

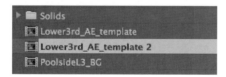

3 Select the duplicate. Press the Return (Enter) key to highlight its name. Change the name to **Lower3rd_AE_Dwight**.

4 Double click this composition to open it.

5 In Lower3rd_AE_Dwight, press the K key to jump the playhead to the next visible keyframe.

6 Double-click the Name layer to highlight the text. Change the text to **Dwight Burks**. Press Command+Return (Ctrl+Enter).

7 Double-click the Title layer to highlight the text. Change the text to **Producer, 12FPS**. Press Command+Return (Ctrl+Enter).

8 RAM Preview to verify how it looks.

Let's make a lower third for Heidi.

1 In the Project panel, select Lower3rd_AE_Dwight.

2 Press Command+D (Ctrl+D) to duplicate this composition.

3 Select the duplicate. Press the Return (Enter) key to highlight its name. Change the name to **Lower3rd_AE_Heidi**.

4 Double-click this composition to open it.

5 In Lower3rd_AE_Heidi, double-click the Name layer to highlight the text. Change the text to **Heidi Petty**. Press Command+Return (Ctrl+Enter). Since Heidi is also a producer at 12FPS, the Title layer doesn't need to be changed.

6 RAM Preview to verify how it looks.

Now let's make a lower third for Tyler.

1   In the Project panel, select Lower3rd_AE_Heidi.

2   Press Command+D (Ctrl+D) to duplicate this composition.

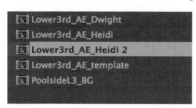

3   Select the duplicate. Press the Return (Enter) key to highlight its name. Change the name to **Lower3rd_AE_Tyler**.

4   Double-click this composition to open it.

5   In Lower3rd_AE_Tyler, double-click the Name layer to highlight the text. Change the text to **Tyler Winick**. Press Command+Return (Ctrl+Enter). Since Tyler is yet another producer at 12FPS, the Title layer doesn't need to be changed.

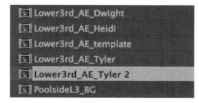

6   RAM Preview to verify how it looks.

Now let's make a lower third for Adam.

1   In the Project panel, select Lower3rd_AE_Tyler.

2   Press Command+D (Ctrl+D) to duplicate this composition.

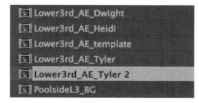

3 Select the duplicate. Press the Return (Enter) key to highlight its name. Change the name to **Lower3rd_AE_Adam**.

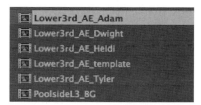

4 Double-click this composition to open it.

5 In Lower3rd_AE_Adam, double-click the Name layer to highlight the text. Change the text to **Adam Shaening-Pokrasso**. Press Command+Return (Ctrl+Enter).

6 Double-click the Title layer to highlight the text. Change the text to **Director, 12FPS**. Press Command+Return (Ctrl+Enter).

7 RAM Preview to verify how it looks.

Finally, let's make a lower third for Filip.

1 In the Project panel, select Lower3rd_AE_Adam.

2 Press Command+D (Ctrl+D) to duplicate this composition.

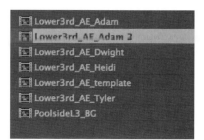

3 Select the duplicate. Press the Return (Enter) key to highlight its name. Change the name to **Lower3rd_AE_Filip**.

4 Double-click this composition to open it.

5 In Lower3rd_AE_Filip, double-click the Name layer to highlight the text. Change the text to **Filip Nikolic**. Press Command+Return (Ctrl+Enter).

6 Double-click the Title layer to highlight the text. Change the text to **Musician, Poolside**. Press Command+Return (Ctrl+Enter).

7 RAM Preview to verify how it looks.

Let's organize the project a little bit.

1 In your Project panel, marquee-select all of the compositions that are outside the Comps folder.

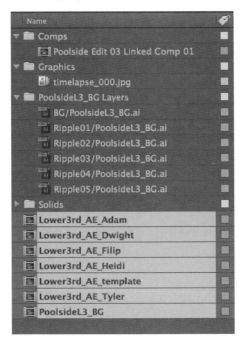

2 Choose and drag these onto the Comps folder, putting them in the folder.

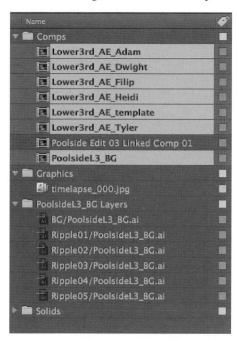

3 While you're tidying up the Project panel, twirl the PoolsideL3_BG Layers folder shut. Select the PoolsideL3_BG Layers folder and drag it into the Graphics folder. Then twirl the Graphics folder shut.

4 Once this is completed, press Command+S (Ctrl+S) to save your After Effects project.

5 Switch to Adobe Premiere Pro by pressing Command+Tab (Alt+Tab).

Using Dynamic Link: from After Effects to Adobe Premiere Pro

Just as you can dynamically link elements from Adobe Premiere Pro to After Effects, you can also link elements from After Effects to Adobe Premiere Pro.

In the following exercises, you will import your animated lower third After Effects compositions into your Adobe Premiere Pro project. Then you will replace your temporary lower third title clips with these animated lower thirds.

Importing After Effects compositions in Adobe Premiere Pro

Now that you have made all of your lower third graphics as separate compositions in After Effects, let's import them to your Adobe Premiere Pro project.

1 In the Adobe Premiere Pro Project panel, select the Graphics bin.

2 Choose File > Import.

3 Navigate to Assets > Lessons > Lesson 05.

4 Select Poolside AE 01.aep, then click Import.

A window for Import After Effects Composition will appear.

5 Twirl open the Comps folder to reveal all of your After Effects compositions inside.

6 Choose Lower3rd_AE_Adam, then click OK.

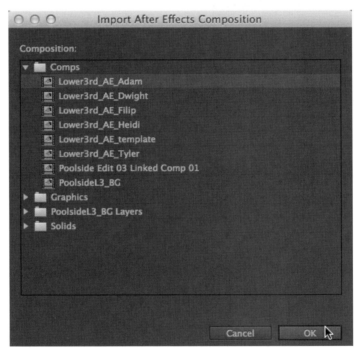

7 The Lower3rd_AE_Adam composition will appear in the Graphics bin.

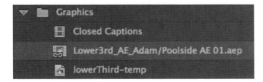

Let's import the rest of the lower third compositions to your Adobe Premiere Pro project by using another, quicker method.

1 With After Effects still open, and your Poolside AE 01 project still open in it, adjust the open application windows in your computer's desktop so that both After Effects and Adobe Premiere Pro are visible on screen together.

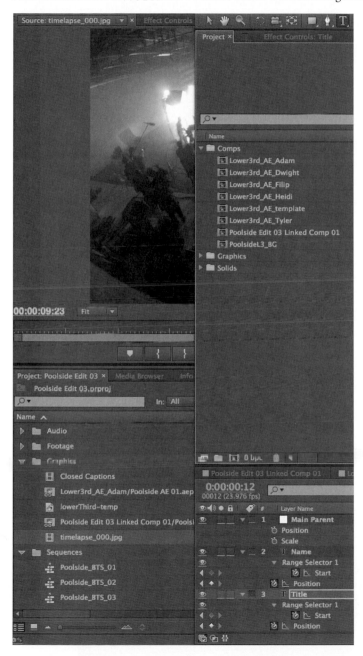

2 In the After Effects Project panel, select Lower3rd_AE_Dwight, hold down the Command (Ctrl) key, and select Lower3rd_AE_Filip, Lower3rd_AE_Heidi, and Lower3rd_AE_Tyler.

Now here's the fun part.

3 Drag the selected comps directly into the Graphics bin in your Adobe Premiere Pro Project panel.

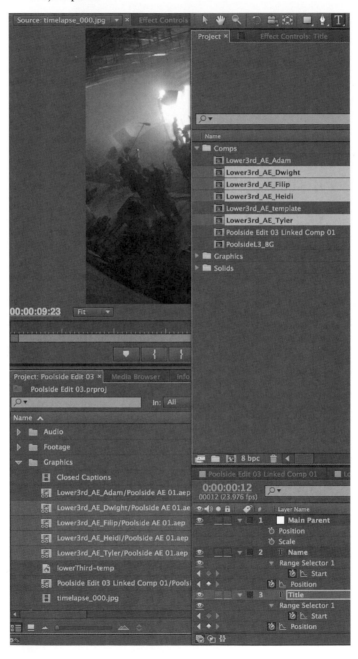

These After Effects compositions will now be imported to your Adobe Premiere Pro project.

1 Press Command+Shift+A (Ctrl+Shift+A) to deselect all.

2 Reset your user interface as needed.

3 In Adobe Premiere Pro, save your project by pressing Command+S (Ctrl+S).

Replacing clips in your Adobe Premiere Pro sequence

Now you will replace all of the temporary lower thirds with the animated ones you just imported.

1 Press the V key to activate the Selection tool.

2 Scrub through the Timeline and locate the lowerThird-temp title clip on Video 4, over Interview-Dwight1-C1.mp4.

3 In the Graphics bin, select Lower3rd_AE_Dwight/Poolside AE 01.aep.

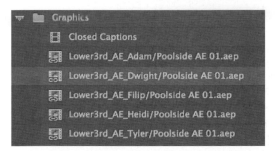

Here is a shortcut for replacing a clip in a sequence with another clip in the Project panel, while preserving the original clip's In and Out points in the sequence but starting with the replacement clip's In point.

4 Hold down the Option (Alt) key, then select and drag Lower3rd_AE_Dwight/ Poolside AE 01.aep onto the lowerThird-temp title clip on Video 4, over Interview-Dwight1-C1.mp4.

5 Scrub the Timeline playhead back a few seconds and press the spacebar to play through the animated lower third.

Notice how the original lower third is now replaced with the animated lower third, with the trimmed Out point of the original left intact in the sequence.

Now let's replace the rest of the lower thirds, starting with Heidi's.

1 Scrub through the Timeline and locate the lowerThird-temp title clip on Video 4, over Interview-Heidi.mp4.

2 In the Graphics bin, select Lower3rd_AE_Heidi/Poolside AE 01.aep.

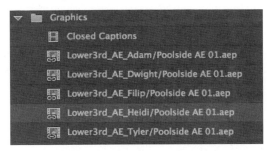

3 Hold down the Option (Alt) key, then choose and drag Lower3rd_AE_Heidi/
Poolside AE 01.aep onto the lowerThird-temp title clip on Video 4, over
Interview-Heidi.mp4.

Now let's replace Filip's temporary lower third graphic.

1   Scrub through the Timeline and locate the lowerThird-temp title clip on
     Video 4, over Interview-Filip.mp4.

2   In the Graphics bin, select Lower3rd_AE_Filip/Poolside AE 01.aep.

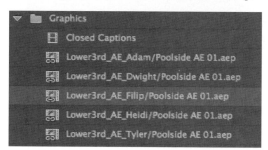

3   Hold down the Option (Alt) key, then choose and drag Lower3rd_AE_Filip/
     Poolside AE 01.aep onto the lowerThird-temp title clip on Video 4, over
     Interview-Filip.mp4.

Now let's replace Adam's lower third.

1 Scrub through the Timeline and locate the lowerThird-temp title clip on Video 4, over Interview-Adam1.mp4.

2 In the Graphics bin, select Lower3rd_AE_Adam/Poolside AE 01.aep.

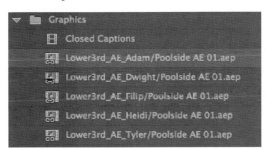

3 Hold down the Option (Alt) key, then choose and drag Lower3rd_AE_Adam/ Poolside AE 01.aep onto the lowerThird-temp title clip on Video 4, over Interview-Adam1.mp4.

Finally, let's replace Tyler's.

1   Scrub through the Timeline and locate the lowerThird-temp title clip on Video 4, over Interview-Tyler1.mp4.

2   In the Graphics bin, select Lower3rd_AE_Tyler/Poolside AE 01.aep.

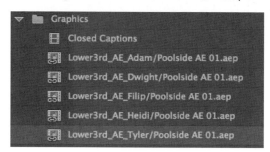

3   Hold down the Option (Alt) key, then choose and drag Lower3rd_AE_Tyler/ Poolside AE 01.aep onto the lowerThird-temp title clip on Video 4, over Interview-Tyler1.mp4.

Dynamic Link updates

Again, one of the obvious advantages of Dynamic Link of an After Effects composition in an Adobe Premiere Pro sequence is that any changes made to that composition in After Effects will automatically update in the corresponding clip (or clips) in your Adobe Premiere Pro sequence.

1 Scrub through the animated lower third graphic Lower3rd_AE_Adam/
   Poolside AE 01.aep on V4.

   Notice how the ripple at the top right of the lower third partially obscures
   Adam's face.

   A lower third graphic should never do that. So let's make a change to that
   graphic in After Effects.

2 Switch to After Effects by pressing Command+Tab (Alt+Tab).

3 In your After Effects Project panel, double-click Lower3rd_AE_Adam to open it.

You will recall that the ripple graphics are in a nested composition, PoolsideL3_BG, in this and all the other lower third compositions. What this means is that, since PoolsideL3_BG is nested in all the other lower third compositions, changing it once will apply that change to all instances of it in the After Effects project. Hence the large obscuring ripple graphic will be fixed in all of the lower third graphics.

1 In Lower3rd_AE_Adam, double-click the PoolsideL3_BG nested composition
   to open it in its own Timeline.

   The ripple layer that appears at the top right of the lower third is Ripple01.
   Let's just turn it off.

2 On the Ripple01 layer, click its visibility switch, which resembles an eyeball.

This turns off the layer's visibility, so that it does not render at all.

3 Select the Timeline tab for Lower3rd_AE_Adam.

4 Scrub through this composition and you will see that the large ripple is no longer visible.

5 Press Command+S (Ctrl+S) to save your After Effects project.

6 Switch to Adobe Premiere Pro by pressing Command+Tab (Alt+Tab).

In your Program Monitor, you will notice that the large ripple graphic in Adam's lower third is no longer obscuring Adam's face.

1 Choose Sequence > Render In To Out to render your Timeline.

2 Play your sequence by pressing the spacebar.

Notice that because all of the lower third compositions used the same animated background, the large ripple graphic that you turned off is no longer visible in any of the lower thirds.

3 In the Adobe Premiere Pro Project panel, twirl the Graphics bin shut.

4 Press Command+S (Ctrl+S) to save your Adobe Premiere Pro project.

In this lesson, you have learned how to create a layered graphic in Illustrator, how to create simple motion graphics with After Effects, and how to dynamically link After Effects compositions in Adobe Premiere Pro.

You're not done with After Effects yet. Keep it open, because in the next lesson, you will incorporate 3D animations with motion graphics.

Review questions

1 What is Dynamic Link, and why is it useful?

2 What does RAM Preview do?

3 How do you modify the timing of a text animation preset?

4 What is the difference between raster and vector artwork?

5 What is a nested composition?

Review answers

1 Dynamic Link greatly speeds up your workflow by allowing you to work seamlessly with the components of digital video in Adobe Creative Cloud. It allows you to work on a project in various applications simultaneously without having to render, export, or import your project files between applications.

2 RAM Preview enables real-time playback of cached, rendered frames of your After Effects compositions.

3 You can modify the timing of a text animation preset by modifying its keyframes in the Timeline.

4 Raster artwork is made up of pixels, and if you scale up in size, your artwork will degrade in image quality. Vector artwork is made up of coordinates and can scale up and down to infinite proportions.

5 A nested composition is a composition that is placed in another composition. The nested composition's original layers are grouped as a single layer.

6 ADVANCED STILL AND MOTION GRAPHICS TECHNIQUES

Lesson overview

In the previous lesson, you learned some basic techniques for creating motion graphics with After Effects. Now it's time to take those techniques to the next level. In this lesson, you'll learn how to

- Create static and animated masks in After Effects
- Create 3D extrusions in After Effects
- Use the 3D Camera Tracker in After Effects
- Add and animate effects in After Effects
- Use blending modes in After Effects
- Apply image sharpening in Photoshop
- Use MAXON CINEMA 4D animations in After Effects

 This lesson will take approximately 180 minutes to complete.

Download this lesson and its project files for this lesson from the Lesson & Update Files tab on your Account page at www.peachpit. com and store them on your computer in a convenient location, as described in the Getting Started section of this book.

Your Account page is also where you'll find any updates to the chapters or to the lesson files. Look on the Lesson & Update Files tab to access the most current content.

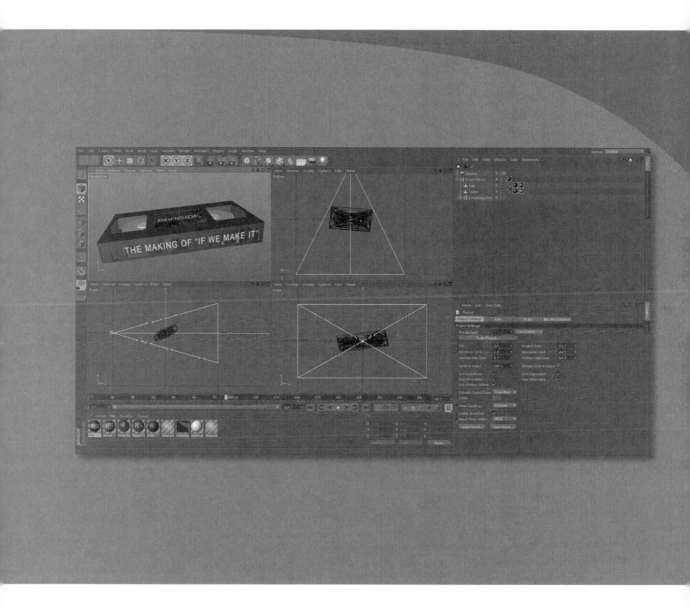

Using MAXON CINEMA 4D Lite

7 WORKING WITH AUDIO

Lesson overview

Creating engaging audio is essential in video production because it produces an emotional context through music and sound design and moves the story forward through dialogue and natural audio. In this lesson, you'll take your skills a step further and learn how to

- Understand the difference between audio clip editing and audio track editing
- Keyframe the relative volume of an audio clip in Adobe Premiere Pro
- Send audio clips between Adobe Premiere Pro and Adobe Audition
- Apply noise reduction to audio clips in Adobe Audition
- Create and export a final audio mixdown in Adobe Audition
- Add a final audio mixdown to a sequence in Adobe Premiere Pro

 This lesson will take approximately 90 minutes to complete.

Download the project files for this lesson from the Lesson & Update Files tab on your Account page at www.peachpit.com and store them on your computer in a convenient location, as described in the Getting Started section of this book.

Your Account page is also where you'll find any updates to the chapters or to the lesson files. Look on the Lesson & Update Files tab to access the most current content.

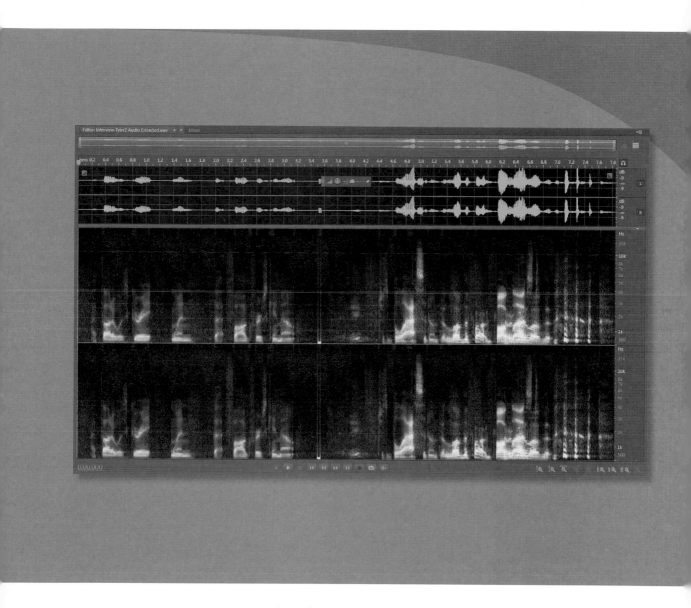

Spectral Frequency Display in Adobe Audition

Beginning this lesson

If you are continuing from the previous lesson, feel free to continue with the Adobe Premiere Pro project you already have open. Skip ahead to "Making your final edit sequence in Adobe Premiere Pro."

If you are starting here

● **Note:** Important! Currently, Adobe Premiere Pro CC does not retain interpret-footage settings on clips even though those clips don't need relinking. Refer to the Getting Started section "Interpret frame rate of linked files" for steps on fixing this issue so you can follow this lesson.

If you are starting at this lesson, generate your own Adobe Premiere Pro project file from a copy of one provided for you.

1   Navigate to the Assets > Lessons > Lesson 07 folder on your hard drive.

2   Double-click to open the Adobe Premiere Pro project Lesson07_Start.prproj.

3   In Adobe Premiere Pro, choose File > Save As.

4   Navigate to the Lesson 07 folder on your hard drive. Name your Adobe Premiere Pro project file **Poolside Edit 05**. Click Save.

Making your final edit sequence in Adobe Premiere Pro

Because you are continuing with a previous version of this edit, you'll first save a new version of your sequence. This allows you to go back to the previous version if need be and is a recommended best practice in the video editing workflow.

1   In the Project panel, twirl open the Sequences bin.

▶ **Tip:** Press Command+C (Ctrl+C) to copy. Press Command+V (Ctrl+V) to paste. This will make a duplicate of this sequence outside of the Sequences folder.

2   Click the Poolside_BTS_04 sequence to select it. Choose Edit > Copy to copy it to your clipboard. Then choose Edit > Paste.

3   To modify the name of the sequence, click the name of the sequence to select it.

Potential error messages

When opening an Adobe Premiere Pro project file that was last saved on a different computer, you may encounter a couple of error messages. Don't panic!

One such error message will tell you that the local scratch disk is not in the same place.

● **Note:** This sidebar also appeared in Chapter 1 and is repeated here for your convenience if you have not followed these chapter lessons in order.

If this happens, choose File > Project Settings > Scratch Disks; then, for all settings in the Scratch Disks window, click the Browse button and navigate to a local folder on your hard drive where you want Adobe Premiere Pro to save your Captured Video and Audio, your Video and Audio Previews, and your Project Auto Saves.

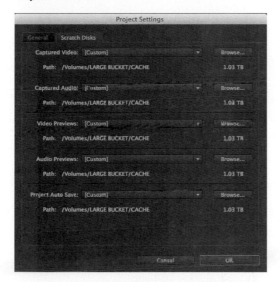

Another error message you may encounter is one that tells you that there is a missing renderer.

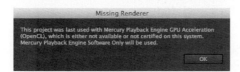

This just means that the project file was last saved on a machine that was using a graphics processing unit (GPU) that is not present on the current machine. Again, don't panic. Just click OK and carry on.

4 Change the name of the sequence to **Poolside_BTS_05**, press Return (Enter), and then drag it into the Sequences folder.

5 Double-click the Poolside_BTS_05 sequence to load it in your Timeline.

Note that the sequence appears in a new tabbed Timeline in front of your original sequence.

For this lesson, you do not need to have multiple Timelines open simultaneously, so let's close the one you won't be working in.

6 In the Timeline, click the Poolside_BTS_04 tab to select it.

7 Press Command+W (Ctrl+W) to close this sequence.

The new sequence is now the only one visible in the Timeline, which will ensure that you are working on the most recent iteration.

8 Press Command+S (Ctrl+S) to save your Adobe Premiere Pro project.

Monitoring audio

If you're editing audio with the Creative Cloud applications, it's important to use recommended methods and quality equipment. You should make sure that the audio in your Timeline is not too loud or too soft and that there isn't any unwanted noise. A simple way to determine if your Timeline audio is too soft is to listen to your playback and compare it to another mastered audio source—for example, a video playing on a website or music playing in an MP3 application. If, by comparison, your Timeline audio is too soft, then consider adjusting your Timeline audio settings to a higher level. To determine if your Timeline audio is too loud, play your Timeline while listening closely with headphones on, all the while paying close attention to your Audio Meters panel (covered in the next section of this chapter). If you hear distortion, or if your Audio Meters ever peak into the red indicators, then your audio is too loud. If this is the case, then adjust your Timeline audio settings to a higher level.

You also want to ensure that what you are hearing in your Timeline is what end users will experience when they hear the finished content. To do this, you must work with quality studio monitors (or speakers) and studio headphones to guarantee that your audio sounds the way you want it to under optimal conditions.

Bear in mind that end users may not be using the best equipment, so you should also listen to your audio using equipment that is not of the highest quality. For example, monitor your audio with inexpensive earbuds that come with an MP3 player, or perhaps use the internal speakers of a laptop. Consider who your listeners are and anticipate their listening environment.

Above all, trust your ears! If you're hearing anomalies or artifacts such as distortion or unwanted noise, end users will probably hear them, too. Consider making the appropriate adjustments.

Understanding audio tools in Adobe Premiere Pro and Adobe Audition

Adobe Premiere Pro and Adobe Audition both offer tools for editing audio, including

*   The Audio Mixer in Adobe Premiere Pro, which gets its look and functionality from Adobe Audition

*   An enhanced Audio Meters panel in Adobe Premiere Pro

*   Easy transfer of audio clips between Adobe Premiere Pro and Adobe Audition

*   Noise-removal effects in Adobe Audition

*   A new Audio Clip Mixer in Adobe Premiere Pro

*   Mute and Solo buttons in Adobe Premiere Pro

Before you do anything in Adobe Premiere Pro, you need to change your workspace, set your preferences, and open the Audio Mixer.

Changing your workspace in Adobe Premiere Pro

Your workspace is an assortment of panels that displays a graphical representation of your controls. Adobe Premiere Pro comes with a set of preset workspaces that were designed to maximize productivity based on certain tasks.

Up until now, you've been using the workspace for editing. Because you'll be working with audio in this lesson, it's best to change your workspace in Adobe Premiere Pro to help streamline your work. To change your workspace, follow these steps.

1 Choose Window > Workspace > Audio.

2 Choose Window > Workspace > Reset Current Workspace. Click Yes in the window that appears.

Notice that by doing this, your user interface has changed slightly. Most notably, the Audio Clip Mixer panel is now prominent. You'll explore the Audio Clip Mixer later in this lesson.

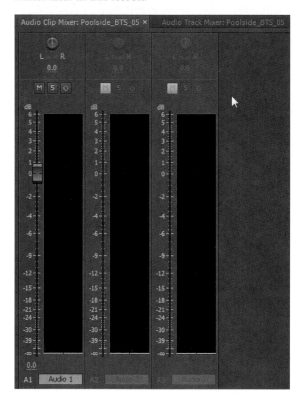

Let's add another panel to your workspace.

3 Choose Window > Audio Meters. The Audio Meters panel appears in the workspace.

4 Hover your mouse pointer between the Timeline and the Audio Meters panel until the mouse pointer changes shape. Drag to the left to stretch the Audio Meters panel horizontally.

5 Now scrub your playhead across the Timeline.

Notice that if the Audio Meters panel is stretched wider than its height, the green meters bounce horizontally, whereas if the height of the Audio Meters panel is longer than its width, the meters bounce vertically. This feature allows for very precise readings on audio levels.

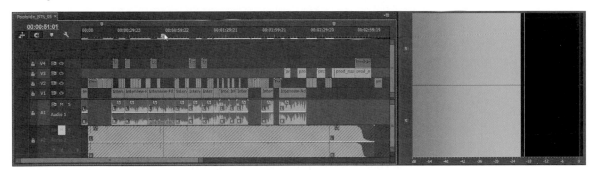

If you want to adjust the scale of units, to yield even more precise measurement of volume, right-click the Auto Meters panel to select from a list of options. For instance, you might choose Show Valleys if you want to see a dynamic indicator of a track's minimum loudness of the last three seconds of audio. Or you might want to adjust the sensitivity of the meters by choosing a different decibel (dB) range than the current 60 dB Range.

Customizing the look of the Timeline

In order to allow for maximum control over the way you work, the Timeline interface in Adobe Premiere Pro can be customized to reveal options you need while hiding those you don't. Click the Timeline display settings icon from the Timeline and choose Customize Audio Header.

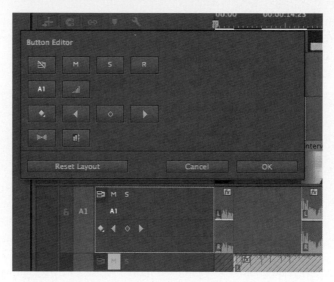

This allows you to choose which buttons will remain present to the left of each audio track or to reorganize them as needed. One of the most useful items to add to your workspace is the Track Meter, which displays a reading of the current output levels on the track, while the main Audio Meters panel displays the master levels.

Stretch your Audio Meters panel so its height is taller than its width.

Verifying your preferences

Your audio monitoring may already be configured properly; however, you should verify your preferences to make sure you can hear your audio output from Adobe Premiere Pro.

Regardless of whether you're listening to your computer's sound through studio monitors or headphones (or earbuds!), set a preference in Adobe Premiere Pro that will use your operating system audio output setting. The same preference panel can be used to configure audio input settings as well for recording a voice-over straight to Adobe Premiere Pro.

1 Choose Premiere Pro > Preferences > Audio Hardware (Edit > Preferences > Audio Hardware) to select your audio monitoring device.

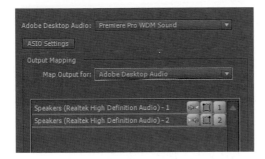

2 Choose your default device and click OK.

Viewing audio waveforms

An *audio waveform* is a graphical representation of the frequency and volume of an audio clip. Generally, where the graphic is short, the volume is low, and when the graphic is tall, the volume is high. If you play your movie and listen carefully as you watch your playhead move across the audio waveform, you can get an idea of when sounds occur just by looking at the waveform.

1 In the Timeline, hover your mouse pointer over the dividing line between Audio 1 and Audio 2 until the mouse pointer changes shape. Click and drag downward to stretch Audio 1 vertically in the interface.

▶ **Tip:** A new way to work the Timeline is to hover the mouse pointer over a track header and use the scroll wheel to adjust its relative size, making it easier than ever to change focus quickly between different video tracks or zoom in closely on an audio waveform.

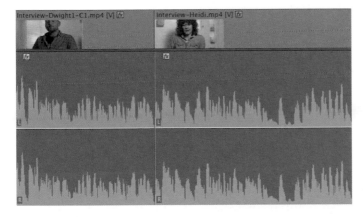

2 Zoom in by pressing the equal (=) key on your keyboard (not the numeric keypad).

3 Play the sequence by pressing the spacebar.

▶ **Tip:** You can zoom in on your Timeline using the equal (=) key. Zoom out by using the minus (–) key.

This blocky graphic shows peaks and valleys over time. This visually represents the microphone's vibration on the capsule when audio is being recorded, as well as the speaker's vibration when the audio is played back.

Opening the Audio Mixer

The Audio Mixer panel in Adobe Premiere Pro has a sleek look that provides fast, accurate visual feedback about your audio track signal levels; it also includes revamped Mute, Solo, and Record buttons (for recording voice-overs), pan controls, and an improved channel strip layout. Now, double-clicking a fader returns it to 0dB, and the Audio Mixer includes separate decibel level scales for the meters and faders. In addition, right-clicking the Audio Mixer reveals context menus that provide a number of options, including the ability to reset the peak level indicators, show valleys at low amplitude points, change the displayed decibel range, and choose between dynamic peak indicators that update every three seconds or static peak indicators that hold the loudest peak until reset or playback is restarted. And—when signal is present—peak levels are displayed numerically below each meter, giving you precise visual feedback about your audio signal levels. Let's open the Audio Mixer.

1 Press Shift+6 to show your Audio Mixer panel.

2 In your Timeline, click the playhead and drag it to the right to scrub through your sequence.

In the audio meters, you'll see a green line moving up and down at varying degrees based on the level of the audio on a given track.

Preparing the music tracks

In a previous lesson, you muted and locked tracks Audio 2 and Audio 3. Now you will unlock and unmute them so that you can hear the music clips in the sequence.

1 Click the Lock icons for Audio 2 and Audio 3 to unlock those tracks.

2 Click the Mute buttons for Audio 2 and Audio 3 to unmute those tracks, as well.

3 Scrub through the Timeline with the playhead and you should hear the music.

  The first long music clip, in Audio 2, is an instrumental version of the Poolside song "If We Make It." The last two music clips, one in Audio 2 and one in Audio 3, are the ending segments of the song; the instrumental ending is in Audio 2 and the vocal ending is in Audio 3. You only need the vocal segment.

4 Right-click the second clip in Audio 2. By default, a clip in the Timeline is enabled, but this state can be toggled. From the context menu, choose Enable, thus disabling it. This clip remains in the sequence but does not render.

5 Scrub the playhead through the Timeline and you will notice that the music clips are set to play too loudly to adequately hear the interview audio.

Adobe Premiere Pro effects

Just as Adobe Premiere Pro offers many effects for video, it also offers many effects for audio. Audio effects can be applied to audio clips in the same way that video effects can be applied to video clips in your Timeline, as demonstrated in Lesson 4. You can apply the following effects and more:

- The **Dynamics effect** provides a set of controls that allow you to adjust audio, including Limiter, Compressor, and Expander settings.

- The **Parametric Equalization effect** allows you to adjust frequencies in relation to a Center frequency. This can be used to simulate a more expensive microphone or reduce an unwanted hiss from a high frequency.

- The **Reverb effect** can apply a simulation of the acoustics of audio playing in a room.

- The **Delay effect** creates an echo of an audio clip's sound. This can be useful to simulate the sound of an audio clip as if it were played in a cavernous space.

- The **Loudness Radar effect**, new in Adobe Premiere Pro, provides a graphical interface for monitoring a clip or track in order to ensure your audio meets broadcast loudness standards. This effect is also available in Adobe Audition. See the "Loudness Radar" sidebar.

These audio effects, and others, are located in the Effects panel within the Audio Effects category.

Loudness Radar

Certain broadcast standards have been enacted to ensure, for instance, that the loudness of TV commercials matches the loudness of the programs that they accompany.

The new Loudness Radar effect, available in both Adobe Premiere Pro and Adobe Audition, gives users a graphical overview of the loudness of an audio clip or an entire audio track over the course of the clip's or track's duration. The user can apply a preset to the effect based on a broadcast standard to make sure that the audio loudness fits within the standard.

For more information about the Loudness Radar effect, visit http://tv.adobe.com/watch/creative-cloud-for-video/adobe-audition-cc-tc-electronic-itu-loudness-radar/.

Track-based effects, which when applied, affect entire tracks, are accessed by clicking the right arrow icon at the top left of the Audio Mixer panel...

...and then by clicking the Effect Selection down arrow button.

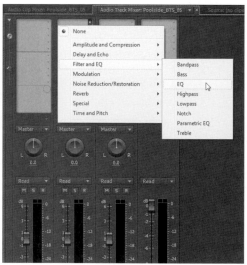

Audio Plug-in Manager

The new Audio Plug-In Manager, found in the Audio preferences, allows you to scan your system for AU and VST plug-ins and load them directly into Adobe Premiere Pro. Mac users will be able to import the plug-in libraries that ship with Apple software.

Clip editing versus track editing

There are two general ways to edit audio during postproduction: clip editing and track editing.

Clip editing entails making changes to the audio of a specific audio clip by adjusting its volume, adding an effect, or performing some other operation. You use clip editing when you want to make changes to a certain clip and not necessarily to any others. Clip editing is common when one clip has a lower or higher volume than the other clips on the given track. It can also be useful when noise is present in one clip but not others. Adjustments made on the clip level are applied only to the clip's instance on the Timeline and will not affect the master clip. Therefore, by moving an instance of a modified clip in the Timeline, any changes applied to it will move with it.

Track editing entails making changes to an entire track, which applies a secondary adjustment to the signal flow of the given track. For instance, by adjusting the volume of an audio track, you can change the output level, which is the compounded volume of the clip(s) and the track.

When you apply automation (i.e., keyframing volume changes over time) to a clip, the time-based changes you make are attached to the clip, regardless of which track it's placed in or whether the clip is moved in the Timeline, whereas automation you apply to a track is independent of clips and is fixed to that track regardless of which clips are on that given track. Although you can apply keyframes to a clip manually, Automation Modes apply keyframes to the track rather than the clip.

Audio gain

The term *gain* refers to the input level of a clip or clips, whereas volume refers to the output level. You can adjust the gain of a clip using the Audio Gain command, accessible by selecting one or more audio clips in the Timeline, and then right-clicking a clip and choosing Audio Gain from the context menu. By adjusting gain, you are compounding this adjustment with the volume of the clip and the track volume.

Set Gain to. Allows you to set the gain of a clip or clips to a specific value.

Adjust Gain by. Allows you to adjust the gain of a clip or clips by a relative amount.

Normalize Max Peak to. Allows you to adjust the peak amplitude of a clip or clips to a value below 0dB; all other peaks in the audio will adjust by an amount relative to that.

Normalize All Peaks to. Allows you to adjust all peaks in the amplitude of a clip or clips to a value below 0dB.

Peak Amplitude. This indicates the selected clip's highest dB level.

Audio clip editing in Adobe Premiere Pro

Editing audio clips in Adobe Premiere Pro is just as simple and intuitive as editing video. Clip volume and duration can be adjusted in the Source Monitor as well as in the Timeline.

Now let's dive into clip editing.

Automating volume with keyframes

You'll be automating the volume of the music clip so that as people are speaking on camera, the music volume is reduced, but it is raised when they are not speaking.

In your Poolside_BTS_05 Timeline, look closely at the Audio 1 track. All of the clips in that track have a white horizontal line. This indicates a clip's current volume level.

1 Hold down Shift and scrub the playhead so that it snaps to the head of Interview-Dwight1-C1.mp4 in track Video 1.

2 With the Selection tool, click the white line for the music clip in Audio 2, and drag downward until your tool tip reads between −3 and −4dB. Notice that it's challenging to achieve a precise result when you're making this adjustment on the Timeline.

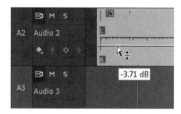

▶ **Tip:** Use Shift+right arrow to adjust your playhead forward five frames. Use Shift+left arrow to adjust your playhead backward five frames.

3 With the music clip in Audio 2 selected, press Shift+5 to open the Effect Controls panel. Click the small triangle icon next to Volume to twirl open the Volume settings. Notice the corresponding volume adjustment for the Level property. Here you can set precise values for your volume adjustments. Change the Volume Level to **−12.0dB**. When you make this adjustment in the Effect Controls panel, Adobe Premiere Pro makes a new keyframe at the current time.

Notice the stopwatch icon next to Level. This is activated by default. If you were to deactivate it, Adobe Premiere Pro would not automatically create new keyframes.

You'll continue to add keyframes to the Volume Level of the music clip on Audio 2 in this fashion. By automating the music clip, you can set different adjustments at different points in time so the music doesn't overpower the interview and the music is prominent when there is no interview audio.

4 Press Shift+right arrow five times, to adjust the playhead ahead 25 frames (or just over one second).

5 In the Effect Controls panel, select the Level value and change it to **−25**; then press Return (Enter). Doing this makes a new Level keyframe.

Look down at Audio 2 in the Timeline and notice that the horizontal line now dips downward between the two keyframes you made.

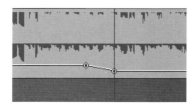

6 Scrub the playhead back a few seconds, then press the spacebar to play the sequence. Notice how the music volume decreases as Dwight starts speaking.

You will perform several more edits to the music clip in Audio 2 so that the music volume increases when there is a gap in the Interview sound bites and decreases as the Interview sound bites resume.

1 Hold down Shift and scrub the playhead so that it snaps to the tail of Interview-Adam2.mp4.gonnaBeAwesome.

2 Press Shift+left arrow five times to adjust the playhead back 25 frames, or just as we hear Adam finish saying "awesome."

3 In the Effect Controls panel, click the empty diamond icon for Level to create a new keyframe at the current time using the current value, which should be −25.

4 Snap the playhead to the tail of Interview-Adam2.mp4.gonnaBeAwesome again.

5 In the Effect Controls panel, select the value for Level and change it to **−12**, then press Return (Enter). This makes a new keyframe at the current time.

6 Snap the playhead to the head of Interview-Tyler2.mp4 in the Timeline.

7 In the Effect Controls panel, click the empty diamond icon for Level to create a new keyframe at the current time with a value of −12.

8 Press Shift+right arrow five times, moving the playhead ahead 25 frames.

9 In the Effect Controls panel, select the value for Level and change it to −25, then press Return (Enter).

10 Scrub the playhead to a few seconds before the sound bite gap in Audio 1 between Interview-Adam2.mp4.gonnaBeAwesome and Interview-Tyler2.mp4; then press the spacebar to preview your audio edits.

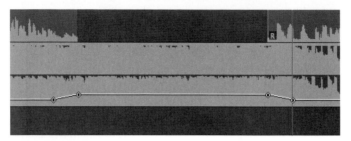

There is one more sound bite gap to fill with music.

1 Snap the playhead to the tail of Interview-Tyler2.mp4.

2 Adjust the playhead back 25 frames by pressing Shift+left arrow five times.

3 In the Effect Controls panel, click the empty diamond icon for Level to create a new keyframe at the current time using the current value of −25.

4 Snap the playhead to the tail of Interview-Tyler2.mp4 again.

5 In the Effect Controls panel, select the value for Level and change it to −12, then press Return (Enter).

6 Snap the playhead to the head of Interview-AdamJeff.mp4.

7 In the Effect Controls panel, click the empty diamond icon for Level, to create a new keyframe at the current time using the current value of −12.

8 Press Shift+right arrow five times to move the playhead ahead 25 frames.

9 In the Effect Controls panel, select the value for Level and change it to −25, then click Return (Enter).

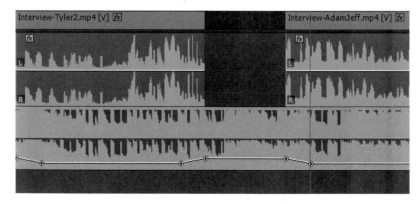

Let's do one last pair of keyframes...

1 Press the spacebar to play the sequence. When you hear Adam finish saying "super-meta," stop playback by pressing the spacebar again.

2 In the Effect Controls panel, click the empty diamond icon for Level to create a new keyframe at the current time using the current value of –25.

3 Snap the playhead to the tail of Interview-AdamJeff.mp4.

4 In the Effect Controls panel, select the value for Level and change it to **–12**, then press Return (Enter).

5 Adjust the playhead back a few seconds; then press the spacebar to play the sequence.

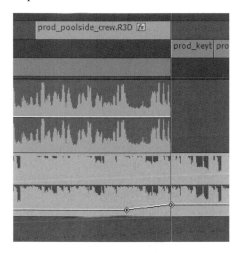

When the instrumental clip in Audio 2 ends, the vocal clip in Audio 3 takes over. You will notice a disparity in their volumes that needs adjusting.

1 Snap the playhead to the head of the vocal clip in Audio 3. Select this clip.

2 In the Effect Controls panel, select the value for Level and change it to **–12**, then press Return (Enter)

Now preview all of the current audio edits in your sequence.

1 Select the Timeline. Press Home to jump to the beginning of your sequence. Press Shift+6 to show the Audio Mixer so that you can see the meters. Press the spacebar to play your sequence. Notice that the green meters for Audio 2 get higher and lower as the Level keyframes for this clip automate upward and downward.

2 Press Command+S (Ctrl+S) to save your project.

Adjusting volume with the Audio Clip Mixer

As you play back the audio, listen closely to the volume of the Interview sound bites. You will notice that some of the Interview sound bites are a bit louder than the others, and they will need some balancing.

To do this, you will use the Audio Clip Mixer.

The Audio Clip Mixer lets you visualize and adjust the volume of an individual clip or clips in your sequence. By pairing audio meters with a fader, the Audio Clip Mixer gives you the ability to select single or multiple clips and make adjustments to the individual clip volume during playback. For users who are more accustomed to audio tools, the Audio Clip Mixer provides a more intuitive interface.

Let's adjust the volume of some of the Interview clips using the Audio Clip Mixer.

1   Press Shift+9 to make the Audio Clip Mixer active.

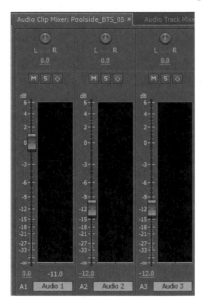

2   Scrub the playhead between Interview-Dwight2.mp4 and Interview-Adam1.mp4 in the Timeline, while looking at the Audio 1 level in the Audio Clip Mixer. Notice that the volume of Interview-Adam1.mp4 is significantly higher.

3 With the playhead placed over Interview-Adam1.mp4, adjust the Audio 1 fader in the Audio Clip Mixer to –7.

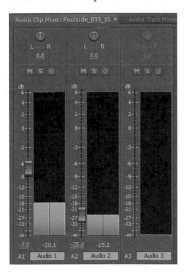

4 Scrub the playhead between Interview-Adam1.mp4 and Interview-Tyler1.mp4. Notice how the latter clip is louder and the levels meter in the Audio Clip Mixer jumps when that clip is playing.

Sometimes when you want a precise value for a clip's audio level, adjusting with the fader can be too clumsy. How about a handy keyboard shortcut?

5 Select Interview-Tyler1.mp4.

6 With the playhead placed over Interview-Tyler1.mp4, adjust the Audio 1 fader to –5 by pressing the left bracket key ([) five times.

Make sure that the clip is selected, or else the keyboard shortcut will adjust the clip volume of all clips in all unlocked tracks at the current time.

The next two Interview clips need adjusting as well.

7 Hover the playhead over Interview-Dancers.mp4 and select this clip. Adjust the clip volume in the Audio Clip Mixer to –5 by pressing [five times.

8 Hover the playhead over Interview-Adam2.mp4.movingSoFast and select this clip. Adjust the clip volume in the Audio Clip Mixer to –5 by pressing [five times.

9 Hover the playhead over Interview-Adam2.mp4.gonnaBeAwesome and select this clip. Adjust the clip volume in the Audio Clip Mixer to –5 by pressing [five times.

10 Finally, hover the playhead over Interview-AdamJeff.mp4 and select this clip. Adjust the clip volume in the Audio Clip Mixer to –5 by pressing [five times.

11 Press Command+S (Ctrl+S) to save your project.

▶ **Tip:** Adjust clip volume of all clips (or only the selected clips) in all unlocked tracks at the current time by plus or minus 1dB; do this by pressing either the [or the] key. Adjust by plus or minus 10dB by pressing Shift and [or], respectively. This can be done during playback.

Audio clip editing in Adobe Audition

Adobe Audition is a cross-platform, high-performance multitrack audio editor with a versatile arsenal of sound-restoration and editing tools, strong integration with Adobe Premiere Pro, and dozens of new features—such as real-time clip stretching, parameter automation, and automatic speech alignment—that increase your efficiency and control.

Although you can use Adobe Premiere Pro in the clip editing and finishing stages of audio production, here you'll be using Adobe Audition for its more robust and efficient tools to resolve issues such as clicks and background noise.

Examining clips for distractions

Let's closely examine the interview audio track to determine what needs to be fixed in the sequence Poolside_BTS_05.

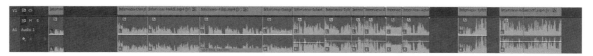

1 In your Adobe Premiere Pro Timeline, mute Audio 2 by clicking its Mute switch so that you can listen closely to the interview audio in Audio 1.

2 Adjust the playhead to 00:01:32:07.

3 Listen closely to Interview-Dwight3.mp4. An audible low-frequency hum is being produced by a poorly grounded microphone or cable. You should remove this noise.

4 Now adjust the playhead to 00:01:51:23.

5 Listen closely to Interview-Tyler2.mp4. Right after Tyler says "first came out" there is an audible click sound. This is distracting and you should also remove it.

You will use now use Adobe Audition to remove these unwanted sounds.

Sending audio clips from Adobe Premiere Pro to Adobe Audition for cleanup

Adobe Premiere Pro allows you to easily send an audio clip to Adobe Audition. First, though, you want to specify where Adobe Premiere Pro will save audio files when it sends them to Adobe Audition.

1 In Adobe Premiere Pro, choose File > Project Settings > Scratch Disks.

2 Click the menu next to Captured Audio and choose Same as Project.

3 Then click OK.

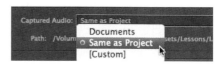

Let's first work with the Interview-Tyler2.mp4 clip. Select that audio clip in your Timeline, right-click it, and then choose Edit Clip in Adobe Audition.

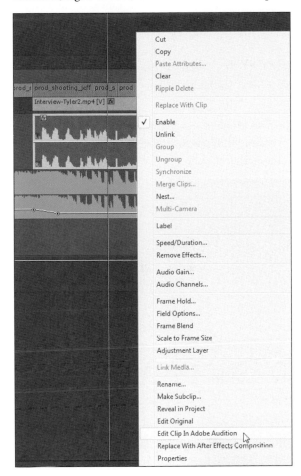

Adobe Premiere Pro automatically renders this as a .wav file and replaces the original audio clip within the Timeline. This new .wav file, Interview-Tyler2 Audio Extracted.wav, will open in Adobe Audition.

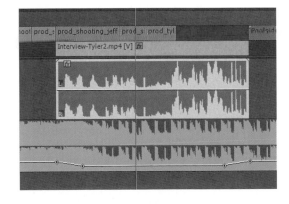

Any changes applied to Interview-Tyler2 Audio Extracted.wav in Adobe Audition will automatically update in your Adobe Premiere Pro sequence.

Understanding the Spectral Frequency Display

In Adobe Audition, Interview-Tyler2 Audio Extracted.wav will appear in the Editor panel. To ensure that you see what this exercise needs you to see, let's choose a workspace and then reset it.

1 Choose Window > Workspace > Default.

2 Choose Window > Workspace > Reset "Default." In the window that appears, click Yes.

At the top of the Editor panel, you'll see a stereo waveform. Below the waveform is the Spectral Frequency Display. It offers a different way of visualizing frequencies and volume in the left and right channels of the clip.

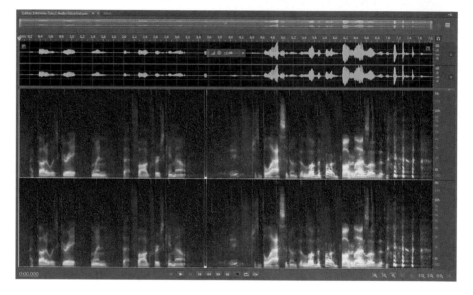

Tip: If you are seeing the waveform and not the Spectral Frequency Display, press Shift+D. This will reveal the horizontal interface divider, which you can then drag upward or downward.

Play the clip and pay close attention to the Spectral Frequency Display. There are separate (but in this case, largely identical) spectra for the left and right audio channels. Frequency is represented on the vertical axis, whereas amplitude is represented by a range of colors and brightness. Notice the range of frequencies displayed on the right side of the Spectral Frequency Display. Also, notice that louder sounds are represented by yellow and orange areas, whereas softer sounds appear red and purple.

As you play the clip a few times, watch the playhead and pay close attention to which areas of the spectrum correspond to the sounds you hear. Try to visually isolate where the click sound is in the spectrum.

Removing transient sounds using the Spectral Frequency Display

The click noise that should be removed from Interview-Tyler2.mp4 is visible in the Spectral Frequency Display as a narrow vertical orange area. You'll remove it using the Hand tool.

1 From the Tools panel at the top, select the Time Selection tool.

2 Adjust your playhead to just before the click sound. Zoom in to the spectrum by pressing the equal (=) key several times.

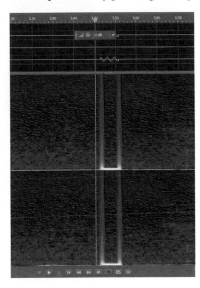

3 Using the Time Selection tool, select the range of the spectrum that contains the click sound.

4 Hover the mouse pointer over this selection and you will see the Time Selection tool temporarily become the Hand tool.

5 With the Hand tool, select and move the selection range to the immediate left of the click sound, so that the click is no longer within the range, but neither is any of the audio spectrum of Tyler speaking.

6 Choose Edit > Copy.

7 Select and drag the selection range back over the click sound, then choose Edit > Paste.

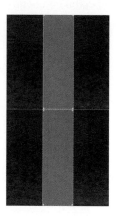

▶ **Tip:** You can also fix clicks and pops in your audio by using the Auto Heal Selection function, Command+U (Ctrl+U).

Doing this replaces the click sound with a split-second of background noise that the viewer won't notice.

Play back the clip from the beginning and verify that the click sound is gone and that the audible voice frequencies or natural noise floor is still intact.

8 Save your .wav file in Audition by pressing Command+S (Ctrl+S).

9 Then switch back to Adobe Premiere Pro by pressing Command+Tab (Alt+Tab).

▶ **Tip:** To switch between open applications, press Command+Tab (Alt+Tab).

10 Play your sequence and notice that the changes you saved in Adobe Audition are indeed applied and that the click sound has been removed.

Removing background noise from your audio

You need to edit one more audio clip in Adobe Audition. Interview-Dwight3.mp4 has a low-frequency hum that is audible as Dwight talks about using a video projector. This time around, you can't simply select and delete an unwanted bit of audio. The low-frequency hum is audible throughout and is interlaced with frequencies that are essential to keeping the quality of dialogue. To remove it, you must select a region of the audio spectrum that represents the room tone, or select the background noise only, which captures a snapshot of these unwanted frequencies. Then you'll use a noise-removal effect in Adobe Audition. The background noise will be removed from the whole clip, leaving the dialogue audio intact.

Based on the edit you currently have in the Timeline, Interview-Dwight3.mp4 has been tightly trimmed to Dwight speaking. To sample some room tone from this clip, you need to temporarily extend the In point of this audio clip.

1 In the Adobe Premiere Pro Timeline, you want to extend the head of the audio but not the video of Interview-Dwight3.mp4. To do this, use the Selection tool to drag the audio portion of Interview-Dwight3.mp4 down to track Audio 3, directly below its current position in the Timeline.

2 With the Selection tool, extend the tail of the audio portion to the right as far as it will go.

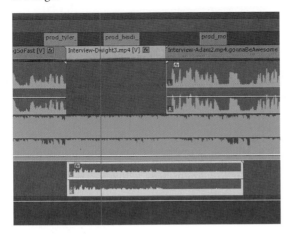

3 Now right-click it, and then choose Edit Clip in Adobe Audition. Again, you should see its replacement audio clip, Interview-Dwight3 Audio Extracted.wav, open in Adobe Audition.

4 Listen to the audio and find a region of time at the end of the clip that is only room tone and no other sounds.

5 You can define your region of selection by setting In and Out points. Adjust your playhead to 0:04.640 seconds and press I to set the In point. Adjust your playhead to 0:05.000 seconds and press O to set the Out point.

6 Choose Effects > Noise Reduction / Restoration > Noise Reduction (process).

7 In the Effect - Noise Reduction window, click the Capture Noise Print button. This will sample the room tone.

8 Now click the Select Entire File button so that any changes you make with the sampled room tone will apply to the entire file.

9 Click the Play button at the bottom of the Effect - Noise Reduction window to hear the audio with the noise removed.

The Noise Reduction slider controls the percentage of noise reduction in the output signal. Fine-tune this setting while previewing audio to achieve maximum noise reduction with minimum artifacts. The Reduce By control determines the amplitude reduction of detected noise.

Noise Reduction is a frequency value, while Reduce By is a decibel value. Basically, you want to capture the frequencies you want to remove while at the same time maintaining integrity of the frequencies that are integral to the sounds you'd like to preserve. It helps to try increasing the Noise Reduction value to the point at which the sound degrades. Listen for destructive qualities to the sound you're trying to preserve, and then ease back the value to a nominal threshold that sounds good to your ears. Use Reduce By to reduce the selected frequencies more or less. It is recommended to use the Noise Reduction and Reduce By values in an inverse fashion.

Remember that the goal here is not to reduce noise completely, but to reduce it so that the speaker is clearer, but still sounds natural. There is a balance between clarity and over-processed audio.

10 Once the noise reduction sounds satisfactory, click Apply.

The Noise Reduction effect offers many capabilities to refine your noise reduction, but in most cases you'll only need to slightly adjust the Noise Reduction and Reduce By properties. Again, trust your ears as you identify the optimal balance between destructive and effective changes.

11 Press Command+S (Ctrl+S) to save your .wav file, and then switch back to Adobe Premiere Pro.

12 Now you need to retrim this audio clip in your Timeline. With the Selection tool, hold down Option (Alt), grab the tail of the audio portion of Interview-Dwight3.mp4, and drag it to the left until it snaps to the edit point between Interview-Dwight3.mp4 and Interview-Adam2.mp4.gonnaBeAwesome.

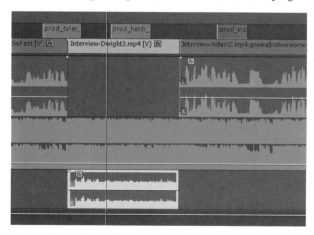

13 Drag the audio portion back up to its original place in track Audio 1.

14 Press Command+S (Ctrl+S) to save your Adobe Premiere Pro project.

Real-time track mixing in Adobe Premiere Pro and Adobe Audition

Just as you have keyframed volume changes to clips over time, you can also keyframe audio tracks and set them up to receive real-time automation so that the volume of an overall track can be increased or decreased regardless of which clip or clips are on the Timeline.

Much like similar tools in other DAWs (digital audio workstations), the Audio Mixer in Adobe Premiere Pro and the Mixer in Adobe Audition allow users to make these volume changes in real time during playback by dragging the fader icon upward and downward. Although this is a great feature and useful in some cases, it records precise keyframes to the track, which yields a large number of keyframes. This amount of keyframes can be managed in the Adobe Premiere Pro Audio Preferences, under Automation Keyframe Optimization.

To do real-time track automation, you need to adjust the mode of the track you want to keyframe from Read to either Latch, Touch, or Write based on the nature of the track automation you want to perform. For music producers and audio engineers, this tool works the same as other digital audio workstations. You play your sequence and adjust an Audio Mixer slider in real-time to generate track keyframes. An audio track in the Timeline can show track keyframes instead of clip keyframes; you simply click the Show Keyframes icon in the audio track, and then choose Show Track Keyframes from the context menu.

Multitrack mixing and finishing in Adobe Audition

At the point in postproduction when your picture is locked—that is, when you have completed the edit and will not make any further adjustments to timing—it is standard procedure to finish the audio mix by balancing levels between tracks and maximizing overall amplitude without introducing distortion.

You'll finish the audio mix in Adobe Audition using its multitrack mixing features. You'll also add a sound effect to the final mix. Then you'll export a final stereo mixdown from Adobe Audition and replace the original clip audio with the final stereo mixdown in the current Adobe Premiere Pro Timeline.

Determine where the sound effect will go

First, let's determine where in the sequence you need to place the sound effect when you add it in Adobe Audition.

In a scenario in which you would need to cue several sound effects to video, you could export a preview video with your sequence audio. That would require a video render of your sequence. For this exercise, that would take an unjustifiably long time, considering you only want to cue one small sound effect to your video.

In Adobe Premiere Pro, adjust the Timeline playhead to 00:00:08:05. This timecode matches the one at the very beginning, when the intro motion graphic shows the visual effect of bad analog TV reception, which lasts for one second.

In Adobe Audition, you will add a sound effect of TV static that will fade up from 00:00:08:05 to 00:00:08:17, and then fade down to 00:00:09:05.

Make note of these timecodes.

Sending your sequence to Audition

Let's send the entire sequence into Adobe Audition.

1   In your Adobe Premiere Pro sequence, make sure that all of your audio tracks are turned on. Click the Mute button for Audio 2 to unmute that track.

2   In the Project panel, in the Sequences folder, select Poolside_BTS_05.

3 Choose Edit > Edit in Adobe Audition > Sequence.

4 In the window that appears, match the settings in the following figure. Click OK.

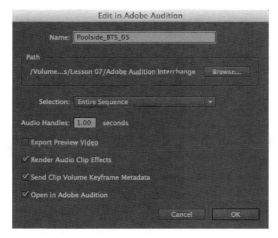

You are exporting preview video with your audio mix so that in Adobe Audition you'll have a visual cue for when to insert a sound effect.

Adobe Premiere Pro exports the audio, and Adobe Audition opens showing all of your tracks and clips from your Timeline.

Note that a few operations happened automatically. All audio clips are exported as .wav files. These are then brought into an Adobe Audition multitrack project with all automation keyframes intact and all effects rendered in the copied audio clips. All original media remains on your computer and will not be affected.

Adding a sound effect

You'll add the sound of TV static to the mix in Adobe Audition.

1 Choose File > Import > File. Navigate to the Audio folder in the Adobe Project Assets folder. Select TV_static.wav and click Open. You'll see this clip in your Files panel.

2 You need to add a new track for the sound effect, so click Multitrack > Track > Add New Stereo Audio Track. This new track appears in the Editor panel below Audio 3.

3 Adjust the playhead to 00:00:08:05 by clicking the timecode value at the bottom left of the Editor panel, typing **8:05**, then pressing Return (Enter).

4 Drag the file TV_static.wav into the Editor panel anywhere in the new audio track and press V to activate the Move tool. Click the TV_static.wav clip in the Editor panel so that its head snaps to the playhead.

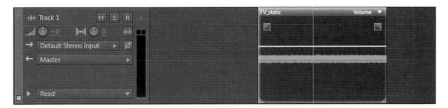

5 Now you need to trim the tail of the sound effect clip. Click the timecode value at the bottom left of the Editor panel, type **9:05**, then press Return (Enter). This moves the playhead to 00:00:09:05, when the visual effect of TV interference stops. With the Move tool, select and drag the bottom right corner of the TV_static.wav clip until the tail of the clip snaps to the playhead.

6 A yellow horizontal line indicates this clip's volume. With the Move tool, select and drag this yellow line to −6dB (give or take 0.1dB).

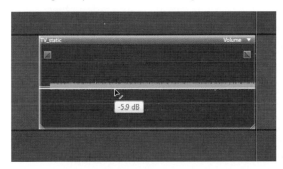

The Zoom tools at the bottom of the Editor panel can be used to expand the tracks horizontally or vertically, making it easier to adjust volume or make time-based edits.

You can also use the equal key (=) to zoom in and the minus key (−) to zoom out.

Now let's fade the clip in and out.

1 Adjust the playhead to 00:00:08:17.

2 Press the equal key (=) until the time range at the top of the Editor panel shows individual frames.

3 Select the clip, if it isn't already selected.

Notice the two square icons at the top left and top right corners of the clip. These allow you to select and drag them to create a fade-in and fade-out, respectively.

4 Select and drag the Fade In icon to meet the playhead. Once there, drag down until the tool tip reads "Fade In Linear Value: 0." This indicates a gradual increase in value, which is consistent with the gradual increase in the visual effect that this sound effect is intended to match.

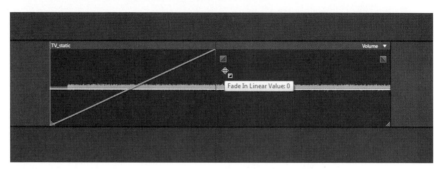

Incidentally, a positive Fade In Linear value would create a fade-in that increases in value more toward the beginning, while a negative value would create a fade-in that increases in value more toward the end.

5 Do the same thing with the Fade Out icon. Select and drag the Fade Out icon inward to meet the playhead, dragging downward so that the tool tip reads "Fade Out Linear Value: 0," again remaining consistent with the gradual decrease in the visual effect that this sound effect is intended to match.

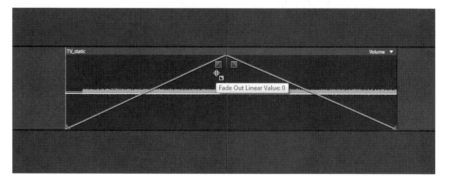

A negative Fade Out Linear Value would create a fade-out that decreases in value more toward the beginning, whereas a positive value would create a fade-out that decreases in value more toward the end.

6 Press Command+S (Ctrl+S) to save your Adobe Audition session. Set your filename as **Poolside_BTS Final Audio Mix.sesx** in the default location. Click OK.

Recording and editing a voice-over

Dialogue can come from many different sources, including on-camera interviews and candid moments captured between subjects. It's common in cases like these for the quality of the audio to be compromised in favor of capturing good video. If you don't intend to use video and only need a voice track to move the story forward, you can use Adobe Premiere Pro and Adobe Audition to capture a voice-over.

To do this, you need a microphone with a digital connection to your host system. This can be as simple as a USB microphone and a laptop, or as complex as a multichannel audio interface with analog microphone pre-amps and analog-to-digital converters. You also need a set of headphones you can use to monitor while you are recording, and a quiet space. It's best to use a cardioid condenser microphone, instead of a dynamic microphone, due to their wider frequency response and increased sensitivity to soft sounds. Configure your audio device in the audio hardware preferences in Adobe Premiere Pro or Adobe Audition. You may also have to adjust settings in the audio preferences for your computer's audio hardware. For example, a Mac user may have to select the specified audio device in the input and output settings in the System Preferences for sound. Once you've configured your device, add a new empty audio track in your sequence and record-enable the selected track in the Audio Mixer. Then click the Record button in the Transport controls of the Audio Mixer.

You can edit voice-over in either Adobe Premiere Pro or Adobe Audition, depending on your needs for sophisticated editing tools and effects. You edit a voice-over in Adobe Premiere Pro much the same way as you edit a video clip, and you can do so in both the Timeline and the Source panel.

Dynamic and condenser microphones

There are two basic types of microphones: dynamic and condenser.

Dynamic microphones are typically used on stage or in noisy environments. Dynamic microphones are more durable and usually cheaper than condenser microphones and do not require their own power source.

Condenser microphones are of higher quality and are more expensive. They are often used for voice-over and music recording in controlled noise-proof environments. They are highly sensitive, and thus susceptible to background noise or other noises, like breathing or nearby traffic. Condenser microphones require their own power source.

Audio track editing in Adobe Audition

Now it's time to do the final multitrack mix. To reiterate, applying changes to a track affects the entire audio output of that track. You'll apply an effect to the music track as well as to the interview track. Then you'll apply an effect to the Master track, which will affect the output of all tracks.

1 Select track Audio 2. Choose Effects > Filter and EQ > Parametric Equalizer to open the Rack Effect window. Set Presets to Loudness Maximizer. This preset boosts the low and high frequencies, leaving the mid-range frequencies between 100Hz and 4kHz (the frequency range of the human voice) unchanged.

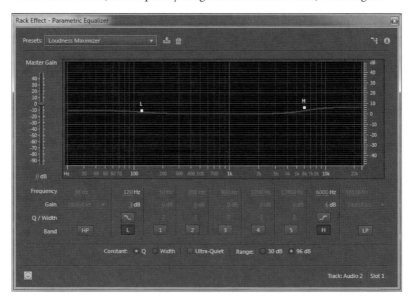

2 Close the Parametric Equalizer window.

3 Select track Audio 1. Rather than go through the menu, this time, go to the Effects Rack panel.

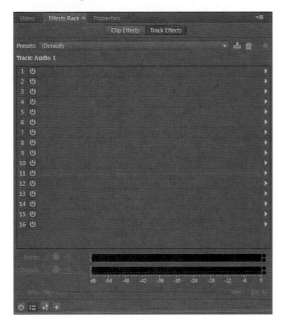

You will see several empty rows, with a number on the left and triangle icons on the right. These rows represent slots where audio effects would show as a list.

4 Click the first triangle icon and a menu will appear. From the menu, choose Filter and EQ > Parametric Equalizer. It will show as the first effect in the rack.

5 In the Rack Effect – Parametric Equalizer window that appears, set the preset to Rap Vocals. This preset enhances the vocal range of audio frequencies by making a subtle increase to frequencies associated with the human voice, while reducing unwanted frequencies so that the resulting vocal sounds are enhanced and distinct. Close the Parametric Equalizer window.

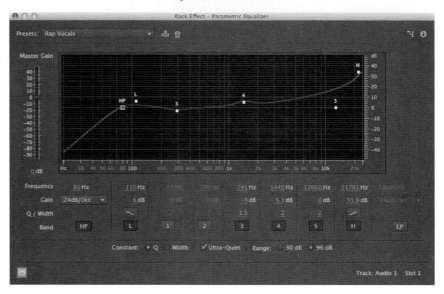

● **Note:** Limiting refers to setting a maximum audio output threshold. With limiting applied, no clip in a track can be louder than this set volume.

6 Select the Master track in the Editor panel. Choose Effects > Amplitude and Compression > Hard Limiter. In the Rack Effect window, set the preset to Limit to −.1dB to ensure that audio in the entire mix is at maximum loudness without clipping or distortion. Close this window.

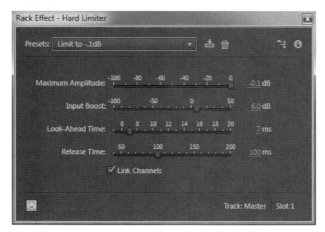

7 Press Command+S (Ctrl+S) to save your Adobe Audition session.

Creating the final audio mix

The final task you want to do in Adobe Audition is export the final audio mix. All of the clips in all audio tracks will get combined into a single audio clip.

1   Choose File > Export > Multitrack Mixdown > Entire Session.

2   In the Export Multitrack Mixdown window, set your filename as **Poolside_BTS Final Audio Mix_mixdown.wav**. Verify that Location is set to the Lesson 07 folder.

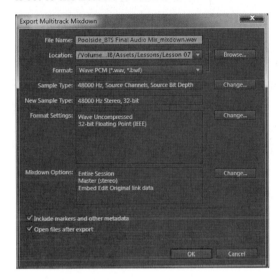

3   Click OK to close the Export Multitrack Mixdown window.

4   Press Command+Q (Ctrl+Q) to quit Adobe Audition.

5   Press Command+Tab (Alt+Tab) to switch to Adobe Premiere Pro.

Sending your final audio mix back to Adobe Premiere Pro

Back in Adobe Premiere Pro, you will create a new sequence for the final audio mix. This is also the final sequence that you will be using in the last two lessons on color correction and exporting your video.

1   In the Project panel, in the Sequences folder, select Poolside_BTS_05. Choose Edit > Duplicate. Select the resulting Poolside_BTS_05 Copy, click it once to make its name editable, and then change it to **Poolside_BTS_Final**. Double-click this to open it. Close the tab for Poolside_BTS_05 in the Timeline to avoid confusion.

Now import the final audio mix that you made in Adobe Audition.

2 Choose File > Import, navigate to your Lesson 07 folder, and select Poolside_
   BTS Final Audio Mix_mixdown.wav. Click Import. Drag the file into the Audio
   bin. Twirl open the Audio bin to reveal it.

▶ **Tip:** To show all
of the clips in your
Timeline, press the
backslash key (\).

3 In the Timeline for Poolside_BTS_Final, hold down Option (Alt) as you draw a
   marquee around all of the audio clips in Audio 1, Audio 2, and Audio 3 to select
   them. Once they are selected, press Delete.

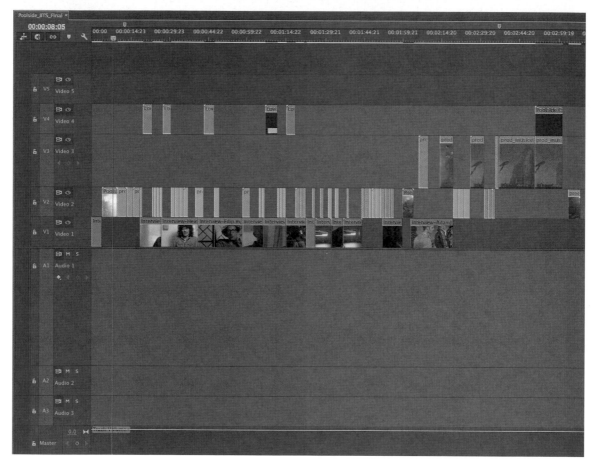

4 Drag Poolside_BTS Final Audio Mix_mixdown.wav from the Audio bin in the
   Project panel into the now-empty track Audio 1. Make sure that its In point is at
   the very beginning of the sequence.

5 Play back your entire sequence and monitor the audio. Pay close attention to
   ensure that the audio is still synced properly with the video. You should now
   have a finished audio mix with optimum amplitude and balancing between
   tracks.

6 In the Project panel, twirl the Audio bin shut.

7 Press Command+S (Ctrl+S) to save your Adobe Premiere Pro project.

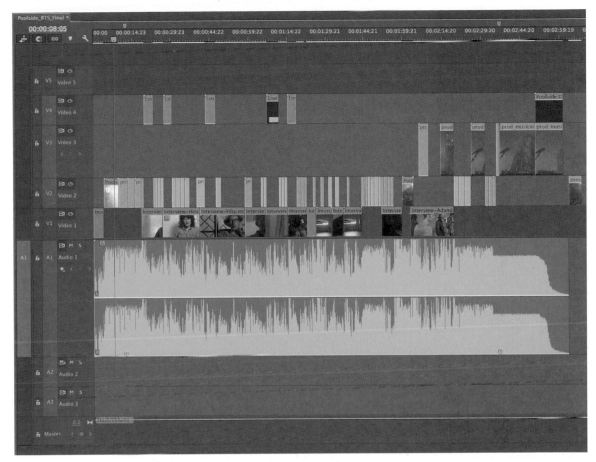

In this lesson, you learned some basic audio editing techniques in Adobe Premiere Pro. You learned how to automate clip volume with keyframes and how to easily adjust clip volume with the Audio Clip Mixer. You also learned some basic audio editing techniques in Adobe Audition, such as noise removal and creating a final audio mix.

In the next lesson, you will learn some useful color correction techniques in Adobe Premiere Pro and SpeedGrade.

Review questions

1 What is the difference between clip editing and track editing?

2 How do you make the volume of an audio clip change over time in a sequence?

3 What new feature in Adobe Premiere Pro allows for adjusting clip volume using a more intuitive audio interface?

4 How do you send a clip from a sequence in Adobe Premiere Pro to Adobe Audition?

5 What is the name of the user interface feature in Adobe Audition that shows an audio clip represented by a range of colors and brightness and simplifies selection and removal of unwanted noise?

6 What audio effect in Adobe Audition allows you to capture a sample of background noise that you can then remove from an entire clip?

Review answers

1   Clip editing entails making changes to the audio of a specific clip by adjusting its volume, adding an effect, or performing some other operation. Track editing entails making changes to an entire track.

2   You make the volume of an audio clip change over time in a sequence by applying Volume Level keyframes to the clip in the Effect Controls panel.

3   The Audio Clip Mixer allows you to adjust the volume of clips in the Timeline using an interface with a levels meter and a fader.

4   Select the audio clip in the Adobe Premiere Pro Timeline, right-click it, and choose Edit Clip in Audition.

5   The user interface feature is the Spectral Frequency Display.

6   The audio effect is the Noise Reduction (process) effect.

8 FINISHING YOUR PROJECT

Lesson overview

In previous lessons, you learned how to add motion graphics created in After Effects to your edit and how to use Adobe Audition to create a final audio mix. The final stages of a video project involve just as much work, but the applications in Creative Cloud can be your guides. In this lesson, you'll learn how to

- Use color correction effects in Adobe Premiere Pro

- Apply color corrections to RED footage in Adobe Premiere Pro

- Apply Lumetri Looks presets in Adobe Premiere Pro

- Create grading presets in SpeedGrade

 This lesson will take approximately 60 minutes to complete.

Download the project files for this lesson from the Lesson & Update Files tab on your Account page at www.peachpit.com and store them on your computer in a convenient location, as described in the Getting Started section of this book.

Your Account page is also where you'll find any updates to the chapters or to the lesson files. Look on the Lesson & Update Files tab to access the most current content.

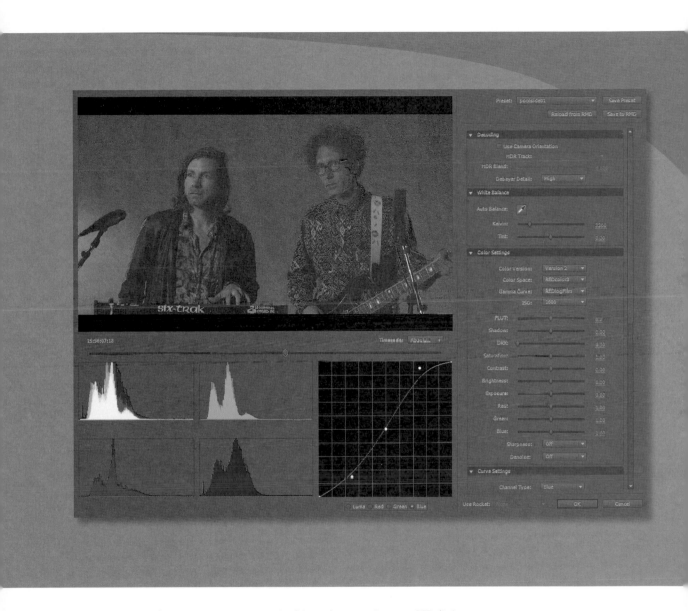

Applying color corrections to a RED clip in
Adobe Premiere Pro

Beginning this lesson

If you are continuing from the previous lesson, feel free to continue with the Adobe Premiere Pro project you already have open. Skip ahead to "The basics of color correction."

● **Note:** Important! Currently, Adobe Premiere Pro CC does not retain interpret-footage settings on clips even though those clips don't need relinking. Refer to the Getting Started section "Interpret frame rate of linked files" for steps on fixing this issue so you can follow this lesson.

If you are starting here

If you are starting at this lesson, generate your own Adobe Premiere Pro project file from a copy of one provided for you.

1 Navigate to the Assets > Lessons > Lesson 08 folder on your hard drive.

2 Double-click to open the Adobe Premiere Pro project Lesson08_Start.prproj.

   You should see the Poolside_BTS_Final sequence open in the Timeline.

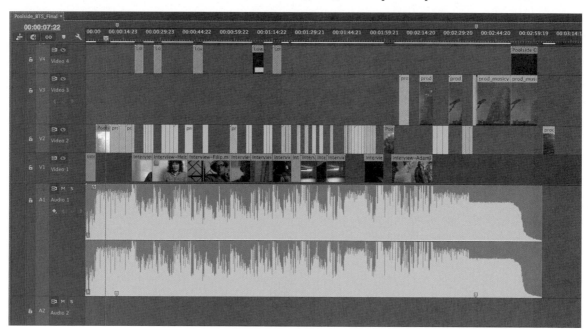

3 Choose File > Save As.

4 Navigate to the Lesson 08 folder on your hard drive. Name your Adobe Premiere Pro project file **Poolside Edit 06**. Click Save.

Potential error messages

When opening an Adobe Premiere Pro project file that was last saved on a different computer, you may encounter a couple of error messages. Don't panic!

One such error message will tell you that the local scratch disk is not in the same place.

● **Note:** This sidebar also appeared in Chapter 1 and is repeated here for your convenience if you have not followed these chapter lessons in order.

If this happens, choose File > Project Settings > Scratch Disks; then, for all settings in the Scratch Disks window, click the Browse button and navigate to a local folder on your hard drive where you want Adobe Premiere Pro to save your Captured Video and Audio, your Video and Audio Previews, and your Project Auto Saves.

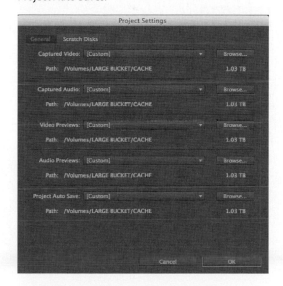

Another error message you may encounter is one that tells you that there is a missing renderer.

This just means that the project file was last saved on a machine that was using a graphics processing unit (GPU) that is not present on the current machine. Again, don't panic. Just click OK and carry on.

The basics of color correction

Before rendering and outputting a final movie, it is standard procedure to spend some time adjusting the color in your video. You should do this to ensure that all video clips in a given sequence are consistent in terms of hue, saturation, and brightness.

Color correction is also a very important step in meeting broadcast standards. It may involve a variety of processes, the most common of which is white balancing. *White balancing* is the process of adjusting the hue of a video so that any object in a shot that appears white in reality also appears white in the video. This is often necessary if lighting exposure was miscalculated during production. Many color-correcting tools come with white balancing controls and/or controls to manually adjust color hue, saturation, and brightness. An example of such a tool would be the Fast Color Corrector effect.

Similar tools for color correction may be used in the process of color grading to achieve stylistic adjustments to hue, saturation, and brightness.

Color grading entails selectively adjusting the color of a video using masks and color-correcting tools to enhance the colors that were captured in-camera. This is done to draw attention to specific subjects in frame and further evoke the desired emotional tone of a story.

For example, color grading can be used to colorize a sequence to make it appear as though it was shot on old film stock or to make a scene that was shot during the day appear to take place during twilight. Color grading can be a simple process driven by presets, or it can be a complex set of operations that is artistic and highly technical.

Using color-correction techniques in Adobe Premiere Pro

In this exercise, you will learn the basics of using the YC Waveform scope in Adobe Premiere Pro, as well as how to perform simple color correcting with the Three-Way Color Corrector effect.

Adobe Premiere Pro comes equipped with a variety of color-correction tools and effects that will serve the needs of most projects.

Before you start color-correcting the clips in Adobe Premiere Pro, we recommend that you change your workspace so that the related panels are showing in your Adobe Premiere Pro interface.

Setting up for color correction

Adobe Premiere Pro, along with the other applications in Creative Cloud, comes with preset workspaces so that you can quickly change your user interface without having to open all of the relevant panels yourself. When you enable a workspace, the relevant panels are placed for you automatically.

There are workspaces in Adobe Premiere Pro for various tasks, including one for color correction.

1 Change your Adobe Premiere Pro workspace by choosing Window > Workspace > Color Correction.

   You want your user interface to correspond to the instructions in this lesson, so reset your Color Correction workspace to its default setting if the workspace has been modified on your system.

2 Each workspace has a default layout of all the panels in the user interface. So that all the figures shown in this lesson match what you are supposed to see, reset this workspace by choosing Window > Workspace > Reset Current Workspace; then click Yes.

3 At the bottom right of the interface, you should see a reference monitor. You want to bring up the YC Waveform monitor in this panel. Click the wrench icon at the bottom right of the reference monitor and choose YC Waveform from the menu.

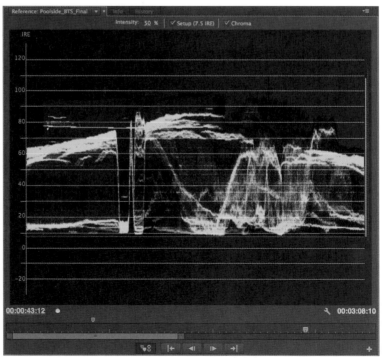

Using the YC Waveform

The YC Waveform displays a graph showing the signal intensity in the video clip. The horizontal axis of the graph corresponds to the video image (from left to right), and the vertical axis is the signal intensity in units called IRE (named for the Institute of Radio Engineers).

The YC Waveform displays luminance information as a green waveform. Bright objects produce a waveform pattern (bright blue areas) near the top of the graph; darker objects produce a waveform toward the bottom. Generally, luminance and chroma values should be about the same and distributed evenly across the 7.5 to 100 IRE range.

The YC Waveform also displays chrominance information as a blue waveform. The chrominance information is overlaid on the luminance waveform.

When you scrub through your Timeline, you should see that the luminance of all of the shots fall within this broadcast-safe range. In projects that use RAW media with an extended dynamic range, the footage may not be broadcast safe and the editor may need to spend considerable time color correcting it. However, in this lesson, you'll use the YC Waveform monitor to make sure that any color corrections that you apply to the clips do not cause the luminance of these clips to fall outside the broadcast-safe range.

Warm and cool colors

Common light sources—for example, household incandescent bulbs, candlelight, halogen, tungsten, and direct sunlight—all have different color temperatures on a spectrum from warm to cool. Lower color temperatures like 2800 K appear warm or contain more oranges and reds, while higher temperatures like 5800 K appear cool with a higher concentration of blue tones. One might use either warm or cool colors intentionally in the final image to achieve a certain mood or indicate a certain time or place.

However, in the event that raw video footage wasn't properly white balanced at the time of recording, the colors in the image might appear differently from how they would look naturally—either too warm or too cool—where what you would naturally perceive as gray instead appears orange or blue, respectively.

Unfortunately, because almost all video systems record compressed video (with the rare exception of RAW file formats such as R3D), attempts to perform white balance color correction in post-production do not yield perfect results 100% of the time. However, tools like the Three-Way Color Corrector effect can make a phenomenal improvement to clips that have an unpleasant color cast over the scene.

Using scopes to monitor color information

Several different scopes are built into Adobe Premiere Pro aside from the YC Waveform. Among them are the RGB Parade, YCbCr Parade, and Vectorscope. Each has a different way of displaying color information, and each has a different usage. Like the YC Waveform, the RGB Parade and YCbCr Parade scopes display a rectangular grid with waveform information, whereas the Vectorscope is characterized by a circular chart.

RGB Parade. In this chart the distribution of the three cardinal colors of light is represented by three respective waveforms. The red, green, and blue patterns indicate the levels of each color channel that make up the image. Ascending on the vertical axis is the value of the color, and the horizontal axis corresponds to the position on the image. You would use this scope to visualize the presence of each color from left to right. For example, an image that is grayscale will show all three charts with the same waveform pattern, because in the absence of color, all RGB patterns are identical.

YCbCr Parade. This chart displays three distinct waveforms, each indicating a different relationship between color and luminance levels. The first of the three is a cyan graph that simply tracks the overall luminance in the image. The middle chart in magenta represents the blue minus luma, and the yellow chart on the right indicates the red minus luma.

Vectorscope. This scope displays the distribution of chrominance in an image. The position of each point on the scope is determined by two variables: hue and saturation. The saturation of the color is displayed on the Vectorscope by the distance of a point from the center, and the direction, or angle, of the point indicates the hue on the color wheel. An image populated by vibrant colors will produce a pattern further outward from the center, while more bleak colors will appear closer to the center of the chart.

Note: The YC Waveform is the only scope that indicates the broadcast-safe threshold for luminance. The horizontal dotted line positioned at 7.5 IRE is the lower limit, meaning that if any part of an image falls below that line, it is too dark for broadcast and should be adjusted accordingly. If an image peaks above the 100 IRE mark, it also must be corrected before it can be broadcasted as it was intended to be viewed.

Using the Three-Way Color Corrector

Next, you'll perform some white balancing on some of the interview clips because these shots appear a bit too warm—that is, the hue of the colors in the shot is a bit too orange/yellow—and could use a bit of overall brightening. Adjust the playhead to the first of these clips in the sequence, Interview-Jeff.mp4, which shows Jeff of Poolside sitting on a couch. This shot was chosen as a casual introduction to the whole video and is immediately followed by the intro graphic and the music. The slightly off white balance of the shot takes away from the warm and inviting tone of the piece.

1   With the Selection tool, select this clip.

2   Press Shift+7 to access the Effects panel. In the Effects panel search field, type **three** to find the effect called Three-Way Color Corrector.

3   Double-click the effect to apply it to the selected clip in your Timeline.

4   Click the X button in the Effects panel search field to clear the field.

5   Press Shift+5 to access the Effect Controls panel and look at the controls for the Three-Way Color Corrector.

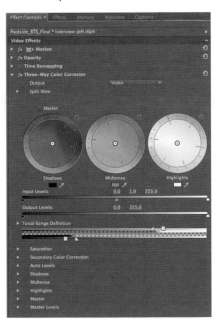

The Three-Way Color Corrector effect

The Three-Way Color Corrector effect makes precise color work directly inside Adobe Premiere Pro easier than it has ever been. Key elements in the effect's interface have been enhanced and repositioned, exposing essential controls the moment you apply the Three-Way Color Corrector to a clip and open the Effect Controls panel.

The Three-Way Color Corrector effect is also GPU-accelerated, so when you have a supported Nvidia or AMD graphics card in your system, or when you're using OpenGL acceleration, you can view results in real time as you work. And thanks to the enhanced Mercury Playback Engine, the Uninterrupted Playback feature lets you make color corrections while your footage plays. Although this can be used on even the most challenging of color-correction jobs, you'll use it for some subtle and simple changes.

Interview-Jeff.mp4 just needs a bit of simple white balancing. In the Three-Way Color Corrector effect controls, you'll see three color wheels, for Shadows, Midtones, and Highlights. Underneath each of these is an eyedropper.

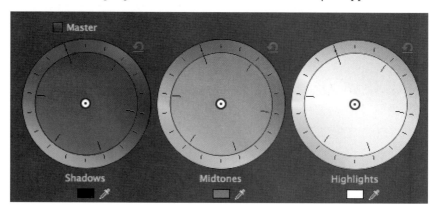

By using these eyedroppers, you sample areas in the current frame that best represent what should be black (for shadows), what should be neutral gray (for midtones), and what should be white (for highlights). The Three-Way Color Corrector will then adjust the color in the clip based on your calibrations. Some adjustment to the color wheels beyond that may be required so the color corrections in one clip match those of another clip shot in the same location and intended to show the same lighting conditions.

Above all else, though, trust your eyes.

6 Click the Highlights eyedropper, and in the current frame showing in the Program Monitor, sample a bright area of the wall behind Jeff.

The wall should look white. Therefore, by sampling it with the Highlights eyedropper, you are calibrating the effect to correct how it shows white.

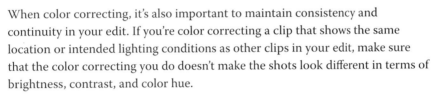

While making the adjustments, also look at the YC Waveform monitor to make sure that the luminance peak doesn't go higher than 100 IRE.

When color correcting, it's also important to maintain consistency and continuity in your edit. If you're color correcting a clip that shows the same location or intended lighting conditions as other clips in your edit, make sure that the color correcting you do doesn't make the shots look different in terms of brightness, contrast, and color hue.

7 Now click the Midtones eyedropper and sample an area of the frame that best represents neutral gray, such as one of the gray shadows on the wall.

8 Finally, click the Shadows eyedropper and sample an area of the frame that best represents black, such as the inside of Jeff's jacket.

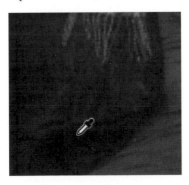

9 To see how this clip looks compared to how it looked before the Three-Way Color Corrector was applied, click the *fx* button next to the effect name. Then click it again to turn the effect back on.

A few more Interview clips need some color correcting. You will use the Three-Way Color Corrector effect on these clips, but rather than apply the effect from the Effects panel, you will simply copy Interview-Jeff.mp4 in the Timeline, paste the attributes of the effect onto these other clips, and then make adjustments to it for each clip.

1 Select Interview-Jeff.mp4 in the Timeline. Press Command+C (Ctrl+C) to copy it to your clipboard.

2 Adjust the Timeline playhead to show Interview-Filip.mp4 on track Video 1. Right-click this clip, then choose Paste Attributes.

The Paste Attributes window appears.

Rather than pasting the clip that you copied, paste any attributes applied to it onto other clips. This method comes in handy when there is more than one set of attributes to paste between clips.

3 Uncheck Scale Attribute Times, Motion, Opacity, and Time Remapping, leaving only Effects and Three-Way Color Corrector checked.

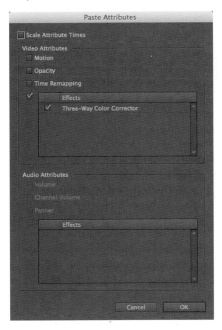

4 Click OK.

5 Press Shift+5 to access the Effect Controls panel and look at the controls for the Three-Way Color Corrector.

Like before, use the eyedroppers to sample a highlight, a midtone, and a shadow.

6 Click the Highlights eyedropper and sample the brightest area in the clip—the light glare on the wooden frame of the room divider behind Filip.

7 Next, click the Midtones eyedropper and sample a gray area of Filip's sweater.

8 Finally, click the Shadows eyedropper and sample a black area, such as the black of Filip's t-shirt.

Although the clip has more of a subtle cool tone to it, it needs further adjustment. Adjusting the brightness with the Input Levels should do the trick.

In the Three-Way Color Corrector effect controls, underneath the color wheels and eyedroppers, you will see a control for Input Levels, with three sliders. The slider on the left calibrates the maximum darkness of the clip, the middle slider calibrates the midtone brightness of the clip, and the slider on the right calibrates the maximum brightness of the clip.

The three numbers above the Input Levels slider correspond to the three sliders.

9 Click the right slider, drag it to the left, and adjust its corresponding value to 202 so that the spectral area in the YC Waveform doesn't go above 100 IRE.

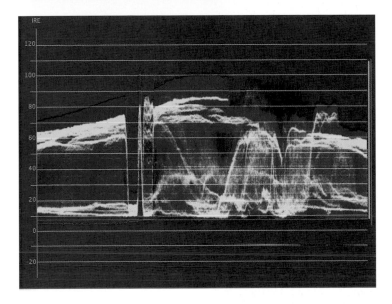

This adjustment brightens up the Interview-Filip.mp4 clip.

Next, you'll perform a similar operation on Interview-Dwight2.mp4. This time, you will copy and paste the effect.

1 With Interview-Filip.mp4 selected, in the Effect Controls panel, select the effect name for Three-Way Color Corrector. Press Command+C (Ctrl+C) to copy it.

2 Adjust the Timeline playhead to show Interview-Dwight2.mp4; then select this clip. Press Command+V (Ctrl+V) to paste the Three-Way Color Corrector onto this clip.

3 Press Shift+5 to access the Effect Controls panel and look at the controls for the Three-Way Color Corrector.

4 Click the Highlights eyedropper and sample a bright area of the wall behind Dwight.

5 Click the Midtones eyedropper and sample a medium-toned shadow on the wall.

6 Then click the Shadows eyedropper and sample a dark area inside Dwight's collar.

7 Finally, adjust the right Input Levels slider to 193, or to a value that sets the top part of the spectrum in the YC Waveform at 100.

Just a couple more...

1 Adjust the Timeline playhead to show Interview-Adam1.mp4; then select this clip. Press Command+V (Ctrl+V) to paste the Three-Way Color Corrector onto this clip.

● **Note:** You may want to temporarily turn off track Video 4 by clicking the Toggle Track Output icon to hide the lower third graphics. Be sure to turn it back on again after finishing this exercise!

2 Press Shift+5 to access the Effect Controls panel and look at the controls for the Three-Way Color Corrector.

3 Click the Highlights eyedropper and sample a bright area of the wall behind Adam.

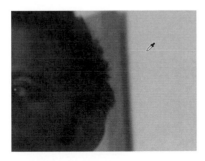

4 Click the Midtones eyedropper and sample the gray bit of wall behind Adam's head.

5 Then click the Shadows eyedropper and sample a dark area inside Adam's collar.

6 Finally, adjust the right Input Levels slider to 200, or to a value that sets the top part of the spectrum in the YC Waveform at 100.

Third-party color correction effects for Adobe Premiere Pro

There is a wealth of color correction effects for Adobe Premiere Pro from third-party vendors. These are definitely worth exploring to expand the color correction techniques you can apply with Adobe Premiere Pro.

Boris FX. www.borisfx.com/fx

Red Giant Software's Magic Bullet Looks. www.redgiant.com/products/all/magic-bullet-looks/

Red Giant Software's Magic Bullet Colorista II. www.redgiant.com/products/all/magic-bullet-colorista-ii/

DV Shade's EasyLooks. www.dvshade.com/easylooks/

Frischluft's Fresh Curves. www.frischluft.com/curves/index.php

Technicolor's Color Assist. www.technicolorcinestyle.com/

32-bit color

Many of the color correction effects in Creative Cloud are able to take advantage of ultra high precision 32-bit color. A huge step up from 24-bit true color, which produced roughly 16 million colors, is 32-bit deep color, which is capable of producing over a billion different colors. In the Effects > Color Correction window, you will notice that several effects display an icon with the number 32 to the right. This means that Adobe Premiere Pro processes an incredibly rich color depth while performing the specified effect, allowing editors to feel confident that their color correction is not hurting the original image or creating unwanted artifacts.

Finally, you'll color correct Interview-Tyler1.mp4.

1 Adjust the Timeline playhead to show Interview-Tyler1.mp4; then select this clip. Press Command+V (Ctrl+V) to paste the Three-Way Color Corrector onto this clip.

2 Press Shift+5 to access the Effect Controls panel and look at the controls for the Three-Way Color Corrector.

This time, reset the effect to its default settings, because the settings that you had copied before may not be a good starting point for this clip.

3 Click the Reset button at the top right of the Three-Way Color Corrector controls.

4 Click the Highlights eyedropper and sample a bright area of the wall behind Tyler.

5 Click the Midtones eyedropper and sample a medium-toned area on the wall in the far right of the shot.

6 Then click the Shadows eyedropper and sample a dark area on the side of the speaker behind and to the left of Tyler.

7 Press Command+S (Ctrl+S) to save your project.

For simple white balancing operations, the Three-Way Color Corrector effect is a very useful tool.

Color Finesse in After Effects

There may be instances when you will be working primarily in After Effects, not Adobe Premiere Pro, in which case it might suit your workflow to do your color-correcting in After Effects. The Synthetic Aperture Color Finesse plug-in included with After Effects has excellent color-correction tools, including waveform and vectorscope monitors, histograms, tone curves, and levels adjustments. Even if they are working predominantly in Adobe Premiere Pro, many editors prefer this self-contained color-correction tool, because it is accompanied by the host of tools in After Effects and offers some advantages over the color correction effects in Adobe Premiere Pro.

For instance, Color Finesse has its own separate full interface, with built-in vectorscopes and waveform monitors. Color Finesse can measure and control colors with Hue/Saturation/Lightness settings, Red/Green/Blue settings, and even Cyan/Magenta/Yellow settings, for easy conversion of print color values to video color values. Color Finesse has both histogram and curves controls, giving users choices between these and color controls they may already be familiar with from working in Photoshop. In fact, Color Finesse even allows users to import curve color control presets from Photoshop to allow their video colors to maintain consistency with colors in their still images, which is something that the RGB Curves effect in Adobe Premiere Pro cannot do.

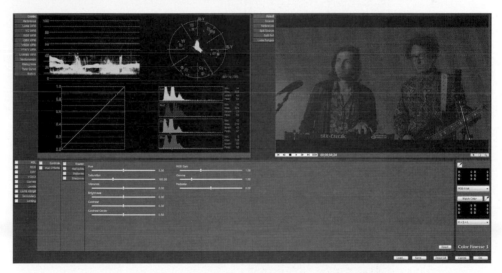

Integrating color corrections to RED footage

As you now know, footage captured on the RED camera is extremely versatile in its ability to pack a wealth of dynamic exposure data into the raw video files. In addition to allowing you to pull a terrific, balanced exposure from RED clips in post-production, the uncompressed footage also lends itself to a precise and uncompromised color correction process. By providing a low-contrast picture with a variable color temperature, raw footage shot on the RED camera is a perfect blank palette for an intensive color treatment, allowing you to go places with your color design that you simply cannot achieve on lossy video capture devices.

Let's give the RED music video clips a distinct look from that of the documentary footage. You will use the Source Settings of the RED clips to adjust exposure and color contrast.

1   Adjust the Timeline playhead to the clip prod_musicvid_raw01.R3D in track Video 3, and select this clip.

2   Right-click this clip, then choose Reveal in Project from the menu.

3   In the R3D bin, right click on prod_musicvid_raw01.R3D and choose Source Settings from the menu.

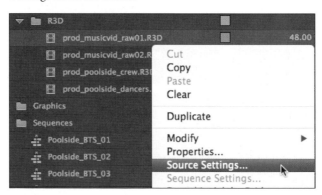

The RED R3D Source Settings window will appear, and it can be daunting at first glance.

At the top left, you will see a video frame of the clip you will be adjusting. Directly below that is a slider that allows you to scrub through the clip.

Below that are four histograms; one for each of the red, green, and blue channels, and one showing all those plus a histogram of the clip's luminance (or Luma, as it's referred to here).

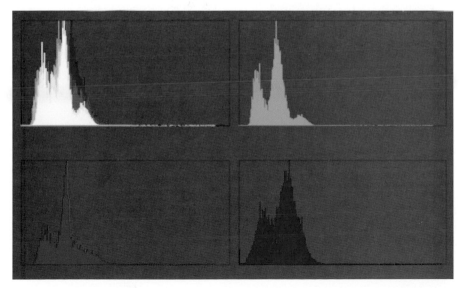

To the right of the histograms is a curves graph, with three white dots in it. These dots (from bottom left to top right) allow you to adjust the lows, midtones, and highlights, respectively, of the Luma, as well as the Red, Green, and Blue color channels.

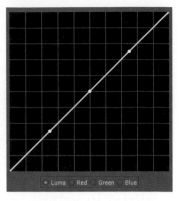

The top right of the Source Settings window is a Preset menu that lists any R3D color correction presets that may exist on your computer. A button for Save Preset allows you to save a preset of your own.

You can save your R3D color correction settings as Red Metadata, or RMD, files, as well as reload these settings from an existing RMD file. These RMD files can then be brought into another R3D editing program, such as REDCINE-X.

Below the Preset settings, on the right side of the Source Settings window, is an array of settings that you can adjust to make color corrections. Relevant to the following exercise, there are

> **Color Settings,** which allow you to adjust overall settings for Brightness, Contrast, Saturation, and so on.

Curve Settings, which give you numerical settings for adjustments you make to the curve graph mentioned earlier. By adjusting the Curve Settings values, the curve graph is adjusted accordingly.

Color space and gamma correction

In the RED R3D Source Settings window, you can change the *color space* of the given clip: a setting that does not exist in non-RAW video clips. Familiar color space presets like sRGB and Adobe 1998, as well as the proprietary REDcolor, REDcolor2, and REDspace, are available, and you can toggle them as needed, or you can save them into custom presets. These different color space settings allow you to conform the video clip to whichever system of color interpretation your project requires. In addition to the color space presets, you have Gamma Curve options you can use to override the gamma curve with a standard preset, such as REDgamma, REDgamma2, REDlogFilm, and several others.

Let's make some adjustments to this .R3D clip and then save the adjustments as a preset.

1   Under the Color Settings, you will see a Gamma Curve menu. Make sure this is set to REDgamma3.

2   In the ISO menu, choose 1600. This will, in effect, simulate the look of a faster-exposed film and brighten the image.

3   Next, under the Curve Settings, make sure the Channel Type menu is set to Luma.

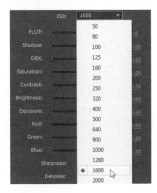

Since the lighting and exposure of this shot are fairly good to begin with, all you need to do is adjust the contrast on the Luma as well as the Red, Green, and Blue color channels.

1   Select the value for Lights Y and enter a value of **0.95**. Select the value for Darks Y and enter a value of **0.15**.

Notice that doing this changes the curves graph.

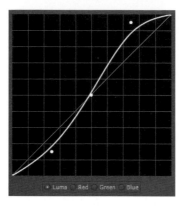

Conversely, you can adjust the graph itself by clicking and dragging the graph points. This method is probably more intuitive when you are experimenting.

You are free to adjust the Red, Green, and Blue color channels by applying curves to their respective graphs. Otherwise, continue entering values as follows.

2   Click the Channel Type menu and choose Red. Enter the same values as before—Lights Y to **0.95** and Darks Y to **0.15**.

3   Click the Channel Type menu and choose Green. Again, enter the same values—Lights Y to **0.95** and Darks Y to **0.15**.

4   Click the Channel Type menu, choose Blue. Set Lights Y to **0.95** and Darks Y to **0.15**, as before.

Notice how changing these settings affects the curves graph.

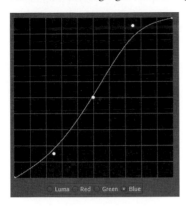

Now you will save these settings as a preset.

1 At the top right of the Source Settings window, click the Save Preset button.

2 A Choose Name dialog appears. In the Please Name This Preset field, type **Poolside01**, then click OK.

3 Finally, click OK at the bottom right of the Source Settings window.

Adobe Premiere Pro allows you to change Source Settings to multiple clips. Since the remaining .R3D clips were shot with the same camera, under the same lighting conditions, the same settings you applied to the first .R3D clip should work fine.

1 In the Project panel, type into the search field **.R3D**. This finds all of the .R3D clips. Marquee-select prod_musicvid_raw02.R3D, prod_poolside_crew.R3D, and prod_poolside_dancers.R3D.

2 Right-click any of these selected clips and choose Source Settings from the menu.

3 The RED R3D Source Settings window appears again. Choose Poolside01 from the Preset menu at the top right, then click OK.

This applies the Poolside01 Source Settings preset to the remaining .R3D clips that you selected.

4 In the Project panel, click the X button on the right side of the search field to clear the field. Twirl the R3D bin shut, then twirl the Footage bin shut.

5 Press Command+S (Ctrl+S) to save your project.

About SpeedGrade

SpeedGrade is a high-end color-grading application that is part of Adobe Creative Cloud. SpeedGrade lets you handle technical grading tasks like matching shots and creating consistent color across a scene. The GPU-accelerated, 64-bit Lumetri™ Deep Color Engine delivers real-time playback as you grade footage regardless of its resolution or frame size. SpeedGrade supports file-based workflows and includes support for RAW and high dynamic range (HDR) footage. HDR support retains the bit-depth of your image files, whereas the ability to work directly with RAW images—recorded straight from the camera sensor—lets you pull details from blacks and highlights that might otherwise have been crushed or blown out.

The color correction presets that come bundled with SpeedGrade also come bundled with Adobe Premiere Pro as effect presets. In the following exercises, you will apply one of these presets, called Lumetri Looks, to your edit.

How do you apply an effect to your entire sequence? One way is to apply the same effect, using the same settings, to every clip in your sequence. This works, but it is highly inefficient, because if you decide to change the effect on one clip, you have to go through every other clip and make the same change. Tedious! A more efficient way would be to apply an *adjustment layer.*

Adjustment layers in Adobe Premiere Pro

If you've read Lesson 6, you learned about how to use adjustment layers in After Effects. They are also available in Adobe Premiere Pro, and they work basically the same way.

In Adobe Premiere Pro, an adjustment layer is a special kind of clip that you create natively in the application. That is, it's a clip that you don't need to import. By placing an adjustment layer on a video track above other video tracks that have video clips in them, and then applying an effect (or effects) to the adjustment layer, those effects will render on all visible clips in all tracks below the adjustment layer.

In this exercise, you will create an adjustment layer and place it in your sequence.

1   Select the Project panel to make it active.

2   Choose File > New > Adjustment Layer.

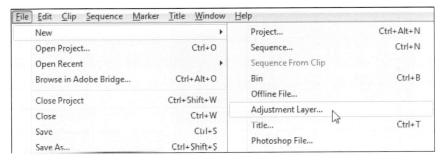

3   An Adjustment Layer window appears. The Video Settings should default to your sequence settings: 1920 pixels wide, 1080 pixels high, 23.976 fps (frames per second), and square pixel aspect ratio. Click OK.

4 The adjustment layer appears in your Project panel.

5 Select the Timeline panel and scrub the playhead to the beginning of the sequence.

6 Select the adjustment layer in the Project panel and drag it into the Timeline, onto track Video 5, so that its In point snaps to the playhead.

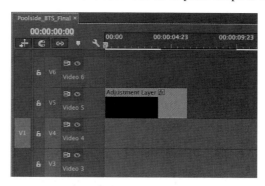

You want the adjustment layer to have the same duration as your sequence. However, it is currently only about six seconds long.

▶ **Tip:** You can zoom in on your Timeline using the equal (=) key. Zoom out by using the minus (–) key.

7 Select the Out point of the adjustment layer and drag it to the right so that it snaps to the Out point of the last clip in your sequence, prod_ sweepingConfetti_60fps.m4v.

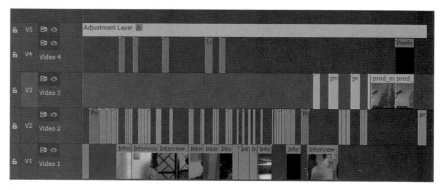

An adjustment layer is invisible. If you scrub the playhead through your sequence, you will not see it rendered in the Program Monitor. If you apply one or more effects to the adjustment layer, however, you will see them rendered on all visible clips in all tracks below it.

Lumetri Looks

Now you will apply a SpeedGrade preset to the adjustment layer.

1 Press Shift+7 to access the Effects panel. You will see groups of effects, including a group called Lumetri Looks.

2 Twirl open the Lumetri Looks effect group, and you will see four groups of presets within, called Cinematic, Desaturation, Style, and Temperature. These names basically describe the looks that these presets create when applied to a clip.

   Let's use one of these Lumetri Looks to decrease the overall saturation of the entire sequence, except for the RED clips. This makes the colors of the RED clips "pop" more when compared to the rest of the clips.

3 Move the Timeline playhead to 00:00:39:00 to show Interview-Heidi.mp4.

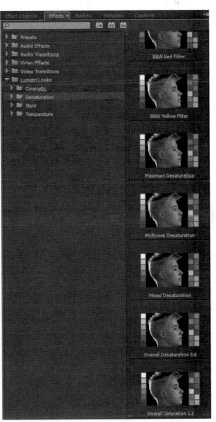

4 Select the Desaturation group folder, and a column of thumbnails appears in the Effects panel. These thumbnails provide a visual clue of how the Looks will appear.

5 Select the thumbnail for Overall Desaturation 0.6; then drag it onto the adjustment layer.

   Notice how the Look preset gives the clip of Heidi a subtle decrease in saturation. But this look takes out too much of the color saturation.

Let's create a Look preset in SpeedGrade using this clip as sample media. To do this, you send this clip of Heidi to SpeedGrade and use it to test out a modified Look.

1 In the Timeline, right-click Interview-Heidi.mp4. A menu appears.

2 From the menu, choose Reveal in Project.

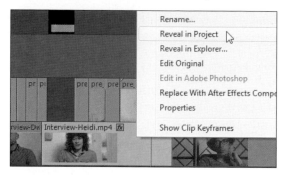

3 The Interview bin opens in the Project panel with Interview-Heidi.mp4 selected.

4 Choose File > Send to Adobe SpeedGrade.

5 A file navigation window appears. Navigate to the Assets > Lessons > Lesson 08 folder. Leave the File name as is and click Save.

6 A Send to Adobe SpeedGrade window appears and a progress bar animates. When that is complete, Adobe SpeedGrade opens and you see the clip of Heidi in SpeedGrade's monitor.

Sending a sequence from Adobe Premiere Pro to SpeedGrade

It's possible to send an entire sequence to SpeedGrade by clicking a sequence icon in the Project panel and choosing File > Send to Adobe SpeedGrade. This command first exports a .dpx sequence for all of the source media found in the selected sequence and then shows all clips in a corresponding Timeline in SpeedGrade. Using this method, you create a new copy of the media, which occupies hard drive space. Alternatively, SpeedGrade supports the import of edit decision lists (EDLs) and thus allows you to apply color grading to instances of the original media without doing an intermediate render.

To create an EDL, select the sequence in your Project panel, and then choose File > Export > EDL. To import this EDL to SpeedGrade, click the Open SpeedGrade project icon at the top left of the interface, change the session type from Composition files to EDL Conform files, navigate to where your EDL file is, select it, then click Open.

Creating a custom Look in Adobe SpeedGrade

Across the horizontal center of the SpeedGrade interface is a Timeline with a playhead. Directly below that is a row of tabs, labeled Timeline, Clip, Look, Stereo 3D, Audio, and Pan & Scan.

1   Click the Look tab.

You then see an array of controls at the bottom of the interface. At the bottom left, you see a Layers panel.

Next to that, taking up most of the bottom of the interface, is a panel for adjusting Input Saturation, Pivot, Contrast, Temperature, Magenta, and Final Saturation. You can apply changes to these properties by switching between Overall, Shadows, Midtones, and Highlights controls.

At the bottom of this panel, you will also see tabs for various Look Examples.

2 Click the tab for ..\settings\looks.

3 Press Shift+Return (Shift+Enter) twice so that you see numerical properties for Contrast and Final Saturation.

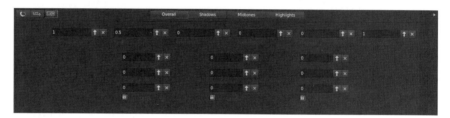

Let's create a custom Look with a slightly increased saturation.

4 Select the value for Final Saturation and change it to **0.8**.

Now save and export this custom Look.

1 At the bottom right of the Layers panel, click the icon for Save Look.

2 You then see an Untitled Look preset in the ..\settings\looks panel.

3 Select the name, change it to **Poolside01**, then press Return (Enter).

4 Quit SpeedGrade by pressing Command+Q (Ctrl+Q).

5 Switch to Adobe Premiere Pro by pressing Command+Tab (Alt+Tab).

▶ **Tip:** Use Command+Tab (Alt+Tab) to switch between open applications.

Applying your custom Look in Adobe Premiere Pro

Now you will apply your custom Look to the adjustment layer in your sequence.

1 Select the adjustment layer in the Timeline.

2 Press Shift+5 to access its Effect Controls. There, you should see the Lumetri effect.

3 To the right of the Lumetri effect name, click the Setup icon.

4 Navigate to where the Poolside01 Look preset you made in SpeedGrade is saved. In Mac OS, navigate to Users > (your username) > Documents > Adobe > SpeedGrade > 7.0 > Settings > Looks. In Windows, navigate to Users > (your username) > AppData > Roaming > Adobe > SpeedGrade > 7.0 > Settings > Looks. Select Poolside01.look and click Open.

This replaces the Look preset that you applied before with the one you created in SpeedGrade.

Cutting the adjustment layer

You don't want the Lumetri Look preset to render on the RED clips in the Timeline because you don't want them to desaturate.

What you can do is simply make cuts in the adjustment layer so that it is not on a track above the RED clips, and therefore the effect applied to the adjustment layer will not render on the RED clips.

1   Adjust the Timeline playhead to the In point of prod_poolside_dancers.R3D at 00:02:06:02.

2   Press the C key to activate the Razor tool.

3   Snap the Razor tool to the In point of prod_poolside_dancers.R3D and then make a cut to the adjustment layer. Snap the Razor tool to the Out point of prod_poolside_dancers.R3D and make another cut.

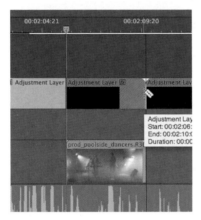

4   Press the V key to activate the Selection tool. Select the portion of the adjustment layer that is directly above prod_poolside_dancers.R3D on track Video 5.

5   Press the Delete key.

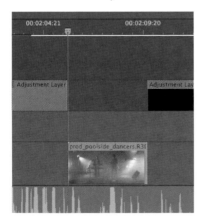

Now make a couple of more cuts to the adjustment layer.

1 Press the C key to activate the Razor tool.

2 Snap it to the In point of prod_poolside_crew.R3D, the next clip on Video 3, and make a cut.

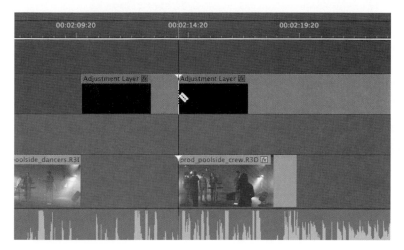

3 Snap the Razor tool to the Out point of prod_poolside_crew.R3D and make a cut.

4 Press the V key to activate the Selection tool. Select the portion of the adjustment layer that is directly above prod_poolside_crew.R3D on track Video 5.

5 Press Delete.

Just a few more cuts…

1   Adjust the Timeline playhead to 00:02:26:04, the In point of prod_musicvid_raw01.R3D, on track Video 3.

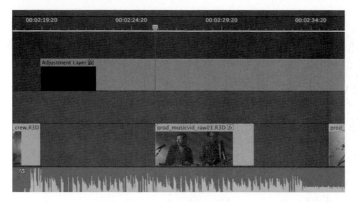

2   Press the C key to activate the Razor tool.

3   Snap it to the In point of prod_musicvid_raw01.R3D and make a cut. Snap the Razor tool to the Out point of prod_musicvid_raw01.R3D and make a cut.

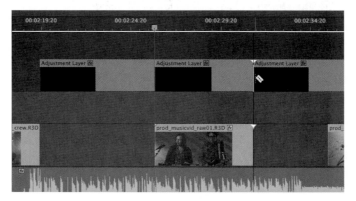

4   Press the V key to activate the Selection tool. Select the portion of the adjustment layer that is directly above prod_musicvid_raw01.R3D on track Video 5.

5 Press Delete.

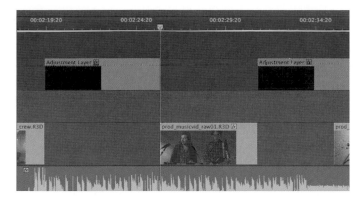

There is one last cut to make to the adjustment layer.

1 Press the C key to activate the Razor tool.

2 Snap it to the In point of prod_confetti_lyrics.m4v, the next clip on Video 3, and make a cut.

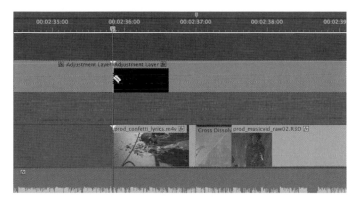

3 Press the V key to activate the Selection tool. Select the end portion of the adjustment layer and press the Delete key.

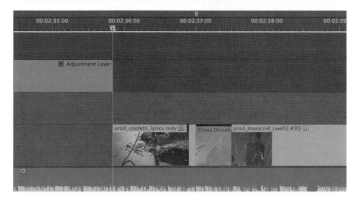

Copying the Lumetri effect

You want the Lumetri effect to be applied to prod_confetti_lyrics.m4v. The reason why you cut the adjustment layer to end right before prod_confetti_lyrics.m4v is because there is a dissolve transition between that clip and a RED clip, and you want the Lumetri effect to fade away accordingly.

Rather than extend the Out point of the adjustment layer and then animate its opacity so that it's timed to the dissolve transition happening on Video 3, a simpler solution is to copy the Lumetri effect and paste it to prod_confetti_lyrics.m4v.

1   Select the adjustment layer and press Shift+5 to make the Effect Controls panel active.

2   Select the Lumetri effect and press Command+C (Ctrl+C) to copy it.

3   In the Timeline, select the prod_confetti_lyrics.m4v clip and press Command+V (Ctrl+V) to paste the effect.

The last clip

Before you proceed with the next lesson, there is one last clip to put in the Timeline. That clip is the Closed Captions clip that you made in Lesson 4.

1   Scrub the Timeline playhead to the beginning of the sequence.

2   Press Shift+1 to make the Project panel active.

3   Twirl the Interview bin shut; then twirl the Footage bin shut.

4   Twirl open the Graphics bin to reveal the Closed Captions clip.

5   Select it, then drag it into the Timeline, above track Video 5. Doing this will automatically make a new track, Video 6. Snap the In point of the Closed Captions clip to the playhead on Video 6.

6   In the Project panel, twirl the Graphics bin shut.

7   Press Command+S (Ctrl+S) to save your project.

You have now completed your edit. You have learned some basic and not-so-basic techniques for color correcting your video in Adobe Premiere Pro and SpeedGrade. Now you are ready to export your video. You will learn how to do that in the following lesson.

Review questions

1 How would you perform white balancing to a video clip in Adobe Premiere Pro?

2 What is a YC Waveform display used for?

3 What is an RMD file?

4 How can you easily find an effect in Adobe Premiere Pro if you know its name but not which effect group it is listed under?

5 How do you send a clip from Adobe Premiere Pro to SpeedGrade?

Review answers

1 One way is to use the Three-Way Color Corrector effect. Use the Highlights, Midtones, and Shadows eyedroppers to sample areas of the video frame that represent what are supposed to look white, neutral midtoned, and black.

2 A YC Waveform display gives you an objective analysis of the luminance of a video frame, regardless of how that frame appears on your computer monitor, which may be calibrated incorrectly.

3 An RMD file is used to store metadata for a R3D video clip, which can then be used by a third-party color correction application.

4 The search field in the Effects panel allows you to find an effect by typing in a keyword; when you do, any effects with that keyword in their names will appear.

5 You select the clip in your Project panel in Adobe Premiere Pro and then choose File > Send to Adobe SpeedGrade.

9 OUTPUT FOR THE WEB AND CREATIVE CLOUD

Lesson overview

In previous lessons, you learned some of the basics of final color correcting your video and creating a final mix of your audio. When your project is complete, you have many different ways to deliver your media to the end user. In this lesson, you'll take your skills a step further and learn how to

- Export a sequence as a movie file in Adobe Premiere Pro
- Apply encoding presets in Adobe Media Encoder
- Render a composition from After Effects
- Perform batch rendering tasks in Adobe Media Encoder
- Create simple customized interactivity in Flash Professional
- Post exports to Creative Cloud
- Promote work on Behance

 This lesson will take approximately 60 minutes to complete.

Download the project files for this lesson from the Lesson & Update Files tab on your Account page at www.peachpit.com and store them on your computer in a convenient location, as described in the Getting Started section at the beginning of this book.

Your Account page is also where you'll find any updates to the chapters or to the lesson files. Look on the Lesson & Update Files tab to access the most current content.

The Export Settings panel in Adobe Media Encoder

Beginning this lesson

If you are continuing from the previous lesson, feel free to continue with the Adobe Premiere Pro project you already have open. Skip ahead to "Final quality control."

If you are starting here

● **Note:** Important! Currently, Adobe Premiere Pro CC does not retain interpret-footage settings on clips even though those clips don't need relinking. Refer to the Getting Started section "Interpret frame rate of linked files" for steps on fixing this issue so you can follow this lesson.

If you are starting at this lesson, generate your own Adobe Premiere Pro project file from a copy of one provided for you.

1 Navigate to the Assets > Lessons > Lesson 09 folder on your hard drive.

2 Double-click to open the Adobe Premiere Pro project Lesson09_Start.prproj.

3 In Adobe Premiere Pro, choose File > Save As.

4 Navigate to the Lesson 09 folder on your hard drive. Name your Adobe Premiere Pro project file **Poolside Edit 07**. Click Save.

Final quality control

At this point in the process of editing a video, you have finished adding any video or images to the edit—in editing lingo, you have "locked picture"—you have completed your final audio mix, and you have performed your final color correction. This is your final chance to make sure everything is OK before exporting your sequence and sending the final deliverable to your client.

You should see the Poolside_BTS_Final sequence in the Timeline. Let's change the Adobe Premiere Pro workspace from the color correction layout to the editing layout.

1 Choose Window > Workspace > Editing.

2 Reset the workspace by choosing Window > Workspace > Reset Current Workspace. In the Reset Workspace window that appears, click Yes.

3 Select the Timeline and press the backslash (\) key to show your entire sequence in the Timeline.

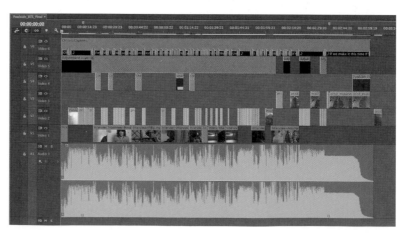

Potential error messages

When you open an Adobe Premiere Pro project file that was last saved on a different computer, you may encounter a couple of error messages. Don't panic!

One such error message will tell you that the local scratch disk is not in the same place.

● **Note:** This sidebar also appeared in Chapter 1 and is repeated here for your convenience if you have not followed these chapter lessons in order.

If this happens, choose File > Project Settings > Scratch Disks; then, for all settings in the Scratch Disks window, click the Browse button and navigate to a local folder on your hard drive where you want Adobe Premiere Pro to save your Captured Video and Audio, your Video and Audio Previews, and your Project Auto Saves.

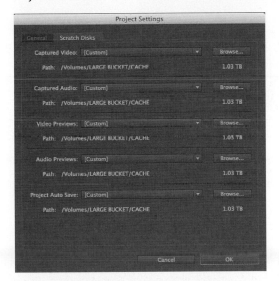

Another error message you may encounter is one that tells you that there is a missing renderer.

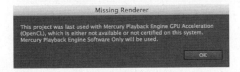

This just means that the project file was last saved on a machine that was using a graphics processing unit (GPU) that is not present on the current machine. Again, don't panic. Just click OK and carry on.

Now you will render your entire sequence so that you can watch it in real time with no skipped frames.

1   First, clear any In and Out points in your Timeline. Right-click the time ruler at the top of the Timeline, and choose Clear In and Out. If this is grayed out, then you don't need to do this. Go to the next step.

2   Choose Sequence > Render In to Out. This brings up the Rendering window that shows a progress bar. Rendering your entire sequence could take several minutes, depending on the speed of your computer. If you have a fast graphics card, the Mercury Playback Engine reduces the need to render your Timeline so that you can play back your sequence at full resolution with no skipped frames. However, in this instance, let's render anyway, just to be sure.

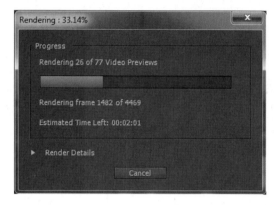

3   When this is complete, your sequence will play back from the beginning.

● **Note:** Adobe Premiere Pro will automatically play back a sequence when finished rendering previews, by default. To change this, choose Premiere Pro > Preferences > General (Edit > Preferences > General) and uncheck "Play work area after rendering previews."

In terms of general rules, as you watch your final rendered sequence, do the following:

•   Watch for any clips or stray frames that don't belong in your sequence.

•   Make sure that the monitor you are watching your sequence on is properly calibrated. Do the colors look as they should?

•   Listen to the audio mix carefully. Does everything sound as it should?

•   Keep an eye on the Audio Meters panel. At any point, do the levels stay peaked in the red?

•   Verify the spelling and text layout of your titles and lower thirds.

•   Verify the spelling of all of your closed captions.

If everything looks and sounds OK, you are ready to proceed with exporting.

Exporting the final output with Adobe Premiere Pro

After editing your video, creating motion graphics and closed captions, finalizing your audio mix, and doing some color correcting, you're ready to export your sequence as a movie file. Before you dive into the finer details of rendering, you'll export the sequence directly from Adobe Premiere Pro using simple presets.

1   With the Poolside_BT_Final sequence in the Timeline, choose File > Export > Media to open the Export Settings window.

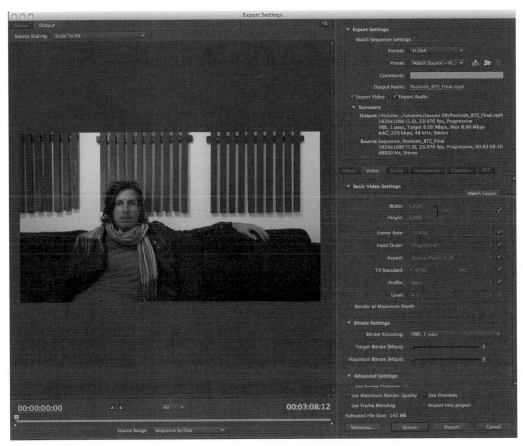

As its name suggests, this window allows you to apply settings to export your sequence as the desired file format using the desired frame rate and frame size with the desired video and audio compression. You can apply all of these settings manually, or you can choose from a list of presets. Let's use presets for this simple render.

▶ **Tip:** Use the keyboard shortcut Command+M (Ctrl+M) to export media from Adobe Premiere Pro.

2   At the top right under Export Settings, choose H.264 from the list of presets in the Format menu. Choose HD 1080p 23.976 from the Preset menu. Select the filename next to Output Name. Name your output **Poolside_BTS_Final**. Navigate to the Assets > Exports folder and click Save.

3   Without changing anything else, click Export at the bottom of the Export Settings window.

An Encoding window appears with a progress bar that shows how much of the render has finished.

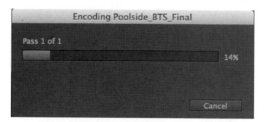

Because the movie is just over three minutes in duration, this render shouldn't take very long. That said, render times will vary depending on the speed of your computer's processor(s), how much RAM is installed in your computer, and whether or not your computer has a supported graphics card for the Mercury Graphics Engine, among other factors.

When your render is finished, you'll find the Poolside_BTS_Final.mp4 movie file in the Assets > Exports folder on your computer's hard drive. You should be able to open this file with the Apple QuickTime player, Windows Media Player, or other supported media player software.

This movie file was rendered using a preset for high-quality video compression for playback on a computer. But what if you wanted to render your Adobe Premiere Pro sequence as an archival-quality copy plus other versions using different export settings without having to render them one at a time directly from Adobe Premiere Pro?

That's when you'd use Adobe Media Encoder. But before you dive into that, let's go over what some of those export settings mean and why they're important.

The .mp4 file type

The .mp4 video format is a cross-platform standard that you can play back on nearly every type of device, from Mac to PC and Linux operating systems, streaming websites, and even an array of mobile and multimedia devices. An integral component of the widespread H.264 format, .mp4 is ideal for exporting for nearly any type of usage.

Understanding compression and other factors for exporting files

Now that you have exported a sequence as a movie file and gotten a glimpse of some export settings, let's detail some important factors you need to bear in mind when you are exporting.

Format. As the demand increases for higher-quality video at quicker loading speeds, industries develop video format standards to continuously improve the way digital video is viewed and shared. Different compression-decompression algorithms (codecs) and file formats use different methods to store color and light information. A standard video compression is H.264, which is used for web streaming on sites such as YouTube and Vimeo. It is the standard compression used in Blu-ray media and is the format that many HD video cameras natively record to, such as several of the latest DSLR models. In most cases, exporting in H.264 is ideal because of its versatility and quality in relation to its file size.

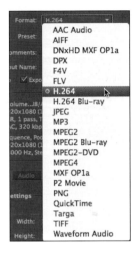

Video Codec. A *codec* is a data compression algorithm that can yield a movie file that still has high image quality, though the actual movie file size isn't unmanageably large. Codecs like the popular H.264 have allowed high definition video to stream on the Internet while maintaining good image quality. Other codecs, like Animation or Apple ProRes, allow for minimal data compression and archival image quality, but yield very large files.

Frame Rate. A video's *frame rate* indicates the number of frames that flash sequentially during one second. For example, at a typical frame rate of 30 frames per second (fps), 30 still images are projected in rapid succession for the duration of a second. Thirty frames per second has become the standard NTSC speed for video in DVD and online media, which was changed to 29.97 fps because of a slight change in broadcast frequency to account for FM (Frequency Modulation) radio interference. The typical frame rate used in film cameras is 24 fps, which is the frame rate that many videographers choose to shoot at in order to emulate the consistency of film. When you export video, make sure to note the frame rate at which the video was originally shot and use it, or else the export might have choppy playback.

File Size. When exporting a video, one of the most important variables you want to control is the file size of the exported file. For instance, YouTube recommends a file size of 2GB or smaller. If you hope for your video to load quickly you'll want it to be somewhat smaller than that. An easy way to control the size of the video file is by manually setting the Target Bitrate and Maximum Bitrate of the export in the Video tab at the bottom right side of the Adobe Media Encoder Export Settings interface. Make sure to note the duration of the video in proportion to your target file size when evaluating the best bitrate to use.

About Adobe Media Encoder

Adobe Media Encoder (AME) is a separate 64-bit software application that saves you time by automating the process of creating multiple encoded versions of source files, Adobe Premiere Pro sequences, and After Effects compositions. AME makes outputting your work to multiple formats and devices a faster, more intuitive process.

Rendering master files

It's a good idea as an editor to have a final export of your edit that could serve as the master file that other copies can be made from. Simply by copying this master file, you can easily and quickly make other copies without having to do all of the raw rendering for each, particularly if your sequence requires a long render.

Therefore, your master file should be of the highest possible quality, because a master file cannot make copies that are of higher image quality than itself. Once you lose image quality of a movie file as a result of data compression or frame size reduction, you cannot regain it. In a worst-case scenario, if your raw project files get lost or corrupted, you still have your master movie file.

Using AME across the suite

Adobe Media Encoder is the central encoding tool used in the Creative Cloud suite of video applications. You'll discover that it is very helpful for video editing tasks, such as

- Exporting final sequences
- Batch transcoding of raw clips
- Batch compression of master files
- Encoding files that are put in a predesignated watch folder
- Uploading an exported file to an FTP server

ProRes + DNxHD

When you are archiving a finished project, it is always a good idea to output to a lossless codec, like the Animation codec. Creating a very large video file called the master file will also allow you to easily down-convert to any lossy file type that you may need down the road. Adobe Premiere Pro CC now comes bundled with the superb ProRes (Mac) and DNxHD (Windows & Mac) codecs, ideal for mastering your project, allowing for compatibility with Apple Final Cut Pro and Avid, respectively.

In this exercise, you'll render a master file of your final Adobe Premiere Pro sequence, but this time you'll use AME. You'll also render other versions of your movie—one for mobile devices and one for the Web—using AME.

1 In Premiere Pro, with the Poolside_BT_Final sequence in the Timeline, choose File > Export > Media.

The Export Settings window appears. Now let's create a preset for minimal data and image compression and no audio compression.

2 Under Export Settings, choose QuickTime from the Format menu. QuickTime is an industry-standard movie file format that is compatible with most nonlinear editing systems, including Adobe Premiere Pro.

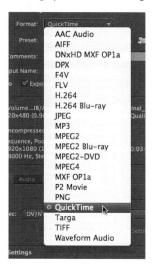

If you are using a Windows system, you must have the QuickTime player installed in order to export QuickTime files from AME. To download this, go here: http://support.apple.com/downloads/#quicktime.

3 In the Video tab below Export Settings, set Video Codec to Apple ProRes 422.

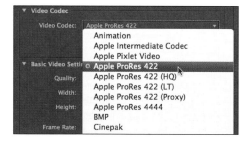

The Apple ProRes codec applies minimal compression to the movie's image quality, thereby making it suitable for yielding a master file. However, it yields a file size that is much bigger than what results from H.264 compression.

4 Make sure that the button to the right of Width and Height is toggled off. If you see a chain link here, click it to toggle it off. If this is on, then resizing one dimension of your output frame automatically adjusts the other dimension in order to maintain a constant aspect ratio.

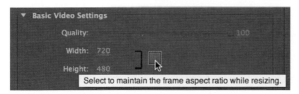

5 Select the value for Width and change it to **1920**. Press the Tab key twice to select the value for Height and change it to **1080**. These denote the frame size of the rendered movie, which you want to be no smaller than your sequence frame size in Adobe Premiere Pro.

6 Set Frame Rate to 23.976. Again, this is the frame rate in your Adobe Premiere Pro sequence, and you want to maintain that. Make sure Field Order is set to Progressive.

7 Set Aspect to Square Pixels (1.0). This refers to whether or not the pixels will be stretched horizontally to meet certain video broadcast standards.

8 Press the Audio tab to access all of the audio exports settings. Set Audio Codec to Uncompressed. Set Sample Rate to 48000 Hz, Channels to Stereo, and Sample Size to 16 bit. These are all standard settings for audio in a movie file that yields optimum quality.

9 Click the Captions tab. From the Export Options menu, choose Create Sidecar File. For File Format, choose Scenarist Closed Caption File (.scc). Set Frame Rate at 29.97 fps DF.

Closed captions standards

Closed captioning is a way of applying toggleable, descriptive text onscreen during a video, primarily for those who are hearing impaired or in the case that the volume is off. Closed captions are not to be confused with *subtitles;* subtitles assume that the viewer can hear but perhaps does not understand the spoken language. Non-verbal elements like descriptions of music and sound design are often included in closed captions, and there are many laws about which types of media must be captioned in order to adhere to disability regulations. Several file types and software encoders for closed captioning are compatible with Adobe Premiere Pro.

Scenarist Closed Caption (SSC) File. The .scc file type, developed by Sonic, provides a packet for applying captions to DVDs or for usage as a sidecar file for playback in many media players. This *sidecar file* is a separate file from the video file, and it can be browsed from within programs like VLC Player, a common multi-platform media player, in order to view the captions with the video. SCC files use the CEA-608 standard, which is only used for SD video and dates back to analog TV broadcast in the 1980s.

MacCaption (MCC) VANC (Vertical ANCillary data space) File. MacCaption is a closed captioning software, developed by the company CPC for the Mac platform, designed to read and write all major captioning formats. For Mac users, MCC files are more versatile than SCC files, with support for both 608 and 708 captioning. The CEA-708 standard allows for multiple fonts, onscreen positions, colors, and sizes. In addition to broadcast HD and SD video, MacCaption encodes captions for web formats like QuickTime, Flash, YouTube, and Windows Media, and also tapeless workflows like MPEG-2 Transport Streams, DVCPRO HD, and XDCAM.

W3c/SMPTE/EBU Timed Text File. SMPTE, or Society of Motion Picture & Television Engineers, is the leading technical society for the motion imaging industry. They have developed Timed Text Format, SMPTE-TT—which provides captioning abilities that can be used primarily on broadband, as well as consumer electronics—taking into account the ability to use data from CEA-608 and CEA-708 captions.

EBU N19 Subtitle File. The EBU (European Broadcast Union) format is an open format intended for subtitle exchange between broadcasters. Files in this format have the extension .stl.

Aspect ratios

The *aspect ratio* of an image refers to the proportion between the width and the height of the frame. Standard aspect ratios used in video are 4:3 and 16:9, which are referred to as fullscreen and widescreen, respectively. Fullscreen is the standard frame size for television broadcast and also the growingly obsolete Standard Definition digital video (DV). The standard HDTV aspect ratio, also known as Full HD, has a frame size of 1920x1080 pixels and is composed of square pixels at the standard widescreen aspect ratio of 16:9. With the growing popularity of HD video sizes such as 720x1080 pixels, the widescreen ratio is preferred over the older fullscreen.

Because different cameras record at different sizes and have varying ways of capturing pixels in an image, it is critical to input the correct aspect ratio settings when exporting your media, or else your image may appear stretched or have an unwanted crop. Some cameras that capture to tape tend to record pixels slightly stretched in order to conform a fullscreen image to a widescreen image. However, for the purposes of displaying video on the Web, it is optimal to use Square Pixels, because this is the standard used on every type of computer video monitor and mobile device. If your video comes out stretched, make note of the size of the frame and the pixel size selected in the Export Settings.

Saving a preset

Now let's save all of these settings as a preset that can be used again later.

1   At the top of the Export Settings window, select the filename next to Output Name. Navigate to the Assets > Exports folder and name this file **Poolside_BTS_Master.mov**. Click Save.

2   Next to the Preset menu, click the Save Preset button.

3   In the Choose Name window that appears, name this preset **QuickTime ProRes 1920x1080**. Click OK.

4   At the bottom of the Export Settings window, next to the Export button, click the Queue button to open Adobe Media Encoder.

A Queue panel lists your Poolside_BTS_Final sequence from Adobe Premiere Pro.

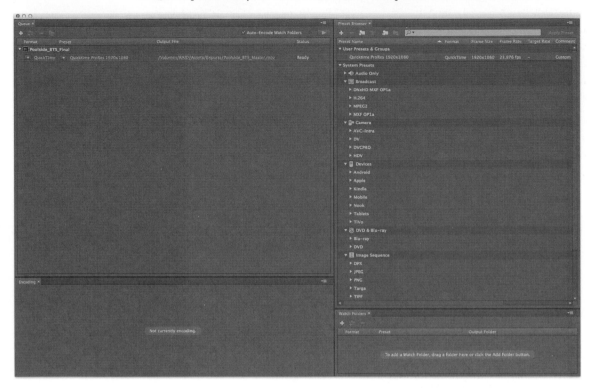

The Queue in Adobe Media Encoder allows you to render several movies at the same time. Not only that, but Adobe Media Encoder can use the Dynamic Link between it and other applications in Creative Cloud. This means that you could have sequences from Adobe Premiere Pro in the Queue as well as compositions from After Effects.

Next to the Queue is the Preset Browser, where you can choose from among dozens of render presets for various devices and outputs.

Before you render your master file, let's add a few more renders to the Queue using various presets.

Encoding video for web and mobile

Not too long ago, the dominant devices for viewing movies were televisions and film projection systems in movie theaters. Today, movies can not only be produced by anybody with a video camera and a computer, but they can be shown on a variety of different devices, including high-definition computer monitors, tablet devices, and smartphones.

To ensure that your movie will download as quickly as possible and look as good as it possibly can on any given device, it's best to create separate rendered movie files that are intended to play on specific types of devices. Since screens for mobile devices and computer monitors vary in size, and since higher-quality movie files are larger files to download, you want to give the end users options so that they can make efficient use of their bandwidth and the capabilities of their movie viewing devices.

Encoding a movie file to be played on a variety of devices requires compressing the raw video in your edited Adobe Premiere Pro sequence to yield a movie file that can be streamed or downloaded as fast as reasonably possible from the Internet, yet still maintain maximum image quality.

In this exercise, you will apply a variety of export presets in Adobe Media Encoder to your final edited sequence in Adobe Premiere Pro to create separate exports for different types of devices.

1   With the Poolside_BTS_Final sequence in the Queue, select it, and then browse through the Preset Browser. Let's apply a render preset to the Queue for Android tablet devices.

2   Under Devices, twirl open Android, and then select the preset Android Tablet - 720p 23.976.

3   Drag this into the Queue, below the one item that's already there.

Doing so creates another render instance in the Queue for your Adobe Premiere Pro sequence.

4   Select the Output File name for this new render, navigate to the Assets > Exports folder, and name this **Poolside_BTS_Final-Tablet**. Click Save.

5 Let's add a render for smartphones. Also under Devices, twirl open Apple, and then select the preset Apple TV, iPad, iPhone 3G and newer - 360p Widescreen 23.976.

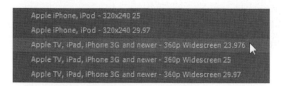

6 Drag this into the Queue so that it's the third item.

This should create yet another render instance.

7 Select the Output File name for this render, navigate to the Assets > Exports folder, and name this **Poolside_BTS_Final-Smartphone**. Click Save.

8 Now let's add another render that could easily be uploaded to YouTube. Under Web Video, twirl open YouTube, and then select the preset YouTube HD 720p 23.976.

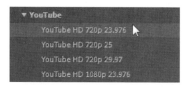

9 Drag this into the Queue so that it's the fourth item.

Another instance will appear.

10 Select its Output File name, navigate to the Assets > Exports folder, and name it **Poolside_BTS_Final-YouTube**. Click Save.

11 Under Web Video again, twirl open Flash, select the preset Web - 1920x1080, 16x9, Project Framerate, 7500 kbps; with the FLV format.

12 Drag this into the Queue.

A fifth instance appears in the Queue.

13 Select its Output File name, navigate to the Assets > Exports folder, and name it **Poolside_BTS_Final-Web**. Click Save.

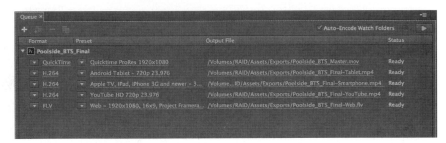

All of your exports are queued and ready to export.

Before you start exporting your Queue, make sure that a setting is activated in your preferences.

14 Choose Adobe Media Encoder > Preferences (Edit > Preferences). In the General preferences, make sure that Enable Parallel Encoding is checked. If it is not, then check it.

With this setting activated, Adobe Media Encoder will render multiple items simultaneously instead of individually. This can be a time saver, particularly when some items in your Queue are shorter in duration and/or less render-intensive than others.

15 Click OK at the bottom of the Preferences window.

16 Finally, click the green Start Queue button at the top right of the Queue panel to begin exporting.

As your exports are rendering, you can see thumbnails of them to monitor for any errors or anomalies.

You will hear a chime sound when Adobe Media Encoder is finished.

As you've witnessed, Adobe Media Encoder allows you to easily set up exports of an Adobe Premiere Pro sequence, using a library of export presets, so that you can make master copies for your archives as well as copies that will play on a variety of web and mobile devices.

Streaming vs. download

There is an important difference between streaming video and downloading video as it relates to creating video for the Web:

- Downloading video involves copying a video file from one computer or server to another. The file then exists locally and can be copied elsewhere.

- Streaming video is video content that is a live playback of the video on a remote server that is then accessed via a web browser by the user. The movie file is not stored locally on the end user's computer and therefore cannot be copied. This is not the same as a Progressive Download, which does cache the video file on the user's computer and allows the user to start watching the video as the video is still downloading.

Archiving your project

When you finish a video project, it is good work practice to archive it properly. This ensures that, should you ever need to revisit the project in the future, you have everything you need in terms of project files and raw media to pick up where you left off.

When you're ready to archive your project, Adobe Premiere Pro and After Effects offer simple ways to bundle your project materials and project files. In Adobe Premiere Pro, use the Project Manager by choosing Project > Project Manager. In After Effects, use the Collect Files feature by choosing File > Dependencies > Collect Files.

Introducing Flash Professional

Flash Professional is an authoring environment that is generally tailored for creating games, websites, animation, and multimedia content for desktop computers and mobile devices.

Creating interactivity with Flash Professional

Although this book can't cover all the tasks you can do with Flash Professional, you can perform a basic task. Let's say you want to embed your movie in a web page without the menu functionality. All you want is the movie with playback controls in a customized skin. To do that is very simple.

1 Open Flash Professional and choose File > New. In the Templates, choose Media Playback, and then choose Title Safe Area HDTV 1080.

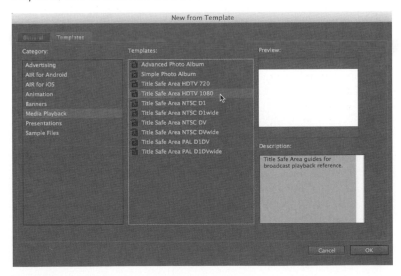

2 Click OK. A new Stage appears with title and action safe guides.

3 Save your project by choosing File > Save As. In the Save As window, navigate to your Assets > Lessons > Lesson 09 folder. Change the default filename to **Poolsite_BTS_Flash01**. Click Save.

Next you want to take an .mp4 export of your movie and bring it directly into your Stage.

4 Choose File > Import > Import Video.

You'll see an Import Video window.

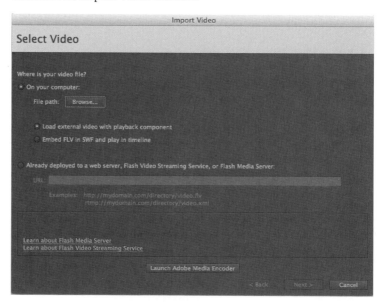

5 Under "Where is your video file?" choose "On your computer" and "Load external video with playback component." Click the Browse button. Navigate to Assets > Exports. Select Poolside_BTS_Final.mp4 and click Open.

6 Back in the Select Video window, click Next, which brings you to the Skinning settings. Choose a Skin preset, click Next, and then click Finish.

You should see an instance of your video in your Stage with playback controls at the bottom.

▶ **Tip:** If you can't see the entire video frame in your stage, choose Fit in Window from the magnification menu at the top right of the Stage panel.

7 To publish this, choose File > Publish Settings. Select Flash (.swf). Set the Output File location as your Assets > Exports folder and name your file **Poolside_BTS_Final-Flash.swf**. Click Publish.

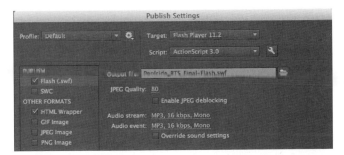

8 In your Assets > Exports folder, you should see Poolside_BTS_Final-Flash.swf ready to be embedded in a web page. If you drag this file into a web browser window, you see your final movie with the playback controls you selected in Flash Professional.

9 Press Command+S (Ctrl+S) to save your Flash project. Press Command+Q (Ctrl+Q) to quit Flash.

As you can imagine, this exercise barely scratched the surface of interactivity you can create with Flash. With Flash, you can create all kinds of interactive media, like games, websites, and mobile applications for the Web, for broadcast, and for tablet and smartphone mobile devices.

For a series of comprehensive tutorials on using Flash Professional, check out *Adobe Flash Professional CC Classroom in a Book* (Adobe Press, 2013).

Uploading and sharing your project using Creative Cloud

With Creative Cloud, you get 20GB of storage or 100GB of storage with a Creative Cloud for teams membership. You can store your files privately, or you can share your files with others by sending them a link to your files on Creative Cloud via email. With a Creative Cloud membership, you can also post your work to the Behance network, where you can create an online portfolio. From there, others can view your work; share your work through online social networks like Facebook, LinkedIn, or Twitter; and even give you feedback with comments on your Behance portfolio. Creative Cloud members also get access to the professional features of Behance, including ProSite, a fully customizable online portfolio that comes with a unique URL. Publishing your creative portfolio online has never been easier.

The following exercises will walk you through the process of uploading a sample still image to Creative Cloud and promoting it on Behance.

Uploading your work to Creative Cloud

Let's upload one of your exports to your Creative Cloud account.

1   Open your web browser and go to https://creative.adobe.com/.

2   Here, sign in to your Creative Cloud account by entering your Adobe ID email address and password, then click Sign in.

3 Now click the Actions button and choose Upload from the drop-down menu.

4 Navigate to your Assets > Lessons > Lesson 09 folder, select sample.psd, then click Open.

Once the image file is uploaded, you will see a thumbnail for it on your Creative Cloud Files page. The icon will have a down-arrow button at its bottom right.

5 Press this icon, and choose Send Link.

6 A Send Link window appears. By default, files are set to Private view so that only you can see them. Click the red lock icon to switch privacy of this file to Public view.

7 With privacy set to Public, check the boxes for Allow Comments and Allow Download.

8 At the bottom of this window, click the envelope icon. You can enter an email address in the text field. It's a good idea to send yourself a link to this file before sending it to anyone else to test if it works.

9 Click the Send Email button.

10 Click the link icon, next to the envelope icon, and click the Copy Link button. You can then paste this link elsewhere, such as in a post to Facebook or Twitter.

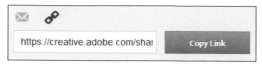

11 Recipients of this link will be able to see a public page for your video. There, they can click the Comments button, fill in the text fields for Name and Email, and click Add Comment to give you feedback.

12 They have another option; they could click the Actions button and choose Download to download your file.

Promoting your project

Once you have uploaded your image to Creative Cloud, you can post it as a Work In Progress to Behance and then promote it online from there.

Linking Behance with your online social networks

In order to seamlessly share your work from Creative Cloud to your Twitter, LinkedIn, Facebook, and Google accounts, you need to link your Behance account with these social networks.

● **Note:** You will need to create a Behance account to complete this exercise. Go to www.behance.net and click Sign Up to create your account.

1   In your web browser, go to www.behance.net and click Log In. You are prompted to enter your login and password info. Fill in the appropriate text fields, then click Log In. In the window that appears, enter your login Email and Password.

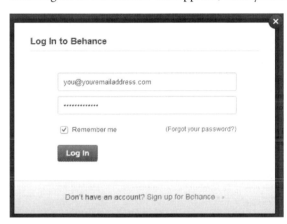

2   Click Log In.

3   Hover over the Me button and choose Invite & Promote.

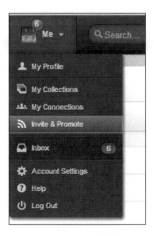

4 On the Invite & Promote page, you see a hyperlink for Linked Accounts. Click this.

5 Here, you see buttons for Link Twitter, Link LinkedIn, Link Google, and Link Facebook. For each that you wish to link to your Behance account, click the appropriate button and follow the instructions.

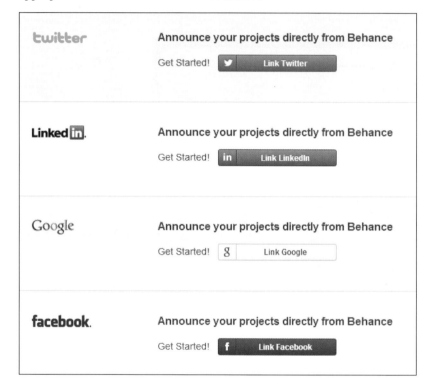

Posting an image to Behance

Now you will post your Work In Progress image to the Behance network.

1 From your Creative Cloud Files web page, find the thumbnail for the sample.psd image file. Click the down-arrow at the bottom right of the file icon and choose Post Publicly from the menu.

2 If you haven't yet linked your Creative Cloud account with your Behance account, a window appears, prompting you to enter your Behance Email and Password. Enter these in the appropriate text fields, then click Link Account.

3 You will then be prompted to enter some information about this work that will accompany it on Behance. By default, New Work will be selected, but if you choose Revision, the Title text field will be replaced by a Choose Existing menu, and from here you would choose a work that is already posted that you want to replace with a revision.

4 In the Title field, type a name for your image.

5 In the Tags field, enter a few searchable keywords that describe the work.

6 You can also enter a comment in the final text field that starts an online discussion about your work.

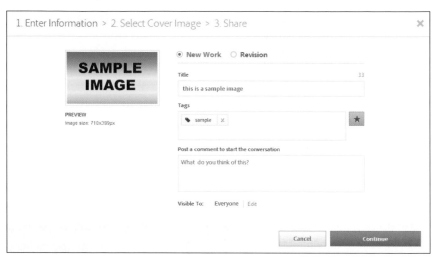

7 Click Continue.

8 Then you are prompted to create a cover image by resizing a square bounding box. Do this.

9 Click Crop Cover & Publish.

10 Finally, the window shows a text field for Promote Your Work. Leave the default text as it is or customize it. To the right of the text field you will see icons for all of the online social networks that are linked to your Behance account, each with

On/Off switches. If you want to disable any of these switches, click them to set them to Off.

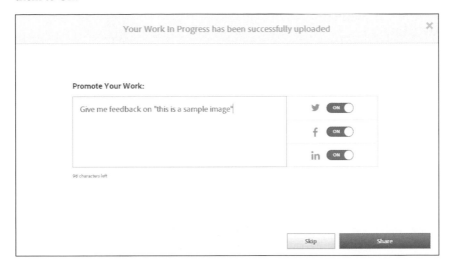

11 Click Share. This posts entries on your linked social networks.

Promoting your work to your online social networks from your Creative Cloud account is simple, and after you do so, your friends and colleagues can view your work and share it with others.

In this book, you have learned some essential workflows for post-production using Creative Cloud.

You have learned how to

- Format a script with Adobe Story
- Apply metadata to assets with Adobe Bridge
- Ingest footage and create an assembly edit with Adobe Prelude
- Edit a video with Adobe Premiere Pro
- Create vector graphics with Illustrator
- Do basic image manipulation with Photoshop
- Create motion graphics with After Effects
- Integrate 3D animations with MAXON CINEMA 4D Lite
- Edit audio with Adobe Audition
- Create color grade presets with SpeedGrade
- Export video with Adobe Media Encoder
- Generate an interactive video with Flash

Now that you have some hands-on experience with these tools, go out and create your own story with them. And have fun!

Review questions

1 How do you export a sequence from Adobe Premiere Pro?

2 How do you apply multiple preset render instances to a queued sequence or composition in Adobe Media Encoder?

3 What would be a good codec to use for exporting an archival high-quality version of a video?

4 How do you give your movie file customized playback controls?

5 How do you upload a work to your Creative Cloud account?

Review answers

1   Choose File > Export > Media, apply Export Settings, and then click Export.

2   Select the queued item, and then drag a preset from the Preset Browser into the Queue for each render instance you want to create.

3   The Apple ProRes codec would be a good codec for archival quality, as it ensures minimal image compression.

4   Create a project in Flash Professional using a Media Playback template.

5   Log in to your Creative Cloud account, click the Actions button, choose Upload from the drop-down menu, navigate to where your file is on your hard drive, and then click Open.

INDEX

Note that Chapters 4 and 6 are included in the files you downloaded with this book. In this index, the index numbers for Chapter 4 begin with a "4" and pages are numbered sequentially for that chapter. The numbers for Chapter 6 begin with a "6."

NUMBERS

2K video compression standard, 53
3D Camera Tracker, 6:43–6:47
3D effects
    activating, 6:26–6:28
    applying extrusions, 6:29
    changing color of extrusions, 6:30–6:37
    Ray-traced 3D renderer, 6:25–6:26
4K video compression standard, 53
32-bit color, 313
64-bit support, in operating systems, 17

A

AAF (Advanced Authoring Format), 4:73
Action
    cutting on, 76
    elements of film script page, 28
Additive Dissolves, 4:42
Adjustment Layers
    in Adobe Premiere Pro, 323–325
    applying custom look in Adobe Premiere Pro, 329
    applying to SpeedGrade preset to, 325–326
    copying LumetriLooks effect, 330–333
    cutting, 330–333
    when to use, 322
Adobe After Effects. see After Effects
Adobe Anywhere service, 4:74
Adobe Audition
    adding sound effects, 282–284
    audio tools in, 255
    cleaning up audio clips, 272–273
    creating final mix, 289
    multitrack editing, 286–288
    multitrack mixing and finishing, 280–282
    overview of, 5
    real-time track mixing, 279
    sending final mix back to Adobe Premiere Pro, 289–291
    spectral frequency display, 251, 274–276
Adobe Bridge
    adding metadata to media files, 26–27
    naming and managing media files, 22
    navigating and previewing media files, 22–25
    overview of, 4, 22

Adobe Creative Cloud. see Creative Cloud introduction
Adobe Flash Professional, 5, 355–358
Adobe ID, 30
Adobe Illustrator. see Illustrator
Adobe Media Encoder. see AME (Adobe Media Encoder)
Adobe Photoshop. see Photoshop
Adobe Prelude. see Prelude
Adobe Premiere Pro
    creating new project in, 54–55
    linking projects containing media files, 9, 11–14
    optimizing performance, 52–53
    overview of, 52
    roles of Creative Cloud components, 5
    sending project to, 46–47
    user interface, 56–58
Adobe Story
    collaborating on script with Adobe Story Plus, 34–35
    creating new A/V script, 29–33
    overview of, 4
    planning and managing production, 35–37
    simplifying formatting of media files, 27–28
Advanced Authoring Format (AAF), 4:73
After Effects
    3D activation, 6:26–6:28
    3D Camera Tracker, 6:43–6:47
    adjustment layers in, 323–325
    advanced techniques, 248–249
    animating backgrounds, 212–213
    animating masks, 6:21–6:25
    animating opacity, 217–219
    animating text, 220–221
    animation presets, 226–230
    Aperture Color Finesse plug-in, 315
    applying extrusions, 6:29
    applying finishing touches, 6:37
    changing color of extrusions, 6:30–6:37
    Collapse Transformations, 216–217
    commonly used effects, 6:60
    Continuous Rasterization, 214–215
    converting vector layer to shape layer, 6:15–6:18
    creating a proxy for compositions, 6:69–6:73
    creating folders, 150

creating new compositions, 191–192, 6:7–6:9
creating new projects, 144
creating text layers, 193–195, 6:10–6:14
displacement map effect, 6:61–6:69
drawing and using masks, 6:19–6:20
Drop Shadow effects, 195–196
duplicating layers, 197–201
dynamic linking, 6, 151, 235, 6:5–6:6
Easy-Ease interpolation of animations, 221–223
editing masks, 6:20–6:21
exporting video frames from Adobe Premiere Pro to, 6:76–6:77
fractal noise effect, 6:54–6:59
Global Performance Cache settings, 16–17, 145–147
graphic from Illustrator used in, 190
importing into Adobe Premiere Pro, 152–153, 236–239
incremental versions, 6:4–6:5
keyframing layer position in, 139
lower third graphics example, 230–235
motion blur effect, 223–225
motion graphics, 157–160
moving and scaling parented group, 207–209
nested compositions, 209–211
nesting and collapsing, 6:40–6:43
Null Objects in, 203–206
optimizing performance of, 144–145
organizing compositions, 6:74
overview of, 5, 138, 143
parenting in, 202–203
Pick-Whip as parenting option, 206
pre-composing, 6:37–6:40
RAM Preview and, 160, 6:7
Ray-traced 3D renderer, 6:25–6:26
re-interpreting frame rate of clip imported from, 153–157
renaming compositions, 6:7
replacing existing clips in Adobe Premiere Pro with imported clips, 239–244
replacing timelapse image with imported After Effects composition, 161–162
shape layers, 6:17
simulating a light leak, 6:48–6:50
simulating TV pixels, 6:51–6:54
snapping layers to frame edge, 6:12
solid layers, 6:56
Transfer Modes, 6:48, 6:51
updating dynamically linked composition, 162–163, 245–246
user interface, 147–149
verifying updates to nested composition, 219
viewing composition in Adobe Premiere Pro, 6:74–6:76

AME (Adobe Media Encoder)
encoding video for web and mobile use, 350–354
Export Settings panel in, 337
overview of, 5, 345
rendering master files, 345–348
saving presets, 349–350
Analog bleed effect, 6:121–6:125
Analyze Content option, Project panel, 84
Animation
of background in After Effects, 212–213
defined, 143
Easy-Ease interpolation of, 221–223
keyframes in, 159
of layers in After Effects, 159–160
of masks in After Effects, 6:21–6:25
of opacity in After Effects, 217–219
playing MAXON animations, 6:103–6:104
presets, 226–230
of shape repeaters in MAXON CINEMA 4D/4D Lite, 6:119–6:120
of text in After Effects, 220–221
Aperture Color Finesse plug-in, 315
Apple Final Cut Pro, 4:73
Archiving projects, 355
Aspect ratio, 349
Assets
asset management, 22, 25
importing as a bin, 64–65
navigating, 59
organizing, 24, 61–62
Audio
adding sound effects, 282–284
adjusting loudness, 270–271
automating loudness, 266–269
creating final mix, 289
effects, 262–264
enhancements, 111
examining clips, 270–271
listening to footage, 68–73
listening to music and sound effects, 79
making audio gaps, 130
microphones, 286
monitoring, 254–255
multitrack editing, 286–288
multitrack mixing and finishing, 280–282
opening Audio Mixer, 260
overview of, 250
preparing tracks, 261
removing background noise, 276–278
removing transient sounds, 275–276
sending clips to Adobe Audition for cleanup, 272–273
sending final mix back to Adobe Premiere Pro, 289–291
spectral frequency display, 274

tools, 255

tracks in Timeline, 96

verifying monitoring preferences, 258–259

voice-overs, 285

waveforms, 111, 259

working with media files, 6–7

workspace for, 256–257

Audio Clip Mixer, 111, 255, 270–271

Audio Gain, 265

Audio Meters, 58, 255, 257

Audio Mixer, 255, 260

Audio Plug-in Manager, 264

Audition. *see* Adobe Audition

A/V script

basic elements of, 28

starting new script in Adobe Story, 29–34

Avid, exchanging projects and, 4:73

B

Background noise, removing, 276–278

Backing up, 17

Batch processing, in Adobe Bridge, 22

Behance network

linking to social networks, 361–362

posting image to, 363–365

posting project to, 358

promoting project via, 361

Best Take comments, 26–27

Bins

creating, 41, 65–67, 4:55

in Creative Cloud interface, 6

importing assets as, 64–65

selecting clips in, 11–12

storing closed caption clip in, 4:66

Bitmap images, 7

Bitrate settings, 344

Boris Continuum Complete AE effects plug-in, 4:46

Boris FX effects plug-in, 312, 4:46

B-roll

adding jump cut to, 4:5–4:9

adding to sequences, 102–105

creating bin for, 65–67

defined, 33

Dynamic Timeline Trimming and, 4:16–4:20

Rate Stretch tool applied to, 4:9–4:16

viewing, 74–76

what it is, 73

C

.c4d file, 6:96–6:99

Cameras

3D Camera Tracker, 6:43–6:47

frames and frame rates, 62–63

RED camera, 4:20–4:22

Capture tool, for tape media, 60

Central Processing Unit (CPU), 4:70

CINEWARE plug-in. *see* MAXON CINEMA 4D/4D Lite

Clip editing

in Adobe Audition, 272

in Adobe Premiere Pro, 266

audio editing options, 265

Clips

adding last, 131–132

adding markers to, 91–94

adding RED clips, 4:24–4:28, 4:33–4:36

adding to sequence, 102–108

applying effects to, 4:43–4:44

applying speed/duration to RED clips, 4:28–4:30

creating subclips, 80–83

ingesting, 38–40

listening to, 68–73

logging clips, 26–27, 40

organizing, 61

pasting effects between, 306–314

previewing, 60, 160–161

reordering on Timeline, 108, 111

selecting, 11–12

sending to Adobe Audition for cleanup, 272–273

shortening music clips, 126–130

snapping for adding to sequence, 112–115

snapping for moving within sequences, 115–126

syncing, 128

trimming, 83, 4:5

viewing, 68, 74–78

working with media files, 6–8

Closed captions, 348, 4:56–4:66

Codecs, 8, 343

Collaboration, in Adobe Story Plus, 34–35

Collapse Transformations, After Effects, 216–217

Color Assist, from Technicolor, 312

Color correction

in Adobe Premiere Pro, 299

Color Finesse plug-in, 315

integrating into RED footage, 315–322

overview of, 298–299

pasting color correction effects between clips, 306–314

scopes, 302

setting up for, 300

Three-Way Color Corrector, 302–306

YC Waveform for, 301

Color Finesse plug-in, 315

Color grading, 298–299, 322

Comments, adding to media files, 26–27, 44–45

CompactFlash, 40

Compatibility issues, video formats and, 7

Compositing, 143

Compute Unified Device Architecture (CUDA), 15–16

Condenser microphones, 286

Continuous Rasterization, After Effects, 214–215

CPU (Central Processing Unit), 4:70

Creative Cloud introduction, 17–18
    component roles, 4–5
    dynamic linking, 6
    linking projects containing media files, 9–14
    overview of, 4
    posting files to, 4:73–4:76
    posting project to, 358–360, 4:72–4:73
    real-time playback and editing, 15–17
    syncing preferences, 4:76–4:77
    user interface, 5–6
    working with media files, 6–8

Cross Dissolve transitions, 4:38–4:42

CTI (current time indicator), Track Targeting and, 4:25

CUDA (Compute Unified Device Architecture), 15–16

Current time indicator (CTI), Track Targeting and, 4:25

D

Damage effects plug-in, 4:46

Delay effect, in audio, 262

Delirium effects plug-in, 4:46

Dialogue, 28

Digieffects effects plug-in, 4:46

Digital asset management software, 22

Digital single-lens reflex (DSLR), 4:20–4:23, 4:30–4:33

Disk cache, 16–17

Disk drives, 53–54, 144

Disk images, backing up, 17

Displacement map effect, 6:61–6:69

Dissolve transitions, 4:37–4:39

DNxHD, for Windows and Mac OSs, 345

Downloading, vs. streaming, 354

Drop Shadow effect, 195–196

Dropped Frame Indicator, 4:71

DSLR (digital single-lens reflex), 4:20–4:23, 4:30–4:33

DV Shade, EasyLooks, 312

Dynamic linking
    between After Effects and Adobe Premiere Pro, 151, 235, 6:5–6:6
    Dynamic Link feature, 6
    updating dynamically linked composition, 162–163, 245–246

Dynamic microphones, 286

Dynamic Timeline Trimming, 4:16–4:20

Dynamics effect, in audio, 262

E

Easy-Ease interpolation, 221–223

EasyLooks, DV Shade, 312

EBU N19 Subtitle File, closed caption standards, 348

Edit points, on Timeline
    adjusting playhead position, 127
    creating subclips and, 81–83
    extending out point when creating dissolve, 4:39–4:42
    selecting portion of clip to ingest, 38–39
    snapping between, 112
    snapping to, 115

Editing
    adding closed caption, 4:56–4:66
    adding markers for, 94–95, 133
    adding reaction shots, 131
    adding RED clips, 4:24–4:28, 4:33–4:36
    advanced techniques, 136–137
    applying effects, 4:43–4:46
    applying speed/duration settings, 4:28–4:30
    audio options, 111, 265, 286–288
    completing rough edit, 134
    creating bins for, 65–67, 4:55
    Dynamic Timeline Trimming, 4:16–4:20
    extract, 100–101
    importing assets as a bin, 64–65
    importing footage for, 59–60
    incorporating RED footage, 4:20–4:22
    Insert edits, 109–110
    interpreting footage, 62–63
    jump cuts, 4:5–4:9
    linear vs. nonlinear, 52
    listening to footage and, 68–73
    listening to music and sound effects and, 79
    marking audio gaps, 130
    moving frames forward/backward, 106–108
    multicam, 133
    muting and locking tracks, 97–98
    optimizing performance, 52–54
    overview of, 50–51, 4:1–4:2
    overwrite edits, 108–109
    posting project or files to Creative Cloud, 4:72–4:76
    preparing for, 95–96
    preserving rough edits, 4:2–4:3
    Project panel and, 61–62
    Rate Stretch tool, 4:9–4:16
    real-time playback and, 15–16
    RED vs. DSLR, 4:22–4:23
    refining story, 126
    relinking with Link & Locate feature, 84–88
    rendering Timeline, 4:70–4:72
    ripple delete, 99–100
    ripple edits, 98

sequences, 88–91
snapping between edit points, 112
syncing and, 4:30–4:33, 4:76–4:77
Timeline components and, 96
titles, 4:47–4:54
transitions, 4:37–4:42
trimming clips, 4:5
user interface features for, 56–58
viewing footage, 67–68
Warp Stabilizer effect, 4:67–4:70
workspace for, 56–58
Effects
adding to clips, 4:43–4:46
adding transitions, 4:37–4:42
audio effects, 262–264, 282–284
commonly used, 6:60
Effects Controls panel, 310, 4:33
Ellipse tool, 178–179
Emotion, 76, 131
Encoding video, for web and mobile use, 350–354
Error messages, Adobe Premiere Pro, 10, 141, 4:3, 6:3
Export Settings panel, in Adobe Media Encoder, 337
Exporting, with Adobe Premiere Pro, 341–342
Extract edits, 100–101
Extrusions
applying, 6:29
changing color of, 6:30–6:37

F

Fast Color Corrector effect, 298
Favorites tab, Adobe Bridge, 22
Files
managing RED clips, 4:31
media files. *see* Media files
posting to Creative Cloud, 4:73–4:76
sharing via Adobe Story, 35–36
size consideration in exporting, 344
Final Cut Pro (Apple), 4:73
Flash Professional, 5, 355–358
Folders. *see also* Bins
Adobe Bridge, 22
creating in After Effects, 150
understanding Creative Cloud interface, 6
Fonts, serif vs. sans serif, 4:55
Footage
B-roll, 33
copying and transcoding, 40
interpreting, 62–63
listening to, 68–73
stabilizing, 4:67–4:70
viewing, 59, 67–68
Formats
audio, 6–7

compatibility and, 7
factors to consider in exporting, 343
video, 6
Formatting menu, Adobe Story, 27–28
Fps (frames per second), 62–63
Fractal noise effect, After Effects, 6:54–6:59
Frame rates
DSLR vs. RED, 4:22
factors to consider in exporting, 344
re-interpreting frame rate of clip imported from After Effects, 153–157
video clips, 62–63
Frames, 62
Frames per second (Fps), 62–63

G

Gain, Audio Gain, 265
Gaussian Blur effect, 4:44–4:46
Global Performance Cache, 16, 145–147
GPUs (graphics processing units)
CUDA (Compute Unified Device Architecture) and, 15–16
error message for missing renderer, 10, 141, 4:3
graphics cards, 16
Mercury Playback Engine and, 4:70
performance optimization and, 54
Gradient fill, 170–175
Graphics
creating bin for, 4:55
creating track for, 4:49–4:50
importing from Illustrator into After Effects, 190
storing closed caption clip in graphics bin, 4:66
Graphics cards, 16, 144
Graphics processing units. *see* GPUs (graphics processing units)

H

H.264
artifacts and noise and, 4:20
factors to consider in exporting, 343
video codecs, 8, 53
Hard drives, 53–54, 144
Hardware requirements, for Adobe Premiere Pro, 52
HD (high-definition), 53, 4:20
HDR (high dynamic range) footage, 322
Highlights, Three-Way Color Corrector, 304–305, 307–308, 310–312, 314
Histograms, color correction and, 317–318
Hover scrubs, 60, 74

I

Icon View, 4:6
Illustrator
    applying gradient fill, 170–175
    creating background shapes, 168–169
    creating groups of shapes, 177–178
    creating images, 164–166
    creating lower third backgrounds, 168
    drawing circles, 178–179
    duplicating layers, 185–189
    duplicating shapes, 180–183
    grouping shapes, 183–184
    importing lower third background into After
        Effects, 190
    layers, 176
    Mercury Performance System and, 17
    overview of, 5, 164
    user interface, 167
Image formats, 6:78
Images, posting to Behance network, 363–365
Importing, with Media Browser, 59–60
In points. *see* Edit points, on Timeline
Increments, 6:4–6:5
Insert edits, 109–110
International Standards Organization (ISO),
    4:20–4:21
Interpret footage, xvi
ISO (International Standards Organization),
    4:20–4:21

J

Jump cuts, 4:5–4:9

K

Keyframes, 159, 266–269
Keyword searches, in Adobe Bridge, 22

L

Layers, After Effects
    animating, 159–160
    converting vector layer to shape layer,
        6:15–6:18
    duplicating, 197–201
    nested compositions, 209–211
    shape layers, 6:17
    snapping to frame edge, 6:12
    solid layers, 6:56
    text layers, 193–195, 6:10–6:14
    working with, 157–158
Layers, Illustrator
    duplicating, 185–189
    organizing vector objects by, 176

Layers, understanding Creative Cloud interface, 6
Light leak, simulating, 6:48–6:50
Linear editing, vs. nonlinear, 52
Link & Locate feature, 84–88
Link Media, 12–13
Linking, to social networks, 361–362
List view, 59, 61
Listening
    to footage, 68–73
    to music and sound effects, 79
Locate File window, 13–14
Locking tracks, Timeline, 97–98, 128
Log Notes, Project panel, 62
Logging clips, 26–27, 40
Loudness Radar, 262–263
Lower third background
    applying gradient fill to, 170–175
    creating in Illustrator, 164–166
    creating shape of, 168–169
    finalizing, 230–235
    importing from Illustrator into After Effects,
        190
Lumetri Looks effects, 330–333
LumetriTM Deep Color Engine, 322

M

Mac OSs. *see* OSs (operating systems)
Magic Bullet Suite, 312, 4:46
Margins, safe, 4:48
Markers
    adding final, 133
    adding to clips, 91–94
    adding to frame, 118
    adding to sequences, 94–95
    snapping to, 115
Marquee-selecting, 66, 77–78, 129
Masks, After Effects
    animating, 6:21–6:25
    editing, 6:20–6:21
    overview of, 6:19–6:20
MAXON CINEMA 4D/4D Lite
    analog bleed effect, 6:121–6:125
    animating shape repeaters, 6:119–6:120
    applying materials, 6:105–6:107
    applying shape repeaters, 6:114–6:119
    creating materials, 6:107–6:112
    importing .c4d file into After Effects,
        6:96–6:99
    importing MAXON clip into Adobe Premiere
        Pro, 6:128–6:132
    overview of, 6:1, 6:95–6:96
    playing animations, 6:103–6:104
    rendering proxy for MAXON clip,
        6:126–6:128

replacing existing clips in After Effects with imported clips, 6:112–6:114

user interface, 6:100–6:102

MCC (MacCaption) VANC (Vertical ANcillary data space) File, 348

MCU (medium close up), 32

Media Browser, importing with, 59–60, 64–65

Media Composer, 4:73

Media files

    adding metadata to, 26–27

    adding notes to footage with Prelude, 40

    adding time-based comments, 44–45

    assembling rough cuts, 41–43

    collaborating on script with Adobe Story Plus, 34–35

    creating bins for, 41

    example using Adobe Story for new A/V script, 29–33

    formatting with Adobe Story, 27–28

    ingesting raw footage and metadata with Prelude, 37–39

    linking project containing, 9–14

    naming and managing, 22

    navigating and previewing, 22–25

    organizing by duration, 61

    overview of, 20–21

    planning and managing production with Adobe Story, 35–37

    Prelude and, 37

    sending project to Adobe Premiere Pro, 46–47

    in video production, 6–8

Medium close up (MCU), 32

Memory cards, ingesting video clips from, 40

Mercury Graphics Engine, 17

Mercury Performance System, 17

Mercury Playback Engine, 15–16, 4:70

Metadata, 26–27, 37–39

Microphones, 286

Midtones, Three-Way Color Corrector, 304–305, 307–308, 310–312, 314

Mixes

    creating final, 289

    multitrack, 280–282

    sending final to Adobe Premiere Pro, 289–291

Mobile devices, 350–354

Modify Clip window, Adobe Premiere Pro, 63

Monitoring audio, 254–255, 258–259

Monitoring color information, 302

Motion blur effect, After Effects, 223–225

Motion graphics. see also After Effects

    animating layers, 159–160

    keyframes, 159

    motion graphics artists vs. video editors, 143

    overview of, 157

    working with layers, 157–158

.mp4 files, 342

MPEG-4 video codec, 8

Multicam edits, 133

Music. see also Audio

    listening to, 79

    preparing tracks, 261

    shortening clips, 126–130

Muting tracks, in Timeline, 97–98, 128, 260

N

Nested compositions, 209–211, 219

Nonlinear editing, 52

Notes, adding to footage, 40

Null Objects, in After Effects, 203–206

O

Opacity, animating in After Effects, 217–219

OpenCL (Open Computing Language), 16

OpenGL (Open Graphics Library), 144

Operating systems. see OSs (operating systems)

Optimizing performance, 52–54, 144–145

OSs (operating systems)

    64-bit support, 17

    Creative Cloud membership and, 4

    DNxHD and, 345

    performance optimization and, 53

Out points. see Edit points, on Timeline

Output for Web. see Web output

Overwrite edits, 108–109, 4:26

P

Parametric Equalization, audio effects, 262

Parenthetical element, of film script page, 28

Parenting, in After Effects

    moving and scaling parented group, 207–209

    Null Objects and, 203–206

    overview of, 202–203

    Pick-Whip as parenting option, 206

Performance, optimizing, 52–54, 144–145

Photoshop

    making spine image label, 6:84–6:94

    making VHS tape labels, 6:81–6:84

    Mercury Graphics Engine and, 17

    new features, 6:79

    overview of, 5

    user interface, 6:80–6:81

Pick-Whip parenting option, 206

Pixel Motion Blur effect, After Effects, 225

Pixels, 53, 4:20–4:21, 6:51–6:54

Playback

    adjusting Playback Resolution, 77, 4:23

    Playback Resolution menu in Program Monitor, 4:35

Rate Stretch tool, 4:10
real-time playback and editing, 15–16
Playhead
adjusting playhead position, 126–127
adjusting position of, 101
Playhead, in Timeline, 96
Posterize Time effect, 4:43–4:44
Posting images/projects, to Behance network, 358, 363–365
Post-production phase, of workflow, 3
Pre-composing, After Effects, 6:37–6:40
Prelude
adding notes to footage, 40
ingesting raw footage and metadata, 37–39
overview of, 5, 37
Premiere Pro. *see* Adobe Premiere Pro
Pre-production phase, of workflow, 2
Preview panel, 25
Production, planning and managing, 35–37
Production phase, of workflow, 3
Program Monitor
in Adobe Premiere Pro, 1
enabling/disabling closed captions, 4:60
Extract icon, 101
panels of Editing workspace, 57
safe margins in, 4:48
Select Playback Resolution menu, 4:35
viewing sequence frames in, 89
Project panel
adding B-roll clips to sequence, 102
Analyze Content option, 84
creating new bin, 65–67
of Editing workspace, 57
naming sequences, 90
opening B-Roll bin, 74
organizing assets in, 61–62
Promoting projects, 361
ProRes, Apple, 345
Proxies
creating for compositions, 6.69–6.73
rendering for MAXON clip, 6:126–6:128

Q

QuickTime, 346

R

R3D clips, 77–78. *see also* RED footage
RAID (redundant array of independent disks), 53–54
RAM
Adobe Premiere Pro requirements, 53
After Effects requirements, 144
Global Performance Cache and, 16–17

RAM Preview, 160–161, 163, 6:7
Raster images, 164, 214–215
Rate Stretch tool, 4:9–4:16
Raw footage
adding notes to, 40
ingesting with Prelude, 37–39
RED camera and, 4:20–4:21
SpeedGrade support for, 322
Ray-traced 3D renderer, 6:25–6:26
Razor tool
creating jump cuts, 4:7–4:8
cutting instrumental clip with, 128–129
editing with, 103–105
ripple deletes with, 99
Reaction shots, 131
Record button, Audio Mixer, 260
RED footage
adding clips, 4:24–4:28, 4:33–4:36
applying speed/duration to, 4:28–4:30
color correction, 295, 315–322
vs. DSLR, 4:22–4:23
file management, 4:31
incorporating, 4:20–4:22
syncing with DSLR footage, 4:30–4:33
Red Giant effects plug-in, 312, 4:46
Redundant array of independent disks (RAID), 53–54
relink files, xv
Reverb effect, audio, 262
RGB Parade color scope, 302
Ripple edits/ripple deletes, 98–100, 129, 4:16–4:17
Roll Edit tool, 4:18, 4:39–4:42
Rough edits
assembling rough cuts, 41–43
completing, 134
preserving, 140–142, 4:2–4:3, 6:2, 6:4

S

Safe Margins, in Program Monitor, 4:48
Sans serif fonts, 4:55
Scene heading element, of film script page, 28
Schedules, coordination with Adobe Story, 35–36
Scopes, for monitoring color information, 302
Scratch Disk error message, 10
Scripts
Adobe Story and, 27
basic elements of film script page, 28
collaboration with Adobe Story Plus, 34–35
creating new A/V script, 29–33
Scrubbing, 11
SD, 40
Selection techniques
for clips in bins, 11–12
marquee-selecting, 66, 129

for portion of clip using in/out point, 38–39
Selection tool, 103–105
snapping and, 115–116, 119–120, 124
Track Select tool, 119
Sequences
    adding B-roll clips, 102–105
    adding markers to, 94–95
    creating first, 88–91
    edited sequence in Timeline, 51
    editing final audio sequence, 252–254
    importing image sequence from After Effects
        to Adobe Premiere Pro, 152–153
    modifying name of, 4:2, 4:4
    sending to Adobe Audition, 280–282
    sending to SpeedGrade, 327
    snapping for adding clips to, 112–115
    snapping for moving clips within, 115–126
Serif fonts, 4:55
Shadows, Three-Way Color Corrector, 304–305,
    307–308, 310–312, 314
Shape repeaters, MAXON CINEMA 4D/4D Lite,
    6:114–6:120
Shapes, converting vector layer to shape layer,
    6:15–6:18
Shapes, in Illustrator
    applying gradient fill to, 170–175
    creating, 168–169
    drawing a circle, 178–179
    duplicating, 180–183
    grouping, 183–184
    making groups of, 177–178
Shots element, of film script page, 28
Slip tool, 106–108
Snapping
    adding clips with, 112–115, 117–119,
        121–126
    between edit points, 112
    layers to frame edge, 6:12
    playhead to clip markers, 119–121
    within sequences, 115–116
Social networks, 361–362
Solid layers, After Effects, 6:56
Solo button, Audio Mixer, 260
Sound bites, 68–73
Sound effects, 79, 280, 282–284. *see also* Audio
Source Monitor
    adding clips to Timeline, 4:25
    adding markers to clips, 92
    adjusting playhead position, 126–127
    creating subclips, 80–83
    Insert button, 110
    opening clips, 63
    panels of Editing workspace, 56
    playing/selecting clips, 70–73
    Select Zoom Level menu, 4:32
    trimming clips, 83
    viewing clips, 68, 75–78
    viewing music and sound effects, 79
Source Patching, 4:25–4:26
Spectral frequency display, 251, 274–276
Speech to Text workflow, Adobe Premiere Pro, 84
Speed/duration settings, RED clips, 4:28–4:30,
    4:36
SpeedGrade
    adjustment layers and, 323–326
    for color grading, 322
    creating custom look, 327–329
    dynamic linking and, 6
    overview of, 5
    sending sequence to, 327
SSC (Scenarist Closed Caption) File, 348
Storage
    capacity in Creative Cloud, 4
    integrating with asset management, 25
Story, refining, 126
Streaming, vs. downloading, 354
Subclips, 80–83
Sync Lock, 4:25
Syncing
    clips, 128
    preferences in Creative Cloud, 4:76–4:77
    RED with DSLR footage, 4:30–4:33

T

Tablets, encoding video for, 350–354
Tape, capturing from, 60
Technicolor Color Assist, 312
Text
    animating in After Effects, 220–221
    creating closed captions, 4:56–4:66
    creating text layers in After Effects, 193–195,
        6:10–6:14
    Speech to Text workflow, 84
Three-Way Color Corrector, 302–306
Thumbnails
    adjusting size of, 24
    ingesting video clips with Prelude, 38
    viewing content of Footage folder, 59
Timecode, 4:9–4:10
Timelapse images
    previewing and making final changes to,
        160–162
    re-interpreting frame rate of imported clip,
        153–157
    replacing with imported After Effects
        composition, 161–162
Timeline
    adding B-roll clips to sequence, 106–108
    adjusting playhead position, 127

in Adobe Premiere Pro, 1
components of, 96
creating graphics track, 4:49–4:50
customizing look of, 258
edited sequence in, 51
extract edits, 100–101
insert edits, 109–110
moving frames forward/backward, 106–108
muting and locking tracks, 97–98
overview of, 6
overwrite edits, 108–109
panels of Editing workspace, 58
preparing to edit in, 95–96
rendering, 4:70–4:72
reordering clips on, 108, 111
ripple deletes, 99–100
ripple edits, 98
snapping between edit points, 112
Title Safe/Action Safe guides, 207
Titles, adding, 4:47–4:54
Toggle Track Lock icon, 97, 129–130
Toolbars, in Creative Cloud interface, 5
Tools panel
panels of Editing workspace, 58
Rate Stretch tool, 4:10
Razor tool, 99, 103–105
Selection tool, 103–105
Slip tool, 106–108
Track Select tool, 119
Track Changes, collaboration and, 35
Track Meter, 258
Track Select tool, 119
Track Targeting, 4:25, 4:51
Tracks
audio editing options, 265
creating graphics track in Timeline,
4:49–4:50
multitrack editing in Adobe Audition,
286–288
multitrack mixing and finishing in Adobe
Audition, 280–282
preparing music tracks, 261
in Timeline, 96
Transcoding footage, 40
Transfer Modes, 6:48, 6:51
Transient sounds, removing, 275–276
Transitions, 28, 4:37–4:42
Trapcode Shine effects plug-in, 4:46
Trim Mode, 4:16, 4:18
Trimming
basic trim edits, 102–103
clips, 4:5
Dynamic Timeline Trimming, 4:16–4:20
example of trimming Interview clips, 83
Rate Stretch tool and, 4:9–4:16

TV pixels, simulating, 6:51–6:54
Twirling down/open, navigating Assets folder, 59

U

User interface (UI)
Adobe Premiere Pro, 56–58
After Effects, 147–149
Creative Cloud, 5–6
Illustrator, 167
MAXON CINEMA 4D/4D Lite, 6:100–6:102
Photoshop, 6:80–6:81

V

Vector images, 7, 164, 6:15–6:18
Vectorscope, 302
Video
codecs, 8
compatibility and, 7
encoding for web and mobile use, 350–354
ingesting, 38–40
interpreting, 62–63
tracks in Timeline, 96
working with, 6
Video cards, 16
Video editors, 143
Videotape, capturing from, 60
Voice-overs, 285
Volume, adjusting/automating, 266–271

W

W3c/SMPTE/EBU Timed Text File, 348
Warp Stabilizer effect, 4:67–4:70
Waveforms, audio, 111, 259
Web output
AME (Adobe Media Encoder) and, 345
archiving projects and, 355
aspect ratio and, 349
closed caption standards and, 348
encoding video for web and mobile use,
350–354
Export Settings panel in Adobe Media
Encoder, 337
exporting to Web, 341–344
interactivity with Flash Professional, 355–358
linking to social networks, 361–362
overview of, 336
posting images to Behance network, 363–365
promoting projects, 361
rendering master files, 345–348
saving settings as a preset, 349–350
streaming vs. downloading, 354
uploading projects to Creative Cloud, 358–360

White balancing, 298, 302–306
Windows OSs. *see* OSs (operating systems)
Wipe transitions, 4:42
Workspaces
 for audio, 256–257
 for color correction, 300
 in Creative Cloud interface, 5

Y

YC Waveform, 300–301
YCbCr Parade, 302

Z

Zoom, in/out, 4:7, 4:12

Production Notes

Digital Video with Adobe Creative Cloud was created electronically using Adobe InDesign CS6. Art was produced using Adobe Illustrator and Adobe Photoshop. The Myriad Pro and Warnock Pro OpenType families of typefaces were used throughout this book.

References to company names in the lessons are for demonstration purposes only and are not intended to refer to any actual organization or person.

Images

Photographic images and illustrations are intended for use with the tutorials.

Typefaces used

Adobe Myriad Pro and Adobe Warnock Pro are used throughout the lessons. For more information about OpenType and Adobe fonts, visit www.adobe.com/type/opentype/.

Team credits

The following individuals contributed to the development of this edition of *Digital Video with Creative Cloud Classroom in a Book*:

Writers: Adam Shaening-Pokrasso, Sam Young, and Adam Kennedy
Adobe Press Editor: Victor Gavenda
Senior Editor: Karyn Johnson
Developmental Editor: Corbin Collins
Copyeditor: Rebecca Rider
Production Editor: Maureen Forys, Happenstance Type-O-Rama
Technical Editor: Simon Walker
Compositor: David Van Ness
Proofreader: Scout Festa
Media Producer: Eric Geoffroy
Indexer: Jack Lewis
Cover designer: Eddie Yuen
Interior designer: Mimi Heft

Authors

Adam Shaening-Pokrasso Adam is a director/producer and owner of San Francisco based creative agency, 12FPS. He produces advertising and educational content for technology companies and motion graphics for award-winning documentaries. Adam also exhibits media works around the world and across the interweb.

Sam Young Sam is a video editor and motion graphics artist based in San Francisco. He has produced music videos, corporate promotions, and documentaries. He enjoys coffee.

Adam E. Kennedy Adam is a young filmmaker, photographer, and animator, who often blurs the lines between digital mediums in order to reveal meaningful relationships between art and science. He is known for his "Planet Universe" series in which he creates vibrant planetary imagery from images of old, rusty fire hydrants.

Contributors

Jeffery Paradise (music and talent)
Filip Nikolic (music and talent)
Saturn Jones (dancer)
Jocquese Whitfield (dancer)
Dwight Burks (producer)
Adam Shaening-Pokrasso (director)
Heidi Petty (creative director)
Tyler Winick (art director)
Matthew Rome (director of photography)
Kristina Willemse (assistant camera)
Chad Leto (grip and electric)
Ian Sotzing (grip and electric)
Winston Merchan (production assistant)
Adam Kennedy (production and editorial)
Richard Barley (sound recordist)

All video content produced by 12FPS (12fps.com) at Hampshire Street Studios in San Francisco, CA. Music produced by Poolside (poolsidemusic.com).

WATCH
READ
CREATE

Unlimited online access to all Peachpit, Adobe
Press, Apple Training, and New Riders videos
and books, as well as content from other
leading publishers including: O'Reilly Media,
Focal Press, Sams, Que, Total Training, John
Wiley & Sons, Course Technology PTR, Class
on Demand, VTC, and more.

No time commitment or contract required!
Sign up for one month or a year.
All for $19.99 a month

SIGN UP TODAY
peachpit.com/creativeedge

creative
edge